also by the editors at america's test kitchen

The Complete Mediterranean Cookbook

What Good Cooks Know

Cook's Science

Kitchen Hacks

100 Recipes: The Absolute Best Ways to Make the True Essentials

The Best of America's Test Kitchen (2007–2017 Editions)

The Complete America's Test Kitchen TV Show Cookbook 2001–2017

The New Family Cookbook

The Complete Vegetarian Cookbook

The Complete Cooking for Two Cookbook

The America's Test Kitchen Cooking School Cookbook

The Cook's Illustrated Meat Book

The Cook's Illustrated Baking Book

The Cook's Illustrated Cookbook

The Science of Good Cooking

The New Best Recipe

Soups, Stews, and Chilis

The America's Test Kitchen Quick Family Cookbook

The America's Test Kitchen Healthy Family Cookbook

The America's Test Kitchen Family Baking Book

THE COOK'S ILLUSTRATED ALL-TIME BEST SERIES

All-Time Best Appetizers

All-Time Best Soups

THE AMERICA'S TEST KITCHEN LIBRARY SERIES AND THE TEST KITCHEN HANDBOOK SERIES

Naturally Sweet

Master of the Grill

Foolproof Preserving

Paleo Perfected

The How Can It Be Gluten-Free Cookbook: Volume 2

The How Can It Be Gluten-Free Cookbook

The Best Mexican Recipes

The Make-Ahead Cook

Healthy Slow Cooker Revolution

Slow Cooker Revolution Volume 2: The Easy-Prep Edition

Slow Cooker Revolution

The Six-Ingredient Solution

Pressure Cooker Perfection

The America's Test Kitchen D.I.Y. Cookbook

Pasta Revolution

THE COOK'S COUNTRY SERIES

Cook It in Cast Iron

Cook's Country Eats Local

The Complete Cook's Country TV Show Cookbook

FOR A FULL LISTING OF ALL OUR BOOKS

CooksIllustrated.com

AmericasTestKitchen.com

praise for america's test kitchen titles

"The sum total of exhaustive experimentation . . . anyone interested in gluten-free cookery simply shouldn't be without it."
NIGELLA LAWSON ON *THE HOW CAN IT BE GLUTEN-FREE COOKBOOK*

"This book is a comprehensive, no-nonsense guide . . . a well-thought-out, clearly explained primer for every aspect of home baking."
THE WALL STREET JOURNAL ON *THE COOK'S ILLUSTRATED BAKING BOOK*

"An exceptional resource for novice canners, though preserving veterans will find plenty here to love as well."
LIBRARY JOURNAL (STARRED REVIEW) ON *FOOLPROOF PRESERVING*

"A terrifically accessible and useful guide to grilling in all its forms that sets a new bar for its competitors on the bookshelf. . . . The book is packed with practical advice, simple tips, and approachable recipes."
PUBLISHERS WEEKLY (STARRED REVIEW) ON *MASTER OF THE GRILL*

"The 21st-century *Fannie Farmer Cookbook* or *The Joy of Cooking*. If you had to have one cookbook and that's all you could have, this one would do it."
CBS SAN FRANCISCO ON *THE NEW FAMILY COOKBOOK*

"This book upgrades slow cooking for discriminating, 21st-century palates—that is indeed revolutionary."
THE DALLAS MORNING NEWS ON *SLOW COOKER REVOLUTION*

"The go-to gift book for newlyweds, small families, or empty nesters."
ORLANDO SENTINEL ON *THE COMPLETE COOKING FOR TWO COOKBOOK*

"Some 2,500 photos walk readers through 600 painstakingly tested recipes, leaving little room for error."
ASSOCIATED PRESS ON *THE AMERICA'S TEST KITCHEN COOKING SCHOOL COOKBOOK*

"A one-volume kitchen seminar, addressing in one smart chapter after another the sometimes surprising whys behind a cook's best practices. . . . You get the myth, the theory, the science, and the proof, all rigorously interrogated as only America's Test Kitchen can do."
NPR ON *THE SCIENCE OF GOOD COOKING*

"Carnivores with an obsession for perfection will likely have found their new bible in this comprehensive collection."
PUBLISHERS WEEKLY (STARRED REVIEW) ON *THE COOK'S ILLUSTRATED MEAT BOOK*

"This encyclopedia of meat cookery would feel completely overwhelming if it weren't so meticulously organized and artfully designed. This is *Cook's Illustrated* at its finest."
THE KITCHN ON *THE COOK'S ILLUSTRATED MEAT BOOK*

"Buy this gem for the foodie in your family, and spend the extra money to get yourself a copy too."
THE MISSOURIAN ON *THE BEST OF AMERICA'S TEST KITCHEN 2015*

"The perfect kitchen home companion. . . . The practical side of things is very much on display . . . cook-friendly and kitchen-oriented, illuminating the process of preparing food instead of mystifying it."
THE WALL STREET JOURNAL ON *THE COOK'S ILLUSTRATED COOKBOOK*

"There are pasta books . . . and then there's this pasta book. Flip your carbohydrate dreams upside down and strain them through this sieve of revolutionary, creative, and also traditional recipes."
SAN FRANCISCO BOOK REVIEW ON *PASTA REVOLUTION*

"Further proof that practice makes perfect, if not transcendent. . . . If an intermediate cook follows the directions exactly, the results will be better than takeout or Mom's."
THE NEW YORK TIMES ON *THE NEW BEST RECIPE*

BREAD ILLUSTRATED

A STEP-BY-STEP GUIDE
TO ACHIEVING
BAKERY-QUALITY
RESULTS AT HOME

BY THE EDITORS AT
America's Test Kitchen

Library of Congress Cataloging-in-Publication Data

Names: America's Test Kitchen (Firm), author.
Title: Bread illustrated : a step-by-step guide to achieving bakery-quality
   results at home / by the editors at America's Test Kitchen.
Description: Brookline, MA : America's Test Kitchen, [2016] |
   Includes index.
Identifiers: LCCN 2016016441 | ISBN 9781940352602
Subjects: LCSH: Bread. | LCGFT: Cookbooks.
Classification: LCC TX769 .B77274 2016 | DDC 641.81/5--dc23
LC record available at https://lccn.loc.gov/2016016441

AMERICA'S TEST KITCHEN
17 Station Street, Brookline, MA 02445

Manufactured in the United States of America

10 9 8 7 6 5 4 3 2 1

Distributed by Penguin Random House Publisher Services
Tel: 800–733–3000

Pictured on front cover: Pain d'Epi (page 377), Fluffy Dinner Rolls
(page 63), Seeded Ficelle (page 383), Fig and Fennel Bread (page 327),
Cinnamon Swirl Bread (page 250)
Pictured on spine: Bakery-Style French Baguettes (page 370)
Pictured on back cover: Durum Bread (page 348), Pitas (page 216),
Sourdough Bread (page 359), Whole-Wheat Quinoa Bread (page 110),
No-Knead Brioche (page 99), Kaiser Rolls (page 151)

CHIEF CREATIVE OFFICER: Jack Bishop

EDITORIAL DIRECTOR, BOOKS: Elizabeth Carduff

EXECUTIVE EDITOR: Julia Collin Davison

EXECUTIVE EDITOR: Adam Kowit

EXECUTIVE FOOD EDITOR: Dan Zuccarello

SENIOR EDITORS: Sara Mayer, Anne Wolf

ASSOCIATE EDITORS: Leah Colins, Nicole Konstantinakos,
Sacha Madadian, Sebastian Nava

TEST COOKS: Kathryn Callahan, Afton Cyrus, Joe Gitter,
Katherine Perry, Amanda Rumore

EDITORIAL ASSISTANT: Alyssa Langer

CONSULTING EDITOR: Andrew Janjigian

ART DIRECTOR: Carole Goodman

ASSOCIATE ART DIRECTOR: Jen Kanavos Hoffman

PRODUCTION DESIGNER: Reinaldo Cruz

PHOTOGRAPHY DIRECTOR: Julie Bozzo Cote

ASSISTANT PHOTOGRAPHY PRODUCER: Mary Ball

ASSOCIATE ART DIRECTOR, PHOTOGRAPHY: Steve Klise

SENIOR STAFF PHOTOGRAPHER: Daniel J. van Ackere

PHOTOGRAPHY: Carl Tremblay

FOOD STYLING: Catrine Kelty, Marie Piraino, and Sally Staub

PHOTOSHOOT KITCHEN TEAM:
    SENIOR EDITOR: Chris O'Connor
    TEST COOKS: Daniel Cellucci and Matthew Fairman
    ASSISTANT TEST COOK: Allison Berkey

PRODUCTION DIRECTOR: Guy Rochford

SENIOR PRODUCTION MANAGER: Jessica Lindheimer Quirk

PRODUCTION MANAGER: Christine Walsh

IMAGING MANAGER: Lauren Robbins

PRODUCTION AND IMAGING SPECIALISTS: Heather Dube,
Sean MacDonald, Dennis Noble, and Jessica Voas

COPY EDITOR: Jeffrey Schier

PROOFREADER: Jane Tunks Demel

INDEXER: Elizabeth Parson

contents

welcome to america's test kitchen

This book has been tested, written, and edited by the folks at America's Test Kitchen, a very real 2,500-square-foot kitchen located just outside of Boston. It is the home of *Cook's Illustrated* magazine and *Cook's Country* magazine and is the Monday-through-Friday destination for more than 60 test cooks, editors, and cookware specialists. Our mission is to test recipes over and over again until we understand how and why they work and until we arrive at the "best" version.

We start the process of testing a recipe with a complete lack of preconceptions, which means that we accept no claim, no technique, and no recipe at face value. We simply assemble as many variations as possible, test a half-dozen of the most promising, and taste the results blind. We then construct our own recipe and continue to test it, varying ingredients, techniques, and cooking times until we reach a consensus. As we like to say in the test kitchen, "We make the mistakes so you don't have to." The result, we hope, is the best version of a particular recipe, but we realize that only you can be the final judge of our success (or failure). We use the same rigorous approach when we test equipment and taste ingredients.

All of this would not be possible without a belief that good cooking, much like good music, is based on a foundation of objective technique. Some people like spicy foods and others don't, but there is a right way to sauté, there is a best way to cook a pot roast, and there are measurable scientific principles involved in producing perfectly beaten, stable egg whites. Our ultimate goal is to investigate the fundamental principles of cooking to give you the techniques, tools, and ingredients you need to become a better cook. It is as simple as that.

To see what goes on behind the scenes at America's Test Kitchen, check out our social media channels for kitchen snapshots, exclusive content, video tips, and much more. You can watch us work (in our actual test kitchen) by tuning in to *America's Test Kitchen* or *Cook's Country from America's Test Kitchen* on public television or on our websites. Listen in to *America's Test Kitchen Radio* (ATKradio.com) on public radio to hear insights that illuminate the truth about real home cooking. Want to hone your cooking skills or finally learn how to bake—with an America's Test Kitchen test cook? Enroll in one of our online cooking classes. If the big questions about the hows and whys of food science are your passion, join our *Cook's Science* experts for a deep dive. However you choose to visit us, we welcome you into our kitchen, where you can stand by our side as we test our way to the best recipes in America.

FACEBOOK.COM/AMERICASTESTKITCHEN

TWITTER.COM/TESTKITCHEN

YOUTUBE.COM/AMERICASTESTKITCHEN

INSTAGRAM.COM/TESTKITCHEN

PINTEREST.COM/TESTKITCHEN

GOOGLE.COM/+AMERICASTESTKITCHEN

AMERICASTESTKITCHEN.COM

COOKSILLUSTRATED.COM

COOKSCOUNTRY.COM

COOKSSCIENCE.COM

ONLINECOOKINGSCHOOL.COM

introduction

Bread baking is experiencing a renaissance— and for good reason. The staff of life of civilizations, bread is one of the most ancient prepared foods, likely cooked in its primitive form, the flatbread, from the starch extracts from plant roots and over fire. It's possible that no other food has as rich a history. Today, American professional bakers are increasingly honoring this long history, making beautiful loaves in the tradition of the best European boulangeries. Artisan bakeries are appearing in towns everywhere and becoming welcome centers of communities.

And yet, despite this increased interest in and appetite for bread, baking bread at home can be intimidating and downright disappointing. The alchemy of bread baking is unlike that of any other kitchen project. Stitching together a loaf from the most basic of ingredients—flour, water, yeast, and salt—is satisfying, even relaxing. But the way these ingredients magically turn from a pale lump of dough into a beautifully browned loaf can seem like a total mystery. Not all attempts yield satisfying results and can leave you wondering whether it's really possible to achieve the results we love so much in bakery breads.

With this cookbook, our first devoted solely to bread, we sought to demystify both the art and the science of bread baking. We aggregated our years of experience and employed all of the resources of the test kitchen to exhaustively test loaves of all kinds. Our aim was to come up with an ideal selection of breads and the most foolproof process for making each of them. But bread baking has a unique feel and rhythm; you need to see the process from start to finish to feel comfortable working with dough. That's why we've created a fully illustrated handbook, with every recipe step clearly photographed—essentially a set of hands-on tutorials teaching you how to knead, shape, slash, and bake like a pro. This approach enables bakers of any skill level to produce artisan bakery–quality bread at home.

We've organized the chapters to build in complexity as they progress, so your confidence grows as you bake your way through the book. The first chapter lays down helpful basic methods that are used across all bread making. These workhorse breads also employ smart ways of achieving great results with simple means, such as using beer for fermented flavor or making terrific pizza in a skillet. Flex this skill set as you tackle more challenging recipes in later chapters. The complex-seeming Italian loaf, Pane Francese, in the Upping Your Game with Starters chapter, for example, builds on the same techniques you learned with the soft, tender, multipurpose Classic Italian Bread in the Starting from Scratch chapter, but adds a few flourishes— a sponge, a resting period called autolyse, and a set of folds—for a taste and texture characteristic of rustic breads. It won't be long before you are amazed at what you are able to produce.

Along the way, you'll discover a world of breads, each of which teaches valuable skills. Learn how to divide dough and form the knotted, rosette-shaped Kaiser Rolls. Incorporate butter and eggs into enriched breads like the towering holiday Panettone. Turn your home oven into a pizza oven, or get comfortable working with whole-wheat flour, even grinding your own wheat berries in a food processor for Rustic Wheat Berry Bread. For added assurance, troubleshooting sidebars accompany many of the breads, so you'll know how to avoid common pitfalls.

We hope you'll also take the time to read the book's front section, because it will set you up for success. We believe that understanding what makes bread recipes work will inform your baking, giving you reason to perform each move with purpose. We cover the core techniques like kneading and shaping here, but we also delve into the science and present it in a clear and intelligible way. Bread dough is a living thing, so you'll want to know what the yeast is doing, how gluten creates structure in bread, and what's really going on while your loaf's in the oven. This primer also walks you through how to stock your kitchen with the ingredients and equipment you need to bake the breads in this book.

Bread baking isn't all that enigmatic. As long as you're equipped with the right tools, this worthwhile craft can become a rewarding part of your routine and you can make bread magic in your own kitchen. Let America's Test Kitchen put first-rate bread in your oven and on your table.

understanding
bread

essential equipment

You can make a loaf of bread from start to finish with just your own two hands—but for first-rate results, you're going to want some equipment. Here's our guide to the essentials for making bakery-quality breads.

big ticket items

Instant-Read Thermometer (1) It's helpful to use an instant-read thermometer to check that breads are within a given temperature range before you pull them from the oven. A thermometer also comes in handy for taking the temperature of ingredients. A digital thermometer will tell you the temperature of your food almost immediately. Thermometers with long probes easily reach the center of a loaf. The **Thermo Works Thermapen Mk4** ($99) has every bell and whistle. (For more information on instant-read thermometers, see page 30.)

Stand Mixer (2) A stand mixer, with its hands-free operation, numerous attachments, and strong mixing arm, is a must if you plan on baking bread regularly. Heft matters, as does a strong motor that can knead stiff dough with ease. Our favorite stand mixer is the **KitchenAid Pro Line Series 7-Qt Bowl Lift Stand Mixer** ($549.95). Our best buy is the **KitchenAid Classic Plus Series 4.5-Quart Tilt-Head Stand Mixer** ($229.99). (For more information on stand mixers, see page 16.)

Food Processor (3) Though not necessary for loaves, a food processor brings together pizza dough in a flash. Look for a workbowl that has a capacity of at least 11 cups. With a powerful motor, responsive pulsing action, sharp blades, and a simple design, the **Cuisinart Custom 14 Food Processor** ($199.99) aced all our tests.

Digital Scale (4) Weighing your ingredients ensures consistent results. We prefer digital scales for their readability and precision. Look for one that has a large weight range and that can be "zeroed." The **OXO Good Grips 11 lb. Food Scale with Pull Out Display** ($49.99) has easy-to-read buttons, and its display can be pulled out from the platform when weighing bulky items.

Baking Stone (5) A ceramic baking stone conducts heat and transfers it evenly and steadily to the loaf, encouraging the development of a thick, crisp, nicely browned bottom crust. Look for a model made of clay or stone; it should be big enough to accommodate a large pizza. Our favorite is the **Old Stone Oven Pizza Baking Stone** ($38.69).

the pans we use

Rimmed Baking Sheet and Wire Cooling Rack (6) We bake a number of free-form loaves and buns on a rimmed baking sheet. A light-colored surface heats and browns breads evenly. You'll want more than one thick, sturdy **Wear-Ever Half Size Heavy Duty Sheet Pan (13 gauge) by Vollrath** ($23.25) on hand. (For more information on baking sheets, see page 27.) And you'll also want a wire cooling rack that fits inside for recipes like New York–Style Bagels (page 397), which we bake elevated on a rack. Even more important, cooling loaves on a wire rack allows air to circulate so the bread dries properly and retains a crisp crust. The **CIA Bakeware 12-Inch x 17-Inch Cooling Rack** ($15.95) is an essential.

Bundt Pan (7) Bundt pans turn out attractive sweet breads. Look for defined ridges, a 15-cup capacity, and nonstick, heavyweight cast aluminum. The **Nordic Ware Platinum Collection Anniversary Bundt Pan** ($26.95) creates evenly brown breads that release perfectly.

13 by 9-inch Baking Dish (7) Thick, tempered glass dishes retain heat to ensure deep, even browning on rolls. The **Pyrex Basics 3 Quart Glass Oblong Baking Dish** ($13.95) is sturdy, dishwasher-safe, and scratch-resistant.

13 by 9-inch Baking Pan (7) Sweet treats won't stick to these straight-sided nonstick pans. The **Williams-Sonoma Goldtouch Nonstick Rectangular Cake Pan** ($32.95) produces uniformly golden baked goods.

9-inch Round Cake Pan (7) We use a cake pan for deep-dish pizza, rolls, and sweet loaves. Look for pans with 2-inch-tall straight sides. We like light-toned pans for cake, but you should buy dark, nonstick pans for bread; they radiate more heat for browned breads. Our favorite is the **Chicago Metallic Non-Stick 9″ Round Cake Pan** ($10.97).

Dutch Oven (8) The humid environment created in a covered Dutch oven helps to produce a dramatically open crumb structure and a shiny, crisp crust on breads. The **Le Creuset 7¼-Quart Round French Oven** ($349.99) is the gold standard of Dutch ovens.

Pullman Loaf Pan (9) This pan has a slide-on lid and produces a squared-off loaf with a compact crumb. We bake our versatile Pain de Mie (page 90) and our Pumpernickel (page 299) in a Pullman pan. We use the **USA Pan 13 by 4-inch Pullman Loaf Pan & Cover** ($33.95). (Avoid pans made from uncoated steel.)

8½ x 4½-inch Loaf Pan (9) We prefer 8½ x 4½-inch loaf pans to 9 x 5-inch pans; they produce tall loaves with rounder tops. Light-colored aluminum finishes yield pale loaves, while superdark finishes overbrown bread. The **Williams-Sonoma Goldtouch Nonstick Loaf Pan** ($21) is just right.

Cast-Iron Skillet (10) A cast-iron skillet creates crisp crusts on flatbreads and cornbread. You'll never replace the preseasoned **Lodge Classic Cast-Iron Skillet**. You'll want both the 10-inch ($15.92) and 12-inch ($33.31) pans.

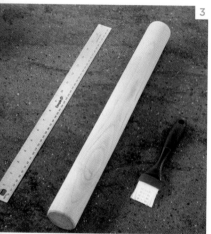

Liquid Measuring Cups (1) It's helpful to have multiple sizes of liquid measuring cups for bread baking. Whisk together your liquid ingredients right in the cup before mixing. The industry-standard **Pyrex Measuring Cup** is unbeatable. We use the 2-cup ($5.99), 4-cup ($11.99), and 8-cup ($12.90) sizes in this book.

Dry Measuring Cups (1) You should be weighing the bulk of your ingredients, but you'll still need a set of measuring cups for small quantities of dry ingredients. Look for heavy, well-constructed, evenly weighted, stainless-steel models, with easy-to-read measurement markings and long, straight handles. We use the very accurate **Amco Houseworks Professional Performance 4-Piece Measuring Cup Set** ($14.95).

Measuring Spoons (1) We prefer heavy, well-constructed steel measuring spoons with long, sturdy, well-designed handles. Choose deep bowls; shallow bowls allow more liquid to spill with the shake of an unsteady hand. **The Cuisipro Stainless Steel Measuring Spoons Set** ($11.95) is our recommended set.

Oven Thermometer (2) It's common for ovens to run hot or cold. The most reliable way to know the exact temperature of your oven is to use a thermometer. The **CDN Pro Accurate Oven Thermometer** ($8.70) has a clear display and attaches to the oven rack securely. Note that it is manufactured in two factories, so your model may not look exactly like the picture.

Ruler (3) A ruler is helpful for measuring how high a proofing dough has risen and for cutting dough into pieces of a certain size. Stainless steel, not wood, is best because it's easy to clean. An 18-inch ruler will handle all kitchen tasks.

Rolling Pin (3) There are many styles of rolling pins: We like the classic French-style wood rolling pins without handles. These pins come straight and tapered. We tend to reach for straight pins, which make achieving even dough thickness and rolling out larger disks easy. The **J.K. Adams Plain Maple Rolling Dowel** ($13.95) has a gentle weight and a slightly textured surface for less sticking.

Pastry Brush (3) We use a pastry brush to paint loaves with egg wash before they enter the oven or to finish baked breads with melted butter. Our favorite pastry brush, the **OXO Good Grips Silicone Pastry Brush** ($6.99), is silicone and far surpasses those with natural bristles, as it is heat-resistant and easy to clean. It sports perforated flaps that trap liquid, and an angled head to reach tight spots.

Bench Scraper (4) This basic tool is handy for transferring bread dough from one surface to another and for cutting dough into pieces. Our winner is the **Dexter-Russell 6″ Dough Cutter/Scraper—Sani Safe Series** ($7.01). It has a comfortable handle, and the deeply beveled edge cuts through dough quickly.

Bowl Scraper (4) The best way to remove or fold sticky dough is with a bowl scraper. This handheld spatula is curved, with enough grip to scrape the bowl clean and enough rigidity to move heavy dough easily. Our favorite models are made of contoured silicone covering a metal insert, like the **iSi Basics Silicone Scraper Spatula** ($5.99).

Serrated Knife (5) You need a good knife to make it all the way through your loaves, from crust to crumb. The well-balanced **Wüsthof Classic Bread Knife, 10 inches** ($89.95), has deeply tapered pointed serrations that slice through bread with ease. (For more information on serrated knives, see page 32.)

Pizza Cutters (5) Wheel-like pizza cutters do the obvious—cut pizza into slices. But they're also helpful for quickly and evenly slicing dough into pieces or strips with clean edges. The clean-cutting **OXO Good Grips 4″ Pizza Wheel** ($12.99) is comfortable to hold and allows for a powerful grip. The blade is 4 inches tall, so it rolls right over towering crusts with ease.

specialty items

Towel-Lined Colander (6) Bakers achieve the symmetrical round loaves known as boules by transferring the dough to shallow woven baskets called *bannetons* (or *brotforms*) for the last rising step before baking. (For more information on bannetons, see page 37.) In this book, we get the same results by using a 5-quart colander (measuring about 11 inches in diameter and 4 inches deep) that has been lined with a linen dish towel to prevent sticking.

Couche (7) To proof artisan-style breads, bakers use a *couche*, made from heavy linen, which keeps the dough's shape intact and its surface uniformly dry as it proofs and rises. Only 100 percent linen cloths will release the dough without sticking or tugging. Our favorite is the **San Francisco Baking Institute 18″ Linen Canvas (Couche)** ($8). (For more information on couches, see page 37.)

Flipping Board (7) To move baguettes from the couche to the oven, professional bakers use a flipping board. A homemade substitute, made by taping two 16 by 4-inch pieces of heavy cardboard together with packaging tape, works equally well. We use the **Baguette Flipping Board** ($12) sold by Breadtopia.

Lame (7) You'll need a curved-blade *lame* to produce the almond-shaped slashes on rustic breads and baguettes. It approaches the dough at a low angle to create a cut with a raised flap. Our favorite is the **Breadtopia Bread Lame** ($9.50).

Pizza Peel (7) A peel is a wide, paddle-like board or metal spatula with a long handle that's useful for sliding pizza and free-form breads into and out of a hot oven. Metal baking peels are particularly easy to clean and store.

Lava Rocks (8) We pour boiling water over disposable pans full of preheated lava rocks, which absorb and retain heat, to create a steamy environment in the oven that helps rustic breads develop a crisp crust. You can find these irregularly shaped rocks, which are used for gas grills, at many hardware stores. (For more information on lava rocks, see page 37.)

Disposable Pans (8) We use disposable pie plates to hold lava rocks. We also use disposable roasting pans to cover loaves baked on a baking stone when we want to trap steam for a thick, crisp crust.

the bread baker's pantry

Once you start baking bread regularly, you'll always want the basics on hand. We've included essential ingredients, plus some that will take your breads to the next level.

flour

Bread starts with the grain, so it's helpful to know what flour to use and when. The main difference among varieties is the amount of protein they contain. More protein leads to more gluten development, which, in turn, translates to chewier bread. For all flours, we prefer unbleached to bleached because bleached flour can carry off-flavors. (Most cake flours, which we do not use in bread baking, however, are bleached.) You can store flour in an airtight container in your pantry for up to one year. Here are the flours we use in this book.

All-Purpose Flour is the most versatile variety. It has a moderate protein content (10 to 11.7 percent, depending on the brand) and is good when you want a relatively tender, soft crumb, like for quick breads, rolls, and sweet breads. We develop our recipes with easy-to-find Gold Medal Unbleached All-Purpose Flour (10.5 percent protein). Pillsbury All-Purpose Unbleached Flour (also 10.5 percent protein) offers comparable results. If you use an all-purpose flour with a higher protein content

(such as King Arthur Unbleached All-Purpose Flour, with 11.7 percent protein) in recipes that call for all-purpose flour, the results may be a bit drier and chewier.

However, there are some recipes for which the higher protein content of King Arthur Unbleached All-Purpose Flour is desirable, such as Croissants (page 403). When we made them with regular all-purpose flour, the dough tore; when we made them with bread flour, the dough was hard to roll. King Arthur all-purpose flour is the perfect compromise. If you cannot find King Arthur all-purpose flour for recipes that call for it, use bread flour.

Bread Flour has a high protein content (12 to 14 percent), which ensures strong gluten development and thus a chewy texture. Because of its structure-building properties, we use it for many of the breads in this book. You cannot substitute all-purpose flour in these recipes; the bread will not be able to support an airy, chewy crumb. We use King Arthur Unbleached Bread Flour in the test kitchen.

Whole-Wheat Flour has a distinctive flavor and texture because it is made from the entire wheat berry unlike white flours, which are ground solely from the endosperm. Whole-wheat flour has a high protein content (about 13 percent), but it behaves differently than white flour, and it can make breads dense. We rely on a combination of white and whole-wheat flours. We use King Arthur Premium Whole Wheat Flour in the test kitchen. Whole-wheat flour contains more fat than refined flours and goes rancid more quickly; store it in the freezer and bring it to room temperature before using it. (For more information on whole-wheat flour, see page 34.)

Rye Flour has an earthy, slightly tangy flavor. It comes in white or light, medium, whole grain, and pumpernickel, and each produces a different bread. The darker the rye flour, the more bran that's been left in after milling. We use light or medium and pumpernickel in this book. Rye flour is low in one of the partial proteins necessary for developing gluten, so you need to cut it with some white flour to avoid dense bread. Store rye flour like whole-wheat flour.

Cornmeal comes in many different varieties. Because the texture and flavor varies, it's important to use the cornmeal variety that a recipe calls for. For example, our Southern-Style Skillet Cornbread (page 44) requires fine or medium stone-ground cornmeal. While coarse stone-ground cornmeal has great texture and strong corn flavor, it does not soften and can make bread gritty.

Semolina Flour is a golden-colored flour that is made by coarsely grinding the endosperm of durum wheat. This Italian flour gives our Sicilian-Style Thick-Crust Pizza (page 192) a creamy crumb. Its coarse texture makes it good for dusting a pizza peel.

Durum Flour is the by-product of semolina production. *Durum* means "hard" in Latin; it's very high in protein, but not in gluten-forming proteins. Like semolina flour, it's associated with pasta. Fine, powdery, and flavorful, the flour is high in beta-carotene and gives bread a golden hue. Be sure to use durum flour for our Durum Bread (page 348); semolina flour gives it a gummy crumb.

chemical leaveners

Quick breads rise with chemical leaveners. There are two varieties, and they can be used alone or in combination.

Baking Soda is an alkali and therefore requires an acidic ingredient in the batter or dough, such as buttermilk, in order to produce carbon dioxide. The leavening action happens right after mixing, so you should bake right away. In addition to leavening, baking soda also promotes browning.

Baking Powder is a mixture of baking soda, a dry acid, and double-dried cornstarch. The cornstarch absorbs moisture and prevents the premature production of gas. Baking powder works twice—when it first comes in contact with a liquid, and again in response to heat. Once its container is opened, it will lose its effectiveness after six months. Our favorite powder is Argo Double Acting Baking Powder.

yeast

Yeast comes in two forms: fresh and dry. We don't use fresh in the test kitchen, as it is highly perishable. There are two types of dry yeast: active dry yeast and instant yeast. We prefer to use instant yeast in our recipes. Store any yeast in the refrigerator or freezer to slow deterioration.

Active dry yeast is treated with heat, which kills the outermost cells. Therefore, it must be proofed, or dissolved in liquid with some sugar, before use. Proofing sloughs off the dead cells and renders the yeast active. To substitute active dry yeast for instant yeast in a recipe, use 25 percent more of it to compensate for the greater quantity of inactive yeast cells. And you'll need to dissolve active dry yeast in a portion of the water from the recipe, heated to 110 degrees. Then, let it stand for 5 minutes before adding it to the remaining wet ingredients.

Instant yeast (also called rapid-rise yeast) is our choice in the test kitchen because it doesn't need to be proofed and can be added directly to the dry ingredients—the result of undergoing a gentler drying process that does not destroy the outer cells. We have also found that it yields breads with a cleaner flavor than those made with active dry because it doesn't contain any dead yeast cells. Storing yeast in the refrigerator or freezer will slow deterioration. To substitute instant yeast for active dry in a recipe, use 25 percent less of it.

liquids

The proportion of liquid in a bread dough corresponds to how hydrated, or wet, it is. Wetter doughs tend to feature irregular holes and a pleasing chew; drier doughs have a tighter crumb structure and a soft chew. (For more information on bread hydration, see page 13.) The type of liquid you use also affects the loaf's structure.

Water is the default liquid in bread baking. When it mixes with flour, the proteins in the flour hydrate and begin to form gluten.

Milk features in a lot of our recipes. The fat in the milk tenderizes the crumb and can weaken the gluten structure; the proteins can contribute to the browning of the loaf.

Beer is, in some ways, like liquid bread: The flavor compounds in beer are similar to those in a bread dough starter. Therefore, its addition can give your bread the more complex flavor of one made with a starter. We use mild-flavored lager, like Budweiser; the fermentation process it goes through allows the bready flavors to come forward.

fats

Fat isn't just for flavor. The presence of fat—even just a tablespoon—can affect the crumb of your bread. When you add fat in large enough amounts, it coats the flour proteins, making them less able to form a strong gluten network; that means tender, less open bread. Here are the fats we use to enrich our breads.

Butter is a must in most enriched bread recipes. We use unsalted butter. (The salt amount in different brands of butter varies; plus, salted butters have a higher water content.) Most unsalted butter contains 81 to 82 percent fat; some European-style butters contain 83 to 86 percent fat (and therefore less water). While this difference isn't noticeable enough in most breads to warrant splurging on premium butter, we recommend it for our Croissants (page 403) and Kouign Amann (page 408). The higher fat content makes the dough easier to manipulate and results in superior layering.

Oil is usually added in small quantities—a tablespoon or so—to add extensibility to doughs and to tenderize breads that don't need to be rich in flavor. Neutral-tasting oil, such as vegetable oil, adds tenderness without changing the dough's flavor. Extra-virgin olive oil, on the other hand, can give bread a slightly earthy flavor, which is great in certain applications. For breads that are baked at superhot temperatures, especially flatbreads, a good amount of oil in dough can also result in a crisp crust: the oil essentially fries the dough in the oven for our Red Pepper Coques (page 208).

Vegetable Shortening is a solid fat that contains no water. As a result, it coats the proteins in flour even more effectively than does butter. We use it in our Fluffy Dinner Rolls (page 63) for superior tenderness, though its flat flavor needs to be bolstered with butter.

eggs

Typically used in sweet doughs, eggs add density to breads. The yolks give doughs richness, and the whites contribute extra structure. We also brush a lot of our breads with a mixture of egg and water (with a pinch of salt). The protein in the white browns the loaf's exterior, and the fat in the yolk makes the crust shiny. The salt in the wash doesn't just give it flavor; it denatures the proteins, making the wash more fluid and easier to brush evenly and gently over delicate doughs.

salt

In bread baking, where you're working only with flour, water, yeast, and salt, the amount of salt you use really impacts flavor. Unless otherwise stated, we use inexpensive table salt in our bread recipes because it is fine-grained and thus dissolves easily. But salt isn't just for flavor; it actually strengthens the gluten network in dough to help make chewy bread. (For more information on the role of salt, see page 12.)

sugar

Many bread recipes call for adding a couple tablespoons of sugar to add subtle sweetness and to help with browning. The most common sugar choices in bread are granulated, for a cleaner flavor, and honey, for an earthier flavor. Note that liquid honey can contribute to the hydration level of the bread dough.

the world of breads

Bread baking has its own language. We talk about the flavor and the texture of a finished loaf of bread in the context of its two main parts: the crumb (the interior of the loaf) and the crust (the exterior of the loaf). The crumb constitutes the bulk of the bread and can be either lean and chewy (the result of using just flour, water, salt, and yeast) or enriched so that is has a more luxurious flavor and soft texture (from the addition of dairy, butter, and/or eggs). The crumb can be tight or closed, meaning it lacks interior holes if the dough contains a relatively low amount of liquid, or it can be open, meaning it features larger and sometimes irregular holes if the dough contains a relatively high amount of liquid. The crust—the browned sheath that encases the crumb—varies across breads as well. It can be soft, golden, and barely detectable, or it can be dark brown and satisfyingly crunchy. We cover a world of breads in this book; below are the main categories and details on their crumbs and crusts.

Quick Breads (1) These easy-to-make loaves rely on chemical leaveners and are often baked in a loaf pan. They require just some hand-stirring, as the goal is to avoid developing a lot of gluten, which can make quick breads tough. They are tender from the addition of lots of butter or oil, and have a cakey closed crumb and no defined crust. We often eat quick breads, like our Quick Cheese Bread (page 41), which features pockets of gooey cheddar, as a snack.

Sandwich Loaves (2) Sandwich bread is yeasted and typically features a soft, tight crumb, as it's often conditioned with tenderizing ingredients. Think about the perfect white sandwich loaf, mild in flavor and a little pillowy, like our American Sandwich Bread (page 86). Baked at a low to moderate temperature, sandwich breads have a thin crust. They're typically baked in a loaf pan, but there are also free-form versions. There are also textural exceptions, such as our Spicy Olive Bread (page 123), which has a little more chew and is more rustic.

Rolls and Buns (3) These small shaped breads often accompany breakfast if they're sweet, or dinner if they're savory. With the exception of our Rustic Dinner Rolls (page 129), which have the crumb structure of artisan bread, rolls are typically tender with a closed crumb and an unassuming golden brown crust. Some are intricately shaped, like Kaiser Rolls (page 151). They can be richly plush, like the butter-packed Parker House Rolls (page 141), or they can be leaner and more milky-tasting, like our Fluffy Dinner Rolls (page 63).

Rustic Loaves (4) The class of breads you find at an artisan bakery are known as rustic loaves. They contain little or no fat and lots of water, and they develop a lot of gluten to support large air pockets. A good rustic loaf has a thick but crisp outer crust that breaks pleasingly to the chewy, complex crumb. Rustic loaves sometimes incorporate a sponge or even a natural starter, like our Sourdough Bread (page 359), for a more open texture and a tangier aroma.

Flatbreads and Pizzas (5) These breads are all about the crust, and they're often meals in bread form. Though there's a lot of variation across the category, these international breads are often rolled thin, sometimes topped, and typically baked on a baking stone. Other times they're pressed into a rimmed baking sheet. Some styles, like focaccia, sport large holes, but the crumb structure is often more even rather than irregular. Thick or rectangular pizzas and flatbreads can be almost cakey—a desirable quality in our Sicilian-Style Thick-Crust Pizza (page 192)—while others are chewy on the inside and supercrisp and charred on the outside, like Thin-Crust Pizza (page 180). Still other flatbreads don't have much of a crumb at all, like Flour Tortillas (page 71).

Enriched Breads (6) A bread that is augmented with butter, sugar, eggs, and/or dairy is considered enriched. This category includes some sweetened, rich, everyday breads like Portuguese Sweet Bread (page 258) and some downright luxurious loaves, like No-Knead Brioche (page 98), which has a soft, tender crumb and a golden hue from the addition of lots of butter and egg yolks. These breads aren't very chewy, as the amount of fat in them impedes gluten development. Their crust is thin and soft.

Laminated Breads (7) Often more like pastry—think Croissants (page 403)—than bread, a laminated bread is one composed of many alternating sheets of fat and dough, which bake into airy breads with many layers. The most traditional way to achieve this is to form a square block of butter that you wrap with a yeasted flour-and-water dough before rolling out and turning multiple times. In the oven, the water in the butter turns to steam, lifting apart the layers of dough, while the fat in the butter provides flavor. The concept of layering fat and dough is similar for recipes like Mallorcas (page 230), where you brush the dough with melted butter before rolling it to separate the layers with fat.

1

2

4

5

6

3

7

bread baking, at a glance

Every yeasted bread is unique, yet virtually all follow the same progression of steps that take it from raw ingredients to finished loaves and rolls. Think of these steps as the key movements of a dance. As you touch, observe, and manipulate more and different doughs, you'll become more in tune with the rhythm of bread baking, and these core steps will become second nature. Each new bread will introduce new twists and flourishes to a pattern you know well and can execute fluidly, giving you a lifetime of better baking. Here, we spell out the essentials of these steps; in the pages that follow, we'll break each one down into more detail, so you're armed with all of our test kitchen knowledge.

The step that gets it all started is **mixing (1)**. This is where you combine your dry and wet goods in the stand mixer to create a shaggy amalgamation of ingredients. This rough mass of dough then becomes smooth during **kneading (2)**. You increase the mixer speed and knead until the dough is elastic, signaling that it has developed an adequate gluten structure. At this point, the dough is ready for the **first rise (3)**. It is during this fermentation period that the yeast creates carbon dioxide bubbles that cause the bread to expand. Once the dough grows to the size indicated in the recipe (usually the dough doubles in size), **dividing and shaping (4)** takes place. You start by pressing down on the dough to deflate it. Then you either divide it (for rolls, buns, or multiple loaves) or shape it whole. The shape will depend on the type of bread you are making; here, we're featuring a basic round boule, which you roll between your cupped hands on a counter until a ball forms. Forming a taut shape ensures an even, lofty final loaf. Then you rest the formed loaf again for a **second rise (5)**. The yeast is redistributed during shaping, so the loaf achieves more volume at this point before baking, when the hot oven causes the bread to expand one more time to its final height. You can test that the loaf is done rising with your knuckle. During **baking (6)**, starches gelatinize to set the crumb, and sugars and proteins caramelize to create a browned, crusty loaf. But the process doesn't end here; there's **cooling and storing (7)**. Most breads must cool fully before you slice and eat them so that the crumb sets to the perfect texture. And if you don't eat the loaf the day you make it, there are guidelines for storing it to ensure that it maintains the best texture.

1 mixing, in depth

At the core of bread baking are the basic ingredients, which begin to morph and change as soon as they meet: The flour hydrates, the yeast awakens, and the gluten proteins that will eventually give bread structure unravel and come together. Bread recipes are carefully formulated. So to start the mixing process, you need to gather and measure your ingredients with care. We forgo measuring cups and spoons (except for ingredients that are measured in small amounts, like salt and yeast, or for mix-ins like raisins and nuts) and use a digital kitchen scale. The ratio of flour to water in your recipe greatly impacts the end result, so accuracy is crucial. Weigh the dry ingredients into one vessel (usually the bowl of the stand mixer) and the wet ingredients into another (usually a liquid measuring cup). Whisk together the dry ingredients to blend thoroughly; do the same for the wet.

Once you weigh and whisk your wet and dry ingredients, it's time to bring them together: We almost always start our breads in the stand mixer fitted with the dough hook attachment. This c- or s-shaped tool can grasp stiffer bread dough, engaging it in a motion that stretches and folds it. While mixing on low speed, slowly stream the wet ingredients into the dry ingredients and mix until a cohesive dough starts to form and no dry flour remains. This will take about 2 minutes. You should scrape the mixer bowl with a rubber spatula as needed to ensure that everything is incorporated.

We add the wet ingredients to the dry rather than the reverse because it prevents pockets of flour from forming and a messy, crusted mixing bowl. Why mix on low instead of just cranking up the mixer and getting it done faster? Kneading is all about building structure, but a more gentle approach is necessary to make sure the ingredients are well distributed and hydrated before that can happen. Mixing also allows the proteins in the flour (more on them in "Kneading, In Depth" on page 14) to become friendly with each other before they cross-link into sheets of gluten. A cohesive but shaggy product signals that the dough has been agitated just enough before kneading.

mixing dough

1 Whisk together the dry ingredients in the bowl of a stand mixer.

2 Whisk together the wet ingredients in a 4-cup liquid measuring cup.

3 Using the dough hook and mixing on low speed, slowly add the wet ingredients to the dry ingredients.

4 Mix until a cohesive dough starts to form and no dry flour remains.

science corner
salt: not just for flavor

Forget to season a dish, and it might taste flat; forget to add salt to dough, and the bread will be not only tasteless but likely dense and crumbly. Salt strengthens gluten; without it, the gluten structure cannot support the carbon dioxide bubbles that expand inside the dough.

don't forget!

DON'T ADD FLOUR The dough should look cohesive but shaggy; it will smooth out during kneading. It's too early to determine if the dough is too sticky, and adding extra flour could compromise the final texture of the loaf.

the science of hydration

Of course you need a liquid to transform flour into dough. And in bread baking, sometimes wetter is better: The more water (or other liquid) in a dough—that is, the more hydrated the dough is—the stronger and more extensible the gluten strands. If the gluten strands are strong and extensible, they can support the starch granules and gas bubbles that hydrate and swell as the dough rises and bakes, giving you an airier bread with good chew. During baking, the water within the dough turns to steam, creating hollow pockets as moisture rushes to escape. Extra water also creates a looser dough, which allows the steam bubbles to expand more easily. In drier dough, gas bubbles have a harder time forming and are more likely to collapse. Getting those gas bubbles to hold their shape until the dough has risen and set in the oven is the key to creating an open, airy crumb.

calculating baker's percentages

Before you can accurately determine how hydrated a bread dough is, you'll need to understand baker's percentages. Professional bakers rely on this method to formulate their recipes. Once you understand them, you'll be able to get a feel for what your dough and baked bread will be like before you even mix them. (They also make scaling recipes up or down a simple matter of multiplication or division.) Baker's percentages present the quantity of each ingredient as a percentage by the weight of the amount of flour, which is always set at 100 percent.

The most important part of a baker's percentage is the weight of the liquid relative to the weight of the flour—the hydration. Sandwich-bread dough, with a typical 60 percent hydration (the weight of the liquid is 60 percent of the weight of the flour), for example, yields a loaf with a tighter crumb, whereas the 80 percent hydration level of rustic breads (the weight of the liquid is 80 percent of the weight of the flour) is responsible for its airy crumb and large, irregular holes.

To calculate the hydration of a recipe, first weigh the flour and liquid. Divide the weight of the liquid by the weight of the flour and then multiply the result by 100. For example, a recipe containing 1¼ cups of water (10 ounces) and 3 cups of all-purpose flour (15 ounces) will have a 67 percent ([10 ÷ 15] × 100 = 67) hydration level, indicating a moderately airy crumb. To find the baker's percentage of other ingredients, follow this procedure, weighing the ingredient, dividing it by the total flour weight, and multiplying by 100.

visualizing hydration levels

We were curious to see what would happen if we took hydration levels to the extreme: Our recipe for Classic Italian Bread (page 55) has a 67 percent hydration level and features modest-size holes. We made a version of it in which we lowered the hydration to 50 percent and another in which we increased the hydration to 80 percent. The 50 percent hydrated loaf had a tight, fine crumb, was dense, and showed little spread or expansion. The 80 percent hydrated loaf, on the other hand, hardly rose, spreading out instead of up, and it featured a loose, open crumb with large, irregular holes. Too much liquid in a recipe can actually dilute and weaken the gluten it typically works so well to build, hindering a bread's ability to rise.

Too dry (50 percent hydration)

Just right (67 percent hydration)

Too wet (80 percent hydration)

2 kneading, in depth

Part of the wonder of bread baking is how many changes in the dough happen without the cook even touching it. It must have seemed like magic to early bakers to watch bread rise and expand of its own accord. But there is one major mechanical step that allows this magic to happen: kneading. Proper kneading incorporates air, distributes ingredients, and, most important, develops gluten, which gives yeasted bread chew. As we learned, mixing starts the process by creating a weak, disorganized matrix of gluten proteins. Then, kneading does the bulk of the work, the mechanical action straightening out these proteins and aligning them so they can cross-link into a strong gluten network. This gluten structure is key: It allows bread to expand without bursting. (For more information, see "The Science of Gluten" on page 18.)

You can knead most bread doughs by hand or in a stand mixer, and we've detailed both techniques. While hand kneading can be a gratifying process, we recommend using a stand mixer with the dough hook attachment for this task. Not only is it easier—the mixer does all the work—but you're more likely to get good results if you use your mixer. Kneading dough by hand can be messy, and many home cooks add a lot of extra flour, which can compromise the texture of the baked loaf. On a practical level, it takes up to 25 minutes—and some well-developed forearm muscles—to knead dough fully by hand, and just about 8 minutes in the stand mixer with the dough hook. However, if you do not own a stand mixer, you can still make a good loaf of bread from most doughs. (We have indicated throughout this book when a dough is just too wet, sticky, or enriched to be kneaded by hand.) The trick is to use a rhythmic, gentle motion that stretches and massages the dough.

kneading in a food processor

For many bread recipes we would caution against the rough treatment of a food processor, which can tear apart the strands of gluten that give bread structure and the ability to rise. But for pizzas, flatbreads, and other doughs where we want chew but the structure is less important, we like to put it to use. Many of these doughs would require 15 to 20 minutes of traditional kneading in the stand mixer to become a shiny, elastic mass—but less than 2 minutes in the food processor. The only exceptions in this category are extremely wet doughs with a hydration level of more than 75 percent, doughs with very large yields. Here's how to ensure the best results.

use metal blades Many food processors come with dull plastic blades meant to mimic the kneading action of a stand mixer. But we found they tend to drag the dough or leave it stuck to the sides of the bowl, out of reach of the stubby blades. A sharp slicing action is essential to forming dough quickly, as the longer you process, the more you risk overheating the dough.

use ice water The forceful action of a food processor creates friction, pumping a lot of heat into dough. To counteract this effect, it's important to use ice water to create a final dough with a temperature around 75 degrees. (Lower temperatures mean the dough will take longer to ferment; higher temperatures can kill yeast.)

kneading in a stand mixer

1 Just after increasing the mixer speed to medium-low, the dough will lack form and will stick to the sides of the bowl.

2 After 4 minutes, the dough will still be tacky, but it will start to pull away from the sides of the bowl and look more uniform.

3 After 8 minutes, the dough will pull away from the sides of the bowl and have a compact form.

4 Knead the dough by hand for 30 seconds to form a smooth, round ball.

kneading by hand

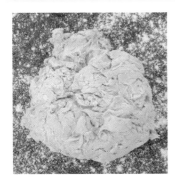

1 After mixing the ingredients, transfer the shaggy dough to a lightly floured counter and shape it into a rough ball.

2 Start each stroke by gently pressing the dough down and away from you with the heel of your hand.

3 Lift the edge of the dough that's farthest away from you and fold the dough in half toward you.

4 Lightly sprinkle the dough with flour as needed to coax the dough into a smooth mass. After about 4 minutes, the dough should look smooth.

5 Press the dough forward again. After about 8 minutes it should begin to turn smooth and elastic.

6 Repeat folding and pressing until the dough is smooth and elastic and forms a ball. This should take 15 to 25 minutes.

stand mixers

A stand mixer is one of the most expensive appliances in your kitchen, but if you're going to bake bread at home regularly, it's something you'll want within your reach. Because of its importance, we've done some of our most extensive testing in the test kitchen with stand mixers so you can make a sound investment. Here's what we've learned.

planetary action is vital Mixers with a stationary bowl and a single mixing arm that uses planetary action work much better than those with a rotating bowl and two stationary beaters because they are much less likely to get clogged up when mixing stiff doughs.

large, squat bowls are best If the bowl is too tall, small batches of dough don't get mixed properly, and scraping down the sides of the bowl is difficult. A wide, shallow bowl is ideal. A mixer that holds less than 4½ quarts is not large enough to hold a batch of bread dough.

consider a bowl lift Tilt-head mixers are fine, but the prolonged running of the motor can cause the latch locking down the tilt head on some mixers to stop working over time.

Our favorite stand mixer is the **Pro Line Series 7-Qt Bowl Lift Stand Mixer from KitchenAid.** This powerful, smartly designed machine handles batches of stiff dough without flinching. We like the bowl-lift design and large vertical bowl handle that aids pouring. At $549.95, this mixer isn't cheap, but it's a worthy investment. Thanks to its power, heft, simple operation, and relatively wallet-friendly price, the smaller sibling, the **KitchenAid Classic Plus Series 4.5-Quart Tilt-Head Stand Mixer** ($229.99), earns Best Buy status.

KitchenAid
Pro Line

KitchenAid
Classic Plus

when is the dough properly kneaded?

There are two ways to determine when you've kneaded dough long enough so that the gluten is fully developed.

1 Does the dough clear the sides of the bowl? If not, keep going. The dough on the left is still sticking slightly. The dough on the right clears the sides of the bowl.

Keep kneading · · · · · · · · · Just right

2 Is the dough elastic? If not, keep going. The dough on the right can be pulled like a rubber band without snapping and springing back into place. The dough on the left lacks elasticity and breaks when pulled, signaling that the gluten proteins have not yet cross-linked into a strong network.

Keep kneading · · · · · · · · · Just right

when should you add more flour to dough?

Sticky dough can be difficult to work with and may require the addition of a small amount of flour to tighten up. But stickiness isn't always bad; wet, high-hydration doughs for rustic breads and sweet doughs enriched with lots of butter or eggs will naturally be more tacky than sandwich bread or dinner roll doughs. Most doughs require the addition of more flour if they fail to clear the sides of the bowl in their kneading time. To ensure you get the proper dough consistency and bread texture, mix in additional flour slowly, 1 tablespoon at a time. And never add more than ¼ cup of extra flour to a recipe.

the no-knead method

While we've outlined the benefits of kneading, you can actually make good bread without this mechanical step with our chewy, open-crumbed, thick-crusted Almost No-Knead Bread (page 52). (We also forgo kneading in our No-Knead Brioche [page 98] and our Rosemary Focaccia [page 353].) Kneading is replaced with a very wet dough and an overnight resting period, which produces gluten slowly—and without any work. Just before baking, the dough is kneaded by hand for less than a minute (just 10 to 15 times), shaped, and baked in a preheated Dutch oven. Because of the long rising time, just ¼ teaspoon yeast is required in our Almost No-Knead Bread recipe. While this amount produces sufficient rise, it doesn't contribute much flavor. Our recipe relies on beer and vinegar to amp up the malty, yeasty flavors in the bread. Try this unique recipe when you want an easy, hands-off way to achieve artisan-style bread.

what happens if you overknead dough?

Proper kneading is essential for developing gluten in doughs, but there can be too much of a good thing. Overkneading causes the dough to become warm and to turn from a wheaty tan color to a dull white, producing baked loaves with a sickly pallor and expired flavors. If the dough is kneaded too long, the action of a stand mixer's dough hook creates too much heat through friction and also kneads excessive amounts of air into the dough, bleaching it of flavor and color in a process called oxidation. Once your dough clears the sides of the bowl and feels smooth and elastic, stop kneading.

don't forget!

DON'T CRANK UP THE MIXER SPEED The motors of even the best home stand mixers can burn out if they're kneading heavy bread dough at too high a speed; plus, kneading at a high speed makes it easy to overknead or rip the gluten network.

SCRAPE DOWN THE BOWL AND HOOK If the whole mass of dough doesn't engage with the mixer attachment, it won't be properly kneaded. Further, if the dough seems to ride up the dough hook instead of staying in the bowl, you'll want to scrape down the hook.

KNEAD BY HAND This final 30 seconds of hand kneading forms the dough into a smooth, round ball for rising.

the science of gluten

what is gluten exactly?

Gluten is the protein developed in bread making that gives bread chew. This elastic protein is formed when two partial proteins present in wheat flour, glutenin and gliadin, bond. Glutenin provides dough with strength, while gliadin provides stretch. Glutenin and gliadin come in contact with water during mixing, in a process called hydration. Moistening the proteins allows them to unwind and become flexible. Then, through mixing, they begin to link up with one another to form long, elastic chains of gluten. Finally, through prolonged kneading, the proteins are aligned and continue to cross-link until the chains combine to form a membrane-like gluten network. Here's an easy way to look at it: Imagine these proteins as bundled-up balls of yarn that need to be unwound and tied together into one longer piece that's then sewn into a wider sheet. In their balled-up state they can't be tied together; first you have to untangle and straighten them. Liquid does the untangling, mixing ties the proteins together, and kneading sews them into a sheet.

why is gluten important?

A strong gluten network provides dough with structure to expand. Starch granules in the flour swell when hydrated, while yeast creates gas bubbles; both of these stretch the network, and it traps the air—much like a balloon—so that the bread develops an airy crumb. Gluten's ability to stretch corresponds with its ability to give bread chew.

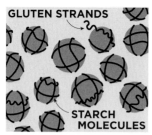

Protein strands glutenin and gliadin wrap around starch granules in flour.

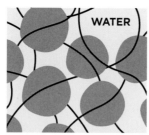

In the presence of water, the strands unwind and link to form a network of gluten.

what does gluten look like?

In the below photos, we isolated gluten in low-protein cake flour and in high-protein bread flour. We did this by creating two basic flour-and-water doughs and rinsing them until all the starch washed away. The cake flour dough (left) formed a very small amount of sticky, weak gluten that cannot be stretched, while the high-protein bread flour dough (right) formed a large ball of highly resilient, rubbery gluten. The bread flour gluten could be stretched very thin without tearing. This structure traps air in breads, providing high rise and good texture.

Gluten in cake flour dough   Gluten in bread flour dough

what affects gluten development?

flour The protein content of the flour you're using determines how much gluten can be developed. More glutenin and gliadin mean more cross-linking and a more elastic network.

water The more water there is in the dough, the more hydrated it will be, meaning that the proteins can unravel more readily to bind into a strong network.

kneading time The longer you knead a dough (to a certain point), the stronger the network will be. Think about the difference between a chewy loaf of bread (that's kneaded for 8 minutes) and a tender muffin (that's simply whisked together).

3 first rise, in depth

Once the dough is done kneading, the visual transformation begins: The dough lightens and rises. You transfer your ball of dough to a greased container and let it sit for a period at room temperature (for most recipes). Yes, the activity of the yeast causes your ball of dough to grow, but on a more technical level the whole mass of dough is fermenting, so we call this first rise bulk fermentation. This is what makes yeasted bread different from quick breads: The characteristics of a good loaf—an airy crumb, a satisfying chew, a tall stature—develop thanks to the interplay between the yeast and gluten during this metabolic process.

Fermentation is arguably the oldest of cooking techniques—when any food sits for a certain period of time, it is going to taste and smell quite different because of the activity of various microbes. Mixing and kneading initiate the fermentation process by distributing the yeast throughout the dough and hydrating it; the yeast must absorb enough moisture to activate. (For more information, see "The Science of Yeast" on page 20.) The dough has a chance to rest, so the gluten, which worked hard during kneading, relaxes, becoming supple. It is within this environment that the yeast cells go to work, consuming sugars in the flour to release carbon dioxide and alcohol. The expansion of carbon dioxide bubbles within this relaxed, elastic dough is like slowly blowing air into a balloon, and the gluten is what holds the gas within the dough. The indicator for when many doughs are properly fermented is when it has doubled in size—the point at which most of the available sugars have been consumed.

don't forget!

GREASE THE CONTAINER If you don't grease the vessel the dough rises in, the dough will stick, and you will rip the gluten network when you try to get the dough out of the bowl or when you fold it.

COVER THE BOWL Covering the bowl with plastic wrap prevents the dough from drying out and forming a skin as it rises.

how can you tell if the dough has "doubled in size"?

How you determine if your dough has doubled in size will depend on the vessel you choose for holding it. A glass bowl is a good choice because you can see through it. But for an even easier indicator, you can place your dough in a straight-sided container and stretch a rubber band around the container at the point double in height from the top of the unrisen dough (left). When the dough reaches the band, it is ready to be manipulated (right).

folding dough

For loaves that require more strength or flavor (typically chewy rustic loaves or butter-laden sweet breads), we gently fold the dough over itself as it rises, a process that brings wayward sheets of gluten into alignment. In addition, folding dough rids it of excess carbon dioxide (which can inhibit yeast activity), distributes gas bubbles evenly, and refreshes the yeast. Recipes vary in the number of folds made, the degree to which the bowl is turned, and how many times the process is repeated, but the approach is the same: Slide a greased bowl scraper (you can also use your fingertips) under the edge of the dough and lift and fold the dough toward the center of the bowl (left). Turn the bowl as instructed by the recipe and repeat the process. Turn the bowl and fold one more time. When you're done, the dough should be shaped like a tight package (right). At this point you let the dough rise for the period of time specified in the recipe, and then repeat the process.

the science of yeast

what is yeast exactly?

Most bakers know that yeast is responsible for making bread dough rise. But fewer bakers know where it comes from or how it's derived. This magical ingredient is a living organism—a unicellular fungus—that's found in the environment on fruits and grains, and even in the air. Its function is to consume sugars and starches and convert them into alcohol, releasing carbon dioxide as a by-product. While essential for bread baking, this yeast activity also initiates fermentation in beverages such as beer, wine, kombucha, and kefir.

what does yeast do?

Yeast plays two roles in bread baking: It provides leavening and creates flavor. The yeast finds its food source in sugar. During fermentation, two enzymes present in wheat, amylase and diastase, break down the flour's complex starch molecules into simple sugars. Upon feeding, the yeast releases carbon dioxide, which allows the loaf to lift and expand; alcohol, which gives the bread flavor; and a multitude of aromatic molecules, which contribute further to the flavor of the bread. This process is called fermentation, and it's what occurs when bread rises. (For more information on fermentation, see page 19.)

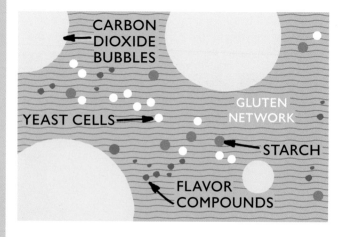

CARBON DIOXIDE BUBBLES

YEAST CELLS

GLUTEN NETWORK

STARCH

FLAVOR COMPOUNDS

what controls the activity of yeast?

As long as it's hydrated and sugar is present, yeast is going make dough expand. But there are various factors that control the extent to which this happens, and at what rate. Knowing how to manipulate each of them will give your bread the best taste and texture.

gluten As we've seen, a strong, elastic gluten network is necessary for containing carbon dioxide and allowing the loaf to expand—like blowing air into a balloon. If the gluten network is poorly developed, the yeast will not be able to do its job, because "the balloon" will not be strong enough to hold in the escaping carbon dioxide. This means not only that underkneaded dough compromises the productivity of yeast, but also that highly enriched doughs experience protracted rise, because large quantities of eggs and fat tenderize the dough. As a result, the dough is simply heavier to lift and has more difficulty retaining gas.

sugar Yeast feeds on sugar, so a bit of sugar in the ingredient list—say a tablespoon or two—creates more available food for the yeast and speeds up its activity modestly. It also ensures that there will be more leftover sugar that is not consumed by the yeast during fermentation, so the crust will be darker in color, and the flavor of the loaf will be deeper. However, adding walloping amounts of sugar to dough will not make your dough rise faster; in fact, it will slow it down. Sugar is hygroscopic, meaning that it holds on to moisture. If there is a lot of sugar in dough, it will subtract from the amount of available liquid needed to hydrate the yeast so it can function. That's why most sweet breads use a higher proportion of yeast. To account for this protracted rise, highly enriched doughs like Panettone (page 266) include more yeast than the amount used in other recipes. Panettone, for example, contains 2.22 percent of its total weight in yeast, while standard doughs contain around 1.50 percent or much less.

salt If there's no salt in the dough, the yeast will ferment much too quickly—salt sets the pace. (For more reasons why you should add salt to your bread dough, see page 12.) But adding too much salt will actually retard fermentation, and you'll end up with a loaf that lacks volume. Yeast contains a bit of water, and if there is an overabundance of salt the yeast will give up too much of the liquid to the salt through osmosis, and this hinders yeast's ability to reproduce.

time and temperature For most breads we recommend using room-temperature liquids and letting the dough rise at a cool room temperature (about 70 degrees), not a warm temperature as some recipes call for. At higher temperatures enzymes break down gluten, forcing the yeast to work harder and faster to make the bread rise. Although you'll see your dough rise faster if you place its container in a warm oven or on a radiator, or if you use liquid that's been heated to a high temperature before adding it to the dough, too much alcohol will be produced because the yeast must digest much more sugar to create enough carbon dioxide to achieve a decent rise. Less available sugar means less surface browning and less flavor, and the additional alcohol adds a boozy, tangy off-flavor tang to the bread. Moreover, overexerting the yeast can result in an uneven rise.

But what happens if dough rises in cold temperatures, in the refrigerator? So-called cold fermentation is actually a boon to many bread recipes, like our airy, tall Panettone (page 266), our chewy Thin-Crust Pizza (page 180), and our open-crumbed Sourdough Bread (page 359). We often let the dough ferment in the refrigerator—sometimes for up to 72 hours—because we've found that we get more flavorful results. Yeast in dough left at room temperature consumes sugars and leavens dough at a relatively fast rate. But then it's spent; it stops producing not just gas but also compounds that give bread flavor. In cool temperatures, yeast produces carbon dioxide more slowly, resulting in a more uniform rise and providing more time for complex-tasting flavor compounds to develop. To demonstrate how temperature affects the rate of carbon dioxide

production in dough, we prepared a yeasted batter and split it into two batches. We placed each in a simple device we fashioned from a test tube and a semipermeable balloon to capture gas. We left one batch out at room temperature and placed the other in the refrigerator, and then monitored the gas production of each at various intervals.

The yeast in the room-temperature batter (top) produced enough gas to fill the balloon within 3 hours but then was spent, while the refrigerated batter (bottom) continued to generate just enough gas to keep the balloon partially filled even after 18 hours.

on the counter

After 3 hours The batter quickly produces enough carbon dioxide to fill the balloon.

After 18 Hours Yeast cells have died and the balloon has collapsed.

in the refrigerator

After 3 hours The batter produces a little carbon dioxide to partially fill the balloon.

After 18 hours The batter continues to produce carbon dioxide at a steady rate.

4 dividing & shaping, in depth

At this point, the dough has slowly morphed into an inflated mass that is double its original size. In most cases, the next step, just before shaping the dough into a loaf, is to deflate the dough. This may seem counterintuitive—didn't you just work to contain all of those expanding gases? The yeast did a lot of work during fermentation—it ate, it expelled gas, it made dough grow. But it's still hungry, and there's more it needs to do for our dough before we bake, so it needs a refresher—and access to more food. When you deflate the dough, the gluten relaxes for better extensibility, the temperature of the dough equalizes throughout, and, most important, the yeast is redistributed so new food sources become available for it to consume, the effects of which are seen after shaping, during the second rise.

Once you deflate the dough, it's time to shape it. The main point of shaping is obvious—to form the dough into the loaf or the rolls it is to become after baking. But the step is also important because it strengthens the bread's structure one last time. Some doughs are shaped into free-form loaves, some fit snugly in a pan, and some are stretched into flatbread. Regardless of the final form, you want to shape all doughs with a gentle but decisive hand so you don't work out too much air. At the same time, though, you want to create surface tension on the dough, developing what is called a "gluten sheath" around the interior network. This sturdy sheath gets inflated like a balloon once again during the second rise and keeps the gases within, allowing the loaf to rise up and not out and to hold on to the carbon dioxide, which will give it an airy crumb. Sealing seams as necessary is the last important part of shaping; this ensures they don't open during baking.

how should you deflate the dough?

Many recipes instruct you to "punch down" the dough after fermentation, but you should take a gentler approach so that you don't knock out all the air that gives your bread holes—only what is necessary. We use two different techniques for deflating dough, depending on the bread. For doughs for sandwich breads, sweet breads, and rolls, like the one on the left, we instruct you to press down with your hands to deflate the dough. While gentle, this technique ensures that larger bubbles of carbon dioxide escape so the loaf is airy but fairly even crumbed. For most rustic, open-crumbed loaves, like the one on the right, we don't recommend deflating in the bowl at all; instead, pat out the dough and use your finger to puncture only unwieldy gas pockets that are larger than 1 inch in diameter so that the dough retains a lot of air.

why did the dough rise unevenly?

Loaves that do not have a taut shape with tightly sealed seams can rise unevenly, bake into an unattractive shape, and expand at random points in the top of the loaf, or "blow out." That's because creating a taut shape on the outside of the loaf forms a gluten sheath. This strong exterior skin sets the structure of the loaf and prevents the carbon dioxide that is formed during the second rise from escaping at weak points in the dough, so it rises uniformly upward.

Messy shaping

Proper shaping

step-by-step shaping

sandwich loaves

Sandwich loaves take the form of their pan, obviously, but that doesn't mean they can be baked without shaping. Rolling the dough into a tight cylinder before transferring it to the pan enforces the gluten structure and prevents the final loaf from being misshapen. To preserve air from the first rise, it is important to work the dough gently; in most cases we use our hands, not a rolling pin, which can overwork the dough. Make sure to lightly flour your hands as well as the counter to keep the dough from sticking. Placing the loaf in the pan seam side down ensures that it doesn't split open as it rises.

1 Shape the dough into a rectangle Press and stretch the dough into a rectangle, with the long side parallel to the counter edge.

2 Roll the dough into a cylinder Roll the dough away from you into a firm cylinder, keeping the roll taut by tucking it under itself as you go.

3 Pinch the seam Pinch the seam closed with your fingers to secure it.

4 Transfer the loaf to the pan Place the loaf seam side down in a greased 8½ by 4½-inch loaf pan.

5 Press in the corners Gently press the dough into the corners of the pan.

rolls

You first divide roll dough into pieces before shaping. You can weigh the pieces as you cut to help create even-size rolls that cook at the same rate. Turning the dough pieces into neat rolls is a largely one-handed affair, and it might require some practice to feel natural. The key is not to flour the counter; you want the dough to stick a bit so the friction between the dough and the counter helps create a round shape. The dough should spin under your hand but not turn over. Keep pieces of dough that you're not shaping under plastic wrap so they don't dry out.

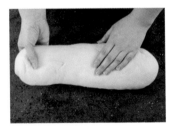

1 Make a log Stretch the dough into an even log.

2 Slice evenly Cut the log into equal pieces and cover them loosely with greased plastic.

3 Stretch and pull Working with one piece of dough at a time, form the dough into a rough ball, stretching it around your thumbs as though you're turning it inside out, and pinching the ends together so that the top is smooth.

4 Drag and roll Place the ball seam side down and, using your cupped hand, drag the dough in small circles until it feels taut and round.

round loaves (boules)

A round boule is a simple shape to execute, but you can't simply shape the blob of dough into a round form before baking it. Pressing the dough flat and then folding it back together builds gluten structure that you need in the loaf. Don't use a rolling pin; you'll risk deflating the dough. The motion of rounding the dough into the final ball shape is akin to working clay on a pottery wheel—you use both hands to shape and tuck the dough.

1 Shape the dough into a round Press and stretch the dough into a round.

2 Fold in the edges Working around the circumference of the dough, fold the edges toward the center of the round until a ball forms.

3 Drag the dough Flip the dough ball seam side down and, using your cupped hands, drag the dough in small circles until the dough feels taut and round.

torpedos

Like with boules, the dough for long, rounded-end torpedos benefits from being pressed flat and then folded inward to build structure. But there a few more steps you need to complete to make these attractive loaves. We then use a stretching process to coax the dough into the right shape. Rolling the loaf seam side down before transferring it to a baking sheet or pizza peel helps the seam close as the loaf rises a second time.

1 Shape the dough into a square Press and stretch the dough into a square.

2 Fold the top corners Fold the top corners of the dough diagonally into the center and press gently to seal. (The dough will look like an open envelope.)

3 Stretch and fold Stretch and fold the upper third of the dough toward the center, and press the seam gently to seal. (The dough will look like a sealed envelope.)

4 Form a rough loaf Stretch and fold the dough in half toward you to form a rough loaf, and pinch the seam gently to seal. Roll the loaf seam side down.

5 Transfer and tuck Gently slide your hands underneath each end of the loaf and transfer it to the prepared baking sheets or pizza peel, being careful not to deflate it.

6 Reshape After moving the loaf, tuck the edges under to form a taut torpedo shape.

bâtards

Much like a torpedo loaf, a bâtard is oblong, but its shape is a bit more refined, with a larger center and attractive pointed ends. Thus, while the process for forming the two loaves is similar, there are a couple of extra steps required for shaping a bâtard. These rustic loaves typically proof on a couche that has been dusted with flour. (For more information on couches, see page 5.)

1 Shape the dough into a square Press and stretch the dough into a square.

2 Fold the top and bottom corners Fold the top and bottom corners of the dough diagonally into the center of the square, and press gently to seal. (The dough will have a diamond shape.)

3 Stretch and fold Stretch and fold the upper and bottom thirds of dough toward the center, and press the seam gently to seal.

4 Form a rough loaf Stretch and fold the dough in half toward you to form a rough diamond-shaped loaf, and pinch the seam closed.

5 Transfer and tuck Gently slide your hands underneath each end of the loaf and transfer it seam side up to the prepared linen couche, being careful not to deflate the loaf.

what if the dough is hard to shape?

Although the gluten relaxes during the dough's first rise, any manipulation of the dough after bulk fermentation can work to bolster the gluten network once again. So as you're shaping, the dough may seem difficult to stretch or roll, and it could potentially snap back to its original position and fail to form the desired shape or to roll out to the correct size. If you experience this during shaping, simply incorporate a rest into the process: Cover the dough on the counter with plastic wrap and let it sit for 10 to 20 minutes until the dough is easy to manipulate once again. This brief rest gives the gluten network time to relax. Be sure to remember to cover the dough so it doesn't form a skin.

don't forget!

MAKE CLEAN CUTS When you divide dough into pieces, every cut you make creates a weak point in the gluten network from which gases can escape. Slicing cleanly—not ripping—through the dough prevents undesirable results.

DIVIDE THE DOUGH EVENLY Even-size dough pieces will rise uniformly. You can weigh pieces to help you.

5 second rise, in depth

Now that the dough has been shaped, it is left to rise a second time, a step called proofing. The goals of proofing are to expand the dough to the appropriate size before baking, relax the dough so the gluten network becomes extensible for rising, make up for any loss of gas bubbles during shaping, and eke out last bits of flavor through additional fermentation. The yeast did most of its work during the first rise, but shaping the dough unlocked more sugars for them to consume, and they create carbon dioxide and alcohol as by-products once again, though to a lesser extent than during the first rise. When properly proofed, the dough will have just the right amount of gas, elasticity, and energy to bake into a well-risen loaf.

In most cases, you transfer the shaped dough either to the vessel in or on which it will bake (this is often a baking sheet), or to a pizza peel, which you'll use to transfer the loaf to a hot baking stone in the oven, to proof so that you handle the delicate dough minimally when it's time to bake. You cover the shaped bread with greased plastic wrap and let it sit (usually at a not-too-warm room temperature, like in the first rise) until it has expanded adequately.

science corner

why do some breads rise in the refrigerator? Some recipes call for transferring the bulk dough to the refrigerator for its first rise, while others do so for a prolonged second rise. At the lower temperature, the yeast releases carbon dioxide more slowly and creates more flavorful sugars, alcohols, and acids. But there's one more benefit to slowing down (or "retarding") the second rise in this way: You can bake loaves or buns in the morning and start your day with fresh bread.

when is the dough properly proofed?

Bake a loaf too soon or too late and the quality of the final bread will not reflect the time you spent making it. Here are the methods we use for determining when dough is properly proofed. Below is a loaf, with a uniform shape, crust, and crumb, that was properly proofed.

Test for volume For free-form breads, you can eyeball when they're ready for the oven. Many doughs will double in size (rustic loaves vary). This process takes anywhere from 30 minutes to 2 hours at room temperature. For sandwich loaves, we include the number of inches a loaf should rise above the pan.

Use the knuckle test A good trick is to make an indentation in the dough with your finger to determine when it's properly proofed. Gently poke the loaf with your knuckle. If the indentation fills in right away, the loaf is underproofed and needs to rise further. Conversely, if the indentation

fails to fill in, the loaf is overproofed. The loaf is perfectly proofed when the indentation springs back minimally and does not fill in completely.

what happens if I bake underproofed dough?

The crust Underproofed loaves will need to rise too much in the oven to open up the crumb properly. Since the crust sets during the first few minutes of baking, the still-rising dough is forced to break through the crust, resulting in an exaggerated crown on the loaf (as below), an unattractive tear in the crust, or even a small attached loaf lump.

The crumb Without enough time to relax, the gluten network will tear rather than stretch in the oven, so carbon dioxide will escape randomly out of torn areas in the network. As a result, the hole structure can be uneven, with large holes at the edges of the loaf and a dense, gummy center.

what happens if I bake overproofed dough?

The crust When a shaped loaf is allowed to rise for too long before baking, the bread reaches its maximum height and then begins to fall because the structure becomes weak and the gases start to escape. Overproofed bread, therefore, will turn out flat and wide, and the slashes (for more information on slashing a loaf of bread, see page 28) barely burst open.

The crumb There is such a thing as too much air. Too much gas builds up when a loaf is overproofed; when the loaf collapses, the crumb compresses and becomes dense, tight, and even.

6 baking, in depth

If you treat dough with care—knead it adequately to develop gluten, let it rise until airy and flavorful, shape it neatly, and proof it perfectly—it is likely to bake into a beautiful loaf. But getting bread ready for the oven and baking it are not hands-off processes. Often, you need to slash loaves with a knife or single-edge razor blade before they're baked so they can rise evenly in the oven. Others benefit from being brushed with egg wash to boost browning, or misted with water to encourage a crisp crust. Some breads bake in pans, others on a baking sheet or on a preheated baking stone; each method gives the crust a different quality. Oven temperatures are variable as well. Sandwich and sweet breads bake at moderate temperatures, while rustic loaves bake at higher temperatures. Sometimes we start breads in superhot ovens to encourage them to rise dramatically, then we turn down the temperature to help set the crumb before the exterior burns. And finally, the last step is being sure to bake your breads until just the right point.

slashing loaves

Slashing a loaf cuts through its gluten sheath, creating designated weak spots in a loaf's surface, which allow the loaf to expand in the right direction in the oven. Without the slashes, the loaf will expand wherever it finds a random weak spot, resulting in an odd shape. For most breads, you can slash with a paring knife or a single-edge razor blade, though we also employ a tool called a lame for the unique slashes on some of our rustic breads. (For more information on lames, see page 5.) We slash either ¼ or ½ inch deep. Act quickly and decisively when slashing; otherwise, the implement will drag, creating messy lines. These are the three major slashing styles we use for the breads in this book; for more advanced slashing techniques, see page 36.

sandwich loaves

Some sandwich loaves do not expand much beyond their prebake height in the oven, so they do not require slashing at all. Others, however, require a slash to eliminate unattractive tears. Make one cut lengthwise along the top of the loaf with a swift, fluid motion, starting and stopping ½ inch from the ends.

round loaves (boules)

The most basic slashing style for a boule is a cross. Make two slashes with a swift, fluid motion along the top of the loaf to form an "X."

torpedos and bâtards

We generally score wide, long loaves with three simple slashes. Make three cuts with a swift, fluid motion across the width of the loaf, spacing the slashes evenly apart.

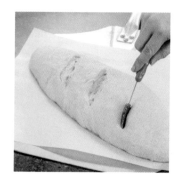

when is the loaf finished baking?

Judging loaf doneness can be tricky. We use two methods—neither of which we rely on alone—to help us out. First, we provide temperature ranges in most of our recipes to guide when to pull loaves out of the oven. In most cases, a properly baked lean bread should register between 205 and 210 degrees; enriched breads should register between 190 and 195 degrees. For some of our lean, rustic-style breads, however, we provide a temperature range of 210 to 212 degrees. The dough for these breads can be quite wet; baking them longer ensures that the center of the loaf is properly set and not gummy. It also helps to ensure an appropriately dark crust. Use an instant-read thermometer to take the bread's internal temperature, sliding the probe all the way to the center of the loaf.

But internal temperature alone is not sufficient proof that bread is fully baked. We've found that color is the ultimate indicator. If you pull a loaf as soon as it comes to temperature, it could have a pale, soft crust and a gummy interior. If you wait until the crust reaches the indicated color, it will have more flavor and a perfectly baked crumb. Bread contains moisture, so the temperature of a loaf's crumb plateaus because it cannot rise above the boiling point of water (212 degrees). That means that bread that registers 210 degrees won't overbake if you leave it in the oven until the exterior is properly browned. Both of the breads below temp within the proper range, yet the loaf on the left has too light a crust and needs to keep baking for better flavor. The loaf on right also temps within the desired doneness range and has a nice finish; it's ready to be pulled from the oven.

Keep baking

Just right

what should the crust look like?

We use four different colors to describe the final exterior appearance of a loaf: light golden brown, golden brown, deep golden brown, and dark brown. Color means flavor, so we generally want more of it on our breads; however, there are some breads, like our Pain de Mie (page 90), that are best with the barest of crusts; you want to sink your teeth right into this light sandwich bread, and so we bake it to a light golden brown. An appealingly golden brown crust signifies that the loaf's exterior will have slightly more presence and flavor. On our Pane Francese (page 285), this color indicates a flavorful crust that's crisp around the ridges but still tender, like a good loaf of basic French bread. A deep golden brown coloring is what gives loaves a homey feel, like on our American Sandwich Bread (page 86). And finally, there's the dark brown loaf. Chewy, thick-crusted artisan-style loaves, like our Pain de Campagne (page 303), sport this coloring that goes along with a substantial crust with crispness and chew.

Light golden brown

Golden brown

Deep golden brown

Dark brown

what if the crust is dark but the interior is still underdone?

Some breads can quickly develop a deep brown, bitter-tasting crust before the center of the loaf finishes cooking. For example, the brown sugar in our Cranberry-Walnut Loaf (page 118) caused the crust to burn during testing. Our solution? Rather than bake at the high temperatures associated with loaves of this kind, we preheated the oven to 450 degrees and then reduced the oven temperature to 375 degrees after 15 minutes of baking. The higher initial temperature gives the bread the oven rise it needs; immediately lowering the temperature allows the loaf to bake through slowly and evenly. If you see a crust getting dark during baking before its due time—this is common for enriched breads like Panettone (page 266)—you can tent the bread with aluminum foil to slow browning.

what pan should you use?

Oven temperature alone doesn't dictate how your crust will turn out. Sandwich breads, rolls, and enriched breads usually bake in specific pans or dishes that give them shape. But there are a few options for free-form breads and flatbreads. A baking sheet is the basic, standard choice; it will evenly brown loaves and will ensure that even the most delicate rolls and buns, like St. Lucia Buns (page 235), don't develop a too-thick crust. For some breads, like our hearty loaf of Deli Rye Bread (page 114) or our blonde Scali Bread (page 294), we stack two baking sheets and line them with insulating aluminum foil to protect the bottom crust from browning too deeply.

On other breads, typically the rustic variety or pizzas, a thicker bottom crust that you can crunch through to a chewy, open crumb is desirable. That's when we employ a baking stone, preheated so it matches the oven's temperature and can store that heat and transfer it to your bread. The blast of heat from below will give your breads an airier crumb and a fire-roasted finish. A baking stone helps our Pane Francese (page 285) develop a satisfying, golden brown crust completely unlike the sad coverings of supermarket French bread.

A final pan option is a covered Dutch oven, which we use for some round loaves to easily achieve a dramatic open-crumbed structure and a shatteringly crisp crust. As a loaf heats, it gives off steam to create a very humid environment inside the Dutch oven. Since moist air transfers heat much more efficiently than dry air does, the loaf heats more rapidly and therefore expands more rapidly, opening up the crumb. Further, as steam condenses on the surface of the bread, it causes starches to create a thin sheath that eventually dries out, giving the loaf a shiny crust that stays crisp.

instant-read thermometer

An instant-read thermometer, coupled with knowledge of how temperature relates to bread's doneness, can help ensure success.

buy a digital model These models are easier than dial-face models to use because you can take a quick look and immediately know the temperature of your loaf.

look for a long stem A long stem is key for measuring the temperature at the very center of a large loaf.

a quick response is vital You don't want to keep your hand in the oven any longer than necessary, so a thermometer that takes more than 5 to 10 seconds to warm up and respond isn't very helpful.

water-resistant is good Kitchen mishaps can occur. If your thermometer is water-resistant, it won't be down for the count if you accidentally drop it in water.

The new **ThermoWorks Thermapen Mk4** ($99) takes all the accuracy and speed of the company's Classic Super-Fast Thermapen ($79) and adds some nifty features: Its display auto-rotates, and it lights up in low light and wakes up when the unit is picked up. It takes a single AAA alkaline battery and is more water-resistant than the Classic, capable of surviving a half-hour bath.

don't forget!

TURN DOWN THE HEAT Many breads' rise and crust benefit from a quick blast of heat. But we often then turn down the temperature to cook the bread through. Don't leave your bread in the oven and forget it: The exterior will burn before the interior cooks.

the science of baking bread

what actually happens to bread in the oven?

We've talked about the science at play when dough is made and prepared for baking. But what's actually happening in the oven? Amylose starches in flour go through a process called gelatinization: Once heated, the starches absorb water until they burst once a loaf reaches its internal doneness temperature. When the starches burst, they set into a solid mass, which forms your bread's crumb. And this is how a ball of soft dough becomes sliceable bread.

But the starches in the dough aren't the only molecules affected by the oven's heat. Throughout the bread-making process, enzymes have been converting some of the starch molecules into sugars—the key to bread's flavor. Sugar's presence is obvious in the brown crust of a baked loaf. Unlike the interior of a loaf of bread, which cannot heat above the boiling point of water (212 degrees), the exterior is exposed to the heat of the surrounding oven, which is hot enough to caramelize the sugars and create a great-tasting crust and flavor compounds that travel inward for a similarly great-tasting crumb. On the inside, all that protein that formed our gluten network breaks down into simpler amino acids as the loaf heats. These cook and combine with other molecules to give the bread a flavorful, clean-tasting crumb.

what is oven spring?

Oven spring is the rise that yeasted dough experiences when it first hits a hot oven. The more "spring," the taller the loaf and the airier the crumb. Baking bread at a higher temperature results in more dramatic oven spring; bread dough is full of water, which will vaporize rapidly and open up the crumb, causing the loaf to expand. To demonstrate this, we baked the well-hydrated Pain de Campagne (page 303) at two different temperatures, 350 and 450 degrees. The difference in the height and crumb of the loaves is clear: The Pain de Campagne baked at the higher temperature is taller and more open—perfect for a rustic bread.

Baked at 350 degrees

Baked at 450 degrees

7 cooling & storing, in depth

The hard work is over, and your reward is a beautifully browned, lofty loaf of bread with an appetite-inducing aroma. But there is one more difficult step: resisting the urge to slice the warm bread! The interior of a loaf needs to cool from the 190 to 210 degrees it was when it emerged from the oven to room temperature. During this time, the starches continue to gelatinize (for more information on gelatinization, see page 31), excess moisture evaporates, and the true flavor of the loaf comes to the fore. We've found that this can take 3 hours for most large loaves. For perfect cooling, take your bread or rolls off their cooking surface or out of the pan and transfer them (after a brief wait, in some cases) to a wire rack so that air can circulate, preventing escaping moisture from softening the crust. Once this wait period is complete, you can finally slice your homemade creation. The tool you use is of utmost importance. Chef's knives may be sharp, but they'll squash the crumb of your loaf as you press down on it. A serrated knife, in contrast, relies on a slicing motion in which the blade is dragged across the bread's surface as it moves down through it, so it preserves the bread's crust and interior holes.

key equipment
serrated knife

A serrated knife, or bread knife, features pointed serrations that allow it to glide through crusty breads and bagels to create neat slices.

look for a 10- to 12-inch blade Knives shorter than 10 inches tend to catch their tips on larger loaves. Also, the blade should be slightly flexible for better maneuverability, yet firm enough to allow for proper control.

a curved blade makes cutting easier A slightly curved blade facilitates a rocking motion to keep knuckles from scraping the cutting board.

go for pointed, not wavy, serrations Pointed serrations give the blade a good grip on the loaf right away, while wavy serrations slide around.

Our favorite serrated knife is the **Wüsthof Classic Bread Knife, 10 Inches** ($89.95). This well-balanced knife with deeply tapered pointed serrations handled every task with exceptional ease and control. But we also highly recommend our Best Buy, the **Victorinox 10¼-Inch Fibrox Pro Serrated (Wavy/Curvy) Bread Knife** ($49.95). Its comfortable, sharp blade and pointed serrations performed almost as well as our top knife, struggling a tad more with crusty bread.

why did my sandwich loaf collapse?

Because sandwich loaves are often baked in a loaf pan, they trap steam and are not yet fully set when they're done baking. Remove the bread from the pan immediately, and the loaf can collapse. Let a sandwich loaf cool in its pan for 15 minutes before transferring it to a wire rack for cooling so the loaf maintains the proper shape.

how should you store bread?

Without preservatives to keep it tasting fresh, homemade bread can quickly stale. In general, you will find that sweet breads, enriched with butter and sugar, and sourdough breads, bolstered with a starter, last longer than the typical lean loaf at room temperature. Here's how to keep different types of bread fresh for as long as possible.

sandwich bread
Sandwich breads are great to have on hand for lunches for a few days. And since they generally don't have thick, crunchy crusts, you don't have to worry about their exteriors softening if you wrap them. Wrap loaves in a double layer of plastic wrap and store them at room temperature for up to three days. Wrapped first in aluminum foil before the plastic, sandwich loaves can be frozen for up to one month. If you don't plan to use the whole loaf at once, slice it and freeze the slices in a zipper-lock bag, thawing individual slices when you want them. While you can thaw slices of bread on the counter, they will taste fresher if you thaw them in the microwave. As frozen bread warms, its starch molecules begin to form crystalline regions, which absorb the water in bread. The process, called retrogradation, will eventually produce a dry, stale texture. The best way to thaw frozen bread is to place the slices on a plate (uncovered) and microwave them on high power for 15 to 25 seconds. This will get the starch and water molecules to break down the crystalline regions, producing soft, ready-to-eat bread.

rustic bread
We've found that storing loaves of rustic bread cut side down on a cutting board works better than wrapping them in paper or plastic. The crust will stay dry, while contact with the board will keep moisture inside the crumb. After 1 day, slice the bread, wrap the slices tightly in aluminum foil, place them in a zipper-lock bag, and freeze them. Thaw the slices at room temperature or in the microwave or oven. Alternatively, if you wrap, bag, and freeze unsliced full loaves or half-loaves, heat the thawed bread, still wrapped in foil, in a 450-degree oven for 10 to 15 minutes, then crisp it by removing the foil and returning it to the oven for a minute or two.

rolls
Rolls and buns are often enriched and thus still taste great after being stored in a zipper-lock bag at room temperature for up to two days. Wrapped in foil before being placed in the bag, rolls can be frozen for up to one month. To reheat rolls, wrap them (thawed if frozen) in aluminum foil, place them on a rimmed baking sheet, and bake them in a 350-degree oven for 10 minutes.

slicing rustic bread

Often, the bread knife fails to cut all the way through the thick bottom crust of artisan-style loaves, leaving you to yank the slice free from the loaf, often tearing it in the process. To get around the problem and cut perfect slices, turn the loaf on its side to cut it. This way, you'll be able to cut through both top and bottom crusts simultaneously.

keep bread out of the refrigerator
Once exposed to air, bread starch undergoes a process called retrogradation. When bread bakes, the starch molecules absorb water and lose their structure, giving fresh bread its moist chew. But as the bread cools and sits, the starch molecules in the bread recrystallize, turning the bread hard and crumbly. Storing bread in the refrigerator to delay staling may seem like a good idea, but this actually shortens the shelf life. The cool temperatures of the refrigerator speed up the retrogradation process.

how to revive stale bread
What if bread has undergone retrogradation? Is it destined for bread crumbs? To revive bread, gradually heat the loaf to the gelation point (about 140 degrees)—but do not heat it to the boiling point of water (212 degrees). In addition, with crusty breads, you also need to supply water to the exterior of the loaf to ensure that the starches can properly soften. Briefly pass crusty bread under cold running water. Wrap the loaf tightly with foil, place it on the middle rack of a cold oven, and heat the oven to 300 degrees. After about 30 minutes (15 to 20 minutes for small or narrow loaves like baguettes), remove the foil and return the loaf to the oven for about 5 minutes to crisp the crust. Note that reheating a stale loaf doesn't free the starches to move around the way that they can in a just-baked loaf, and they recrystallize much more quickly. The effect lasts for only a few hours.

honors class

So far, we've broken down the process of bread baking from start to finish. Once you've performed these steps a few times, you'll see how easy—and rewarding—it is to make bread a part of your repertoire, and you'll know how to navigate and troubleshoot new recipes that come your way. But bread baking is a lifetime education, and there are always new moves you can experiment with to get the results that you see in the windows of the best boulangeries. In this section, we build on the basic routine, introducing more advanced techniques for giving your already-great bread even more flavor and flair.

baking with whole-wheat flour

There are a lot of reasons to introduce whole-wheat flour into your breads: It's healthful, it has nice color, it can give a loaf heartiness, and it boasts a nutty taste that provides bread with great depth of flavor. As the name implies, whole-wheat flour is ground from the whole wheat berry—the outer bran layer, the germ, and the endosperm—whereas white flour is ground from just the endosperm. Because it contains the entire berry, however, baking with whole-wheat flour is a real challenge.

The problem lies with the bran—the very thing that gives whole-wheat flour its character. The fiber in bran has sharp edges that tend to cut the gluten strands, weakening their bonds and making the dough less able to contain gases during proofing and baking. The result is a squat, heavy, crumbly loaf. So what can you do to put healthful whole-wheat breads on your table?

combine whole-wheat flour with bread flour

You should cut the whole-wheat flour in a recipe with some higher-protein bread flour and not with all-purpose flour (unless you're making a soft, fluffy roll, like our Honey-Wheat Dinner Rolls [page 133]). Whole loaves, like our Whole-Wheat Sandwich Bread (page 290) and our Rustic Wheat Berry Bread (page 308), need structure, and the bread flour automatically gives your bread a boost in gluten-forming proteins and therefore gluten development, making up for the structure-compromising activity of the whole-wheat flour.

make it wet

You can soften the whole-wheat flour's bran by letting the bran absorb a lot of water in a highly hydrated dough. This can make the dough a bit more difficult to work with, but it will blunt the bran's sharp edges that cut through gluten strands.

use a soaker

When you have the time, the ultimate way to get whole-wheat flour to behave in a bread recipe is to employ a soaker—simply soak the whole-wheat flour or the whole grain (like in our Rustic Wheat Berry Bread [page 308]) in some of the water or other liquid from the recipe prior to mixing and kneading it with the other ingredients, or before grinding it. A presoak accomplishes three things: First, it softens the bran's edges. Second, its hydrating effect prevents the grains from robbing moisture from the dough, which would toughen the crumb. Third, steeping the grains activates the wheat's enzymes, converting some starches into sugars and, in turn, reducing the bran's natural bitterness and coaxing out a sweet flavor.

On the left is a close-up crumb shot of our Whole-Wheat Sandwich Bread (page 290) made according to our recipe, with a soaker. You can see it has a lighter texture. Its flavor is nutty. The bread on the right was made without presoaking the whole-wheat flour. It has a dense texture and a bitter flavor.

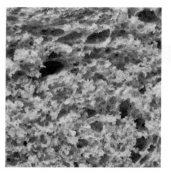

Soaked   Not soaked

baking with sponges

You can certainly make great-tasting bread by adding yeast straight to all of your dry ingredients. But once you've mastered making a "straight" dough, as this is called, it's well worth learning how to take it further to achieve the complex flavor and appealingly rustic texture of bakery loaves. We do this in chapter six of this book by introducing the sponge (also called *poolish* in French, or *biga* in Italian), which is what the professionals use to start rustic-style bread recipes.

A sponge is a mixture of a portion of a recipe's flour, yeast, and water, which is allowed to ferment for at least 6 hours or up to 24 hours before it is added to the bulk of the bread dough. It is for that reason that a sponge is considered a type of pre-ferment. During this pre-fermentation time, the flour's carbohydrates and starches, which have little flavor of their own, break down into a multitude of sugars, acids, and alcohols and develop mildly sour and nutty flavors. Another bonus: The acid developed strengthens a rustic bread dough's gluten network, so that breads made with a sponge have an appealingly open crumb and a welcome chew.

Once the sponge ferments, it's added to more flour, yeast, and water to build a bread dough. Sure, this method adds time to your recipes, but it's hands-off and couldn't be simpler. Working with sponges grows the skills you've already mastered to unlock a whole new world of breads—impressive loaves like the slightly tangy, open-crumbed French country loaf known as Pain de Campagne (page 303) or the Caramelized Onion Bread (page 321) that features sweet and savory caramelized onions swirling through a chewy interior.

what should the sponge look like?
The key to using a sponge is to let it rise (about 2 hours; left) and then wait for it to begin to fall (another 4 hours; right) before using it. The fall is not dramatic, but it indicates that the yeast is active and ready to go. Once the sponge has fallen, it can be held for up to 24 hours at room temperature before using, or it can be refrigerated for several days.

After 2 hours

After 4 hours

baking with starters

While most of the recipes in this book call for commercial yeast, breads can be leavened naturally without any commercial leavener at all by using a sourdough starter. A labor of love that a baker can keep alive indefinitely, a starter begins as a culture that you make yourself. A culture is a mixture of flour and water that contains a "colony" of two organisms—"lactic acid" bacteria (*Lactobacillus sanfranciscensis* and several relatives) and yeasts (*Saccharomyces cerevisiae* or one of several Candida species)—living in harmony. The yeast is derived from the air and from the flour since wild yeast is present on the kernels of wheat; it takes time—two or three days—for them to multiply to the point where they are abundant enough to leaven a loaf of bread. You'll know your culture is ready because it will be bubbly and will have a strong aroma.

Once your culture is established, you then have to feed a portion of it with more flour and water, once every 24 hours, until the culture is pleasantly aromatic and rises and falls within an 8- to 12-hour period after being fed. This takes about ten to fourteen days. But if you're patient, this process will give you a refreshed sourdough starter that you can bake with and maintain.

adding a rest to your dough

We've learned that adequate kneading is necessary to build gluten structure in bread doughs. But if you want to make a rustic bread from a wet dough that has a chewy crumb and the structure to support large, open holes, the standard kneading time often isn't enough. Knead for too long, however, and the dough can oxidize and bake into a pale, stale-tasting loaf. (For more information on overkneading dough, see page 17.) How can we fortify our gluten structure for a superlatively chewy, open crumb? We employ a technique called *autolyse*. In this method, the dry and wet ingredients go through step one of the process, mixing; then, the shaggy dough is left to rest before proceeding with kneading. While the mixture rests, naturally occurring enzymes (proteases) break down the disorganized bonds of gluten, acting like scissors, cutting the coiled-up proteins into smaller segments that are easier to strengthen and align during kneading, so they require less time.

hold the salt
Hold the salt when mixing doughs that will undergo autolyse: Salt hinders both the ability of flour to absorb water and the activity of the enzymes that break down proteins during autolyse. If you add the salt up front, the dough will be sticky and stiff after autolyse. If you wait to add the salt, the dough will get a head start in gluten development and will be supple and smooth.

beautifying your bread

A nicely browned crust and a crumb full of well-formed interior holes are enough to make any homemade bread a sight to behold. But you can recreate the rustic, almost-too-pretty-to-eat loaves that artisan bakeries display at home. We've detailed the hows and whys of crafting your own bread masterpieces.

advanced slashing techniques

While the slashes on loaves are primarily functional (for more information on slashing bread, see page 28), the pattern is open to embellishment. These fun flourishes create beautiful motifs on your loaves. For each design, use a lame and, unless otherwise instructed, hold the blade at a 30-degree angle to the loaf.

for round loaves (boules)

square Make four 6-inch-long, ½-inch-deep slashes with a swift, fluid motion to form a square, with slashes intersecting ½ inch from each end in the corners of the square.

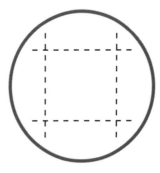

spiral Starting at the center of the loaf, make one ½-inch-deep slash with a swift, fluid motion in one outward spiral, ending the spiral 1 inch from the edge.

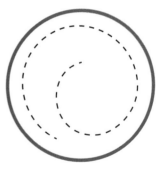

for bâtards

five slashes Make five evenly spaced ½-inch-deep slashes with a swift, fluid motion across the width of the loaf, starting and stopping about ½ inch from the ends. (The central slash should be 6 inches long, the second slashes on either side should be 5 inches long, and the end slashes should be 3 inches long.)

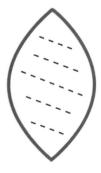

leaf Make three 3-inch-long, ½-inch-deep parallel slashes with a swift, fluid motion at a 45-degree angle in a mirror image on either side of an imaginary line down the center of the loaf, staggering each slash about ¾ inches from the previous slash, starting and stopping ½ inch from the ends, and spacing the slashes about 1½ inches apart.

achieving a crackling crust

Some breads are popped into the oven right after they've completed the second rise. For others, we spray the surface of the dough with water or paint it with egg wash in order to achieve bread with a crisp or shiny crust, respectively. But we also employ a couple of specialty proofing tools and techniques to put the finishing touches on artisan-style rustic breads.

working with a couche

Professional bakers proof some free-form loaves in the folds of a piece of heavy linen known as a couche. The couche has two core jobs: It helps the loaf hold its shape, and it wicks away moisture, keeping the dough's surface uniformly dry as it proofs and rises, helping develop a thin "skin" that bakes up to the perfect crisp, chewy, attractively floured crust.

working with a banneton

Bakers achieve symmetrical round loaves of bread (boules) by transferring the dough to shallow, woven baskets known as bannetons or brotforms for the last rising step before baking. The cloth-lined basket serves two functions: It retains the round shape of the loaf as it proofs, and its breathable construction wicks away moisture from the dough's surface, much like the couche does, for a crispier, browner crust. We've found that you can improvise a banneton at home by lining a 5-quart metal or plastic colander with a linen dish towel and dusting the towel liberally with flour, and we use this simple technique in our recipes. But if you're inclined to purchase these inexpensive baskets, you'll find that they're not just lightweight and convenient; they mark your bread with a beautiful floured spiral. As the dough expands when it proofs, it makes its way into the ridges of the banneton, so the pattern is transferred onto the loaf's surface.

moisture makers: lava rocks and steam pans

For dinner rolls and sandwich loaves, baked either in pans or free-form, a mist of water before baking is an adequate way to get a good crust that's appropriate for these breads. But for thick, crisp-crusted, dramatic-looking rustic loaves, a steamy oven is a bread's best friend. Professional bakers use steam-injected ovens for three reasons. For starters, a moist environment transfers heat more rapidly than dry heat does, allowing the gases inside the loaf to expand quickly in the first few minutes of baking, ensuring maximum volume. At the same time, steam prevents the bread's exterior from drying out too quickly, which would create a rigid structure that limits rise. Finally, as we've learned, moisture converts the exterior starches into a thin coating of gel that eventually results in the glossy, crackly crust that is a hallmark of a great artisan-style loaf.

So how can you make a home oven as steamy as possible? Many recipes suggest adding boiling water or ice cubes to the oven; the problem is that home ovens cannot retain moisture long enough for their impact to be felt on the finished bread. We've come up with a more effective approach: using lava rocks. These irregularly shaped rocks (available at many hardware stores for use in gas grills) have a lot of surface area for absorbing and retaining heat, maximizing the amount of steam produced when boiling water is introduced. We begin using lava rocks in the oven in chapter six, and we highly recommend the technique—we've found that it simply gives you the best bread. To use them, adjust an oven rack to the lowest position. Fill two aluminum pie plates with 1 quart of lava rocks each and place them on the rack before heating the oven. When your bread is ready for the oven, pour ½ cup of boiling water into one of the plates of lava rocks and close the oven door for 1 minute to create an initial burst of steam. Then, working quickly, transfer the loaf to the oven and pour ½ cup of boiling water into the second plate of rocks. This one-two punch ensures that the oven stays steamy for the entire baking time.

starting from scratch
12 foolproof breads that teach the basics

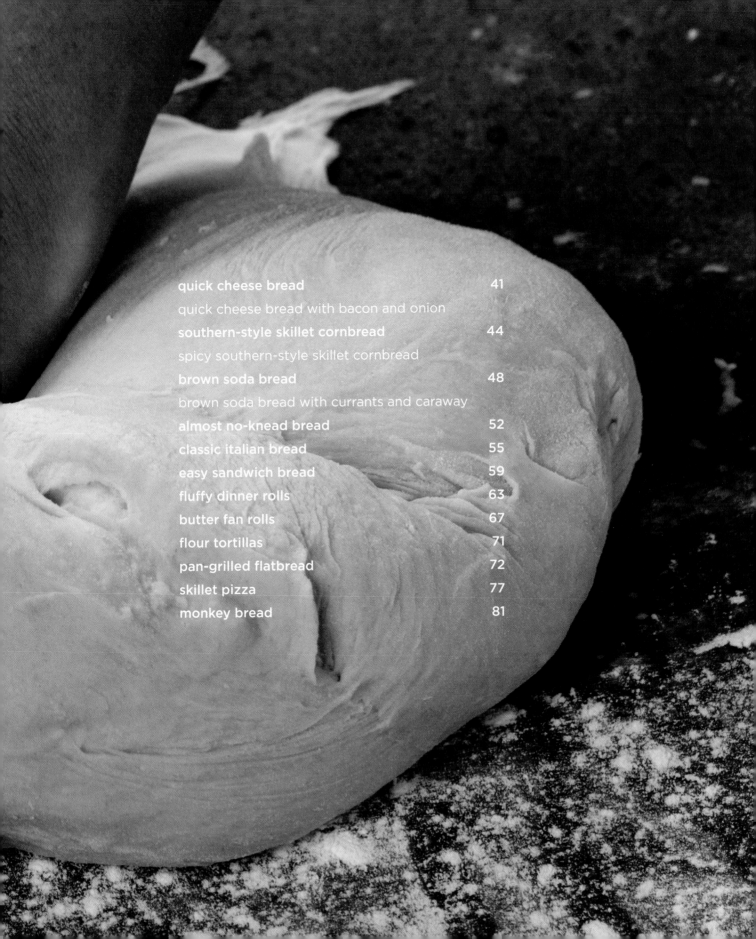

quick cheese bread

makes 1 loaf
baking time 45 minutes
total time 1½ hours, plus 3 hours cooling time
key equipment 8½ by 4½-inch loaf pan

3 ounces Parmesan cheese, shredded (1 cup)

2½ cups (12½ ounces) all-purpose flour

1 tablespoon baking powder

1 teaspoon salt

⅛ teaspoon pepper

⅛ teaspoon cayenne pepper

4 ounces extra-sharp cheddar cheese,
cut into ½-inch pieces (1 cup)

1 cup (8 ounces) whole milk

½ cup (4 ounces) sour cream

3 tablespoons unsalted butter, melted

1 large egg

why this recipe works Bread baking can take time and patience; it often requires activating yeast, kneading, proofing, shaping, and cooking. And while these steps contribute to a beautiful homemade loaf, it's possible to make something special with just a mixing bowl, a spatula, and the quick-bread mixing method. The technique isn't just for sweet breakfast loaves; we employed it to make a stellar savory quick bread that's moist, rich, and hearty, with a bold, cheesy crust—everything you'd want from a loaf of bread. We simply mixed the dry ingredients (flour; salt, pepper, and cayenne for flavor; cheeses; and a generous amount of baking powder to lift this heavy mix) and the wet ingredients (milk and sour cream for creamy flavor and moisture, melted butter for richness, and an egg for structure) separately and then folded them together. As for the cheese, we mixed small chunks (rather than shreds) of extra-sharp cheddar into the dough for pockets of rich, salty flavor throughout. You can substitute a mild Asiago, crumbled into ¼- to ½-inch pieces, for the cheddar. (Aged Asiago that is as firm as Parmesan is too sharp and piquant.) The test kitchen's preferred loaf pan measures 8½ by 4½ inches; if you use a 9 by 5-inch loaf pan, start checking for doneness 5 minutes earlier than advised in the recipe. Use the large holes of a box grater to shred the Parmesan. If, when testing the bread for doneness, the skewer comes out with what looks like uncooked batter clinging to it, try again in a different, but still central, spot. (A skewer hitting a pocket of cheese may give a false indication.) The texture of the bread improves as it cools, so resist the urge to slice the loaf when it's still warm.

continued

1 Adjust oven rack to middle position and heat oven to 350 degrees. Grease 8½ by 4½-inch loaf pan, then sprinkle ½ cup Parmesan evenly in bottom of pan.

2 Whisk flour, baking powder, salt, pepper, and cayenne together in large bowl. Stir in cheddar, breaking up clumps, until cheese is coated with flour. Whisk milk, sour cream, melted butter, and egg together in second bowl.

3 Using rubber spatula, gently fold milk mixture into flour mixture until just combined (batter will be heavy and thick; do not overmix).

4 Transfer batter to prepared pan and smooth top. Sprinkle remaining ½ cup Parmesan evenly over surface.

5 Bake loaf until golden brown and skewer inserted in center comes out clean, 45 to 50 minutes, rotating pan halfway through baking.

6 Let loaf cool in pan for 15 minutes. Remove loaf from pan and let cool completely on wire rack, about 3 hours, before serving.

variation **quick cheese bread with bacon and onion**

Cook 5 slices bacon, cut into ½-inch pieces, in 10-inch non-stick skillet over medium heat until crispy, 5 to 7 minutes. Using slotted spoon, transfer bacon to paper towel–lined plate. Pour off all but 3 tablespoons fat from skillet. Add ½ cup finely chopped onion to fat left in skillet and cook over medium heat until softened, about 3 minutes; set aside. Substitute Gruyère cheese for cheddar and omit butter. Add bacon and onion to flour mixture with cheese in step 2.

troubleshooting

problem The loaf doesn't rise during baking.

solution Don't overmix the dough.

This bread relies on the quick-bread mixing method in which the wet ingredients are gently folded into the dry ingredients with a rubber spatula until just combined and a few streaks of flour still remain. Avoid overmixing as it can encourage too much gluten development, which inhibits rise in quick breads and makes them tough and squat.

problem The bread seems gummy or soggy.

solution Test for doneness with a skewer.

There is a lot of moisture in this recipe, so if you under-bake the loaf the texture will be particularly undesirable. To avoid a dense, wet loaf, don't remove the bread from the oven until a wooden skewer inserted in the center comes out clean. Because this bread is filled with cubes of molten cheese, you may hit a pocket of cheese when testing for doneness. If there appears to be uncooked batter clinging to the skewer, try testing again in a different, but still central, spot.

southern-style skillet cornbread

makes one 10-inch loaf
baking time 12 minutes
total time 1¼ hours
key equipment 10-inch cast-iron skillet

2¼ cups (11¼ ounces) stone-ground cornmeal

1½ cups (12 ounces) sour cream

½ cup (4 ounces) whole milk

¼ cup (1¾ ounces) vegetable oil

5 tablespoons (2½ ounces) unsalted butter, cut into 5 pieces

2 tablespoons sugar

1 teaspoon baking powder

1 teaspoon baking soda

¾ teaspoon salt

2 large eggs

why this recipe works Cornbread is an easy-to-make quick bread, but it means different things to different people. Northerners like their cornbread sweet and light—more cake than bread. Recipes abound for this style, but we wanted to add to our bread repertoire the satisfying skillet-baked cornbread that's popular in the South. Southern-style cornbread should boast hearty corn flavor, a sturdy, moist crumb, and a brown crust. And it definitely shouldn't be sweet—that's veering into Yankee territory. That said, we departed from tradition in some ways. For one, we chose yellow cornmeal rather than the typical white; cornbread made with yellow stone-ground corn-meal had a more potent corn flavor. Toasting the cornmeal in our skillet for a few minutes intensified that flavor. After we toasted it, we created a cornmeal mush by softening the cornmeal in a mixture of sour cream and milk. This ensured that our bread had a fine, moist crumb. We used sour cream in the mush because it added a pleasant tang that worked well with the sweet cornmeal; plus, it reacted with the leaveners to keep this flourless bread from being too dense. And for bread that baked up rich and tender, we whisked two eggs into the batter. When it came to the fat, we skipped the customary bacon fat and instead used a combination of butter (for flavor) and vegetable oil (for its ability to withstand high heat without burning). Greasing the skillet with both and preheating it before adding the batter delivered the rich, crisp, distinctly Southern crust we were after. We prefer a cast-iron skillet, but any ovensafe 10-inch skillet will work. You can substitute any type of fine- or medium-ground cornmeal; do not use coarse-ground cornmeal.

continued

southern-style skillet cornbread, continued

1 Adjust oven rack to middle position and heat oven to 450 degrees. Toast cornmeal in 10-inch cast-iron skillet over medium heat, stirring frequently, until fragrant, about 3 minutes.

2 Transfer cornmeal to large bowl and whisk in sour cream and milk; set aside.

3 Wipe skillet clean with paper towels. Add oil to now-empty skillet, place skillet in oven, and heat until oil is shimmering, about 10 minutes. Using potholders, remove skillet from oven, carefully add butter, and gently swirl pan to melt.

4 Being careful of hot skillet handle, pour all but 1 tablespoon oil-butter mixture into cornmeal mixture and whisk to incorporate. Whisk sugar, baking powder, baking soda, and salt into cornmeal mixture until combined, then whisk in eggs.

5 Quickly transfer batter to skillet and smooth top. Transfer skillet to oven and bake until top begins to crack and sides are golden brown, 12 to 15 minutes, rotating skillet halfway through baking.

6 Let bread cool in skillet for 15 minutes. Remove bread from skillet and transfer to wire rack. Serve warm or at room temperature.

variation **spicy southern-style skillet cornbread**
Whisk 2 minced jalapeño chiles and 2 teaspoons grated lime zest into cornmeal mixture with eggs in step 4.

troubleshooting

problem The cornmeal is still crunchy.

solution Use the right cornmeal and soak it.

It's important to use fine or medium stone-ground cornmeal; coarse-ground cornmeal will not soften properly in this recipe. Additionally, be sure to let the cornmeal soak in the sour cream mixture to soften before you mix the batter so that the bread has a fine, moist crumb. If you skip this step, the cornmeal will retain its hard texture.

problem The cornbread does not release from the skillet.

solution Let the bread rest before removing.

The cornbread must cool in the skillet for 15 minutes before you remove it. This allows the bread time to set up so it releases cleanly from the skillet.

problem The cornbread has a soggy crust.

solution Preheat the skillet.

Preheating the skillet in the oven is what gives this bread its crunchy crust. Don't let the skillet cool off before you add the batter.

brown soda bread

makes 1 loaf
baking time 45 minutes
total time 1¼ hours, plus 3 hours cooling time
key equipment rimmed baking sheet, pastry brush

why this recipe works Robust, moist, and permeated with wheaty sweetness, brown Irish soda bread holds lots of appeal. This quick bread gets its hearty, deeply flavored crumb from the addition of coarse whole-meal flour to the all-purpose flour. For a stateside version, we substituted whole-wheat flour for the hard-to-find whole-meal flour, and to highlight the bread's nutty aspects we added toasted wheat germ. Unfortunately, these ingredients made our bread slightly gummy. To remedy this, we tried upping the baking soda, but it imparted a soapy flavor. Instead, equal amounts of two leaveners, baking soda and baking powder, lightened the bread without creating off-flavors. Acidic buttermilk played double-duty, yielding a moist loaf and reacting with the baking soda for a light crumb. Just a touch of sugar and a few tablespoons of butter added a hint of sweet richness. The dough required only a brief knead, and shaping it was a cinch—we simply patted it into a round. Finally, brushing melted butter on the hot loaf gave this authentic soda bread a rich crust.

2 cups (10 ounces) all-purpose flour
1½ cups (8¼ ounces) whole-wheat flour
½ cup (1½ ounces) toasted wheat germ
1½ teaspoons salt
1 teaspoon baking powder
1 teaspoon baking soda
1¾ cups (14 ounces) buttermilk
3 tablespoons sugar
3 tablespoons unsalted butter, melted

1 Adjust oven rack to lower-middle position and heat oven to 400 degrees. Line baking sheet with parchment paper. Whisk all-purpose flour, whole-wheat flour, wheat germ, salt, baking powder, and baking soda together in large bowl. Whisk buttermilk, sugar, and 2 tablespoons melted butter in second bowl until sugar has dissolved.

2 Using rubber spatula, gently fold buttermilk mixture into flour mixture, scraping up dry flour from bottom of bowl, until dough starts to form and no dry flour remains.

3 Transfer dough to lightly floured counter and knead by hand until cohesive mass forms, about 30 seconds. Pat dough into 7-inch round and transfer to prepared sheet.

4 Using sharp paring knife or single-edge razor blade, make two 5-inch-long, ¼-inch-deep slashes with swift, fluid motion along top of loaf to form cross.

5 Bake loaf until golden brown and skewer inserted in center comes out clean, 45 to 50 minutes, rotating sheet halfway through baking.

6 Transfer loaf to wire rack and brush with remaining melted butter. Let cool completely, about 3 hours, before serving.

variation **brown soda bread with currants and caraway**
Stir 1 cup dried currants and 1 tablespoon caraway seeds into flour mixture in step 1.

almost no-knead bread

makes 1 loaf
resting time 8 hours
rising time 1½ to 2 hours
baking time 55 minutes
total time 11 to 11½ hours, plus 3 hours cooling time
key equipment Dutch oven with lid, instant-read thermometer

why this recipe works Artisan-style bakery loaves—beautifully browned boules with a thick, crisp crust that breaks to a chewy, open interior—take professional skills to make, right? Wrong. Not only is it possible to make a rustic loaf for your table, it's easy, too, with the no-knead method of bread baking. This technique replaces the kneading that develops gluten to give bread structure with a high hydration level—around 85 percent (8½ ounces of water for every 10 ounces of flour)—and an 8- to 18-hour-long (and hands-off) resting period, or *autolyse*. During autolyse, the flour hydrates and enzymes work to break up the proteins so that the dough requires only a brief turn to develop gluten. The dough is then baked in a Dutch oven; the humid environment gives the loaf a dramatic open crumb and a crisp crust. But the breads we tested needed more structure and flavor. To strengthen the dough, we lowered the hydration and added less than a minute of kneading to compensate. We introduced an acidic tang from vinegar and a shot of yeasty flavor from beer. We prefer to use a mild American lager, such as Budweiser, here; strongly flavored beers will make this bread taste bitter.

3 cups (15 ounces) all-purpose flour

1½ teaspoons salt

¼ teaspoon instant or rapid-rise yeast

¾ cup (6 ounces) water, room temperature

½ cup (4 ounces) mild lager, room temperature

1 tablespoon distilled white vinegar

1 Whisk flour, salt, and yeast together in large bowl. Whisk water, beer, and vinegar together in 4-cup liquid measuring cup. Using rubber spatula, gently fold water mixture into flour mixture, scraping up dry flour from bottom of bowl, until dough starts to form and no dry flour remains. Cover bowl tightly with plastic wrap and let sit at room temperature for at least 8 hours or up to 18 hours.

2 Lay 18 by 12-inch sheet of parchment paper on counter and lightly spray with vegetable oil spray. Transfer dough to lightly floured counter and knead by hand until smooth and elastic, about 1 minute.

3 Shape dough into ball by pulling edges into middle, then transfer seam side down to center of prepared parchment.

4 Using parchment as sling, gently lower loaf into Dutch oven (let any excess parchment hang over pot edge). Cover tightly with plastic and let rise until loaf has doubled in size and dough springs back minimally when poked gently with your knuckle, 1½ to 2 hours.

5 Adjust oven rack to middle position. Using sharp paring knife or single-edge razor blade, make two 5-inch-long, ½-inch-deep slashes with swift, fluid motion along top of loaf to form cross. Cover pot and place in oven. Turn oven to 425 degrees and bake loaf for 30 minutes while oven heats.

6 Remove lid and continue to bake until loaf is deep golden brown and registers 205 to 210 degrees, 25 to 30 minutes. Using parchment sling, remove loaf from pot and transfer to wire rack; discard parchment. Let cool completely, about 3 hours, before serving.

classic italian bread

makes 1 loaf
rising time 1½ to 2½ hours
baking time 25 minutes
total time 3 to 4 hours, plus 3 hours cooling time
key equipment pizza peel, baking stone, water-filled spray bottle, instant-read thermometer

why this recipe works You might assume that you have to make a trip to a bakery for good Italian bread, or else settle for pale, doughy supermarket loaves, but making your own from scratch is surprisingly simple. For a classic loaf with a thin, crisp crust and a chewy but tender crumb, we started with bread flour and then focused on our biggest challenge: flavor. We hoped to shorten the rising time for the bread, but that meant we would be reducing the fermentation time, which provides a lot of flavor. To make up for this, we added yeasty tang by using beer as the main liquid in our dough. Preheating our baking stone for an hour gave us a nicely browned crust, and misting the loaf with water before baking helped the exterior of the bread stay supple and encouraged additional rise and a light, tender crumb. We prefer to use a mild American lager, such as Budweiser, here; strongly flavored beers will make this bread taste bitter.

3 cups (16½ ounces) bread flour

1½ teaspoons instant or rapid-rise yeast

1½ teaspoons salt

1 cup (8 ounces) mild lager, room temperature

6 tablespoons (3 ounces) water, room temperature

2 tablespoons extra-virgin olive oil

1 Whisk flour, yeast, and salt together in bowl of stand mixer. Whisk beer, water, and oil together in 4-cup liquid measuring cup.

2 Using dough hook on low speed, slowly add beer mixture to flour mixture and mix until cohesive dough starts to form and no dry flour remains, about 2 minutes, scraping down bowl as needed. Increase speed to medium-low and knead until dough is smooth and elastic and clears sides of bowl, about 8 minutes.

3 Transfer dough to lightly floured counter and knead by hand to form smooth, round ball, about 30 seconds. Place dough seam side down in lightly greased large bowl or container, cover tightly with plastic wrap, and let rise until doubled in size, 1 to 1½ hours.

4 Line pizza peel with 16 by 12-inch piece of parchment paper, with long edge of paper perpendicular to handle. Gently press down on dough to deflate any large gas pockets. Turn dough out onto lightly floured counter (side of dough that was against bowl should now be facing up) and press and stretch dough into 10-inch square.

5 Fold top corners of dough diagonally into center of square and press gently to seal.

6 Stretch and fold upper third of dough toward center and press seam gently to seal.

7 Stretch and fold dough in half toward you to form rough loaf and pinch seam closed.

8 Starting at center of dough and working toward ends, gently and evenly roll and stretch dough until it measures 15 inches long by 4 inches wide. Roll loaf seam side down.

continued

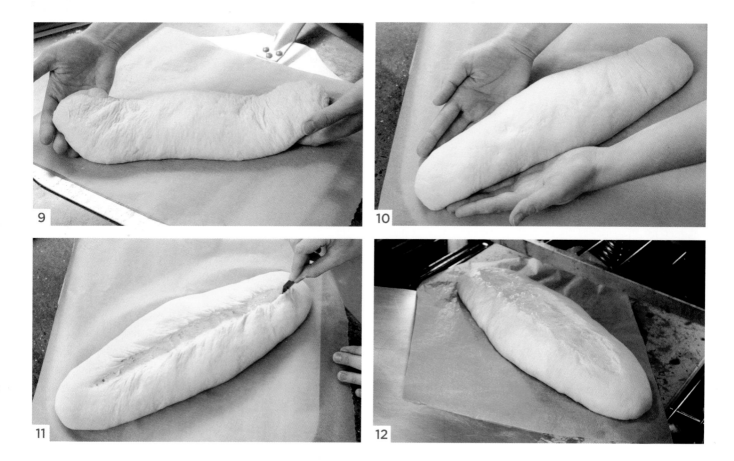

classic italian bread, continued

9 Gently slide your hands underneath each end of loaf and transfer seam side down to prepared pizza peel.

10 Reshape loaf as needed, tucking edges under to form taut torpedo shape. Cover loosely with greased plastic and let rise until loaf increases in size by about half and dough springs back minimally when poked gently with your knuckle, 30 minutes to 1 hour.

11 One hour before baking, adjust oven rack to lower-middle position, place baking stone on rack, and heat oven to 450 degrees. Using sharp paring knife or single-edge razor blade, make one ½-inch-deep slash with swift, fluid motion lengthwise along top of loaf, starting and stopping about 1½ inches from ends.

12 Mist loaf with water and slide parchment with loaf onto baking stone. Bake until crust is golden brown and loaf registers 205 to 210 degrees, 25 to 30 minutes, rotating loaf halfway through baking. Transfer loaf to wire rack; discard parchment. Let cool completely, about 3 hours, before serving.

easy
sandwich
bread

makes 1 loaf
rising time 40 minutes
baking time 40 minutes
total time 2 hours, plus 3 hours cooling time
key equipment stand mixer, 8½ by 4½-inch loaf pan,
pastry brush, instant-read thermometer

2 cups (11 ounces) bread flour

6 tablespoons (2 ounces) whole-wheat flour

2¼ teaspoons instant or rapid-rise yeast

1¼ cups plus 2 tablespoons (11 ounces)
warm water (120 degrees)

3 tablespoons unsalted butter, melted

1 tablespoon honey

¾ teaspoon salt

1 large egg, lightly beaten with 1 tablespoon
water and pinch salt

why this recipe works Many people who might enjoy
making homemade sandwich bread (which beats any store-
bought loaf) don't even try because they think it takes most
of a day. Not so. It's true, however, that "quicker" yeasted
breads can lack the structure necessary for a satisfactory
rise and that their interiors are often coarse. But we
found that we could bake soft, well-risen, even-crumbed
bread that was perfect for any sandwich without kneading or
shaping—and it took just 2 hours to make (with most
of that time being hands-off). To encourage maximum
gluten development in a short amount of time, we used
higher-protein bread flour and made a wet, batter-like
dough; increasing the amount of water enhanced the gluten
structure without requiring prolonged kneading. We also
reduced the fat and sugar slightly and withheld salt until
the second mix, which gave our bread more spring and
lift. Using our mixer's paddle instead of the dough hook
and increasing the speed to medium not only shortened our
mixing time but also gave our loose dough enough
structure to rise into a dome shape—plus, we didn't need
to handle the dough or determine when it was perfectly
kneaded. We highlighted the crust by brushing the loaf
with an egg wash before baking and painting it with melted
butter afterward. The test kitchen's preferred loaf pan
measures 8½ by 4½ inches; if you use a 9 by 5-inch loaf
pan, start checking for doneness 5 minutes earlier than
advised in the recipe. To prevent the loaf from deflating as
it rises, do not let the batter come in contact with the plastic
wrap. We do not recommend mixing this dough by hand.

continued

1 Whisk bread flour, whole-wheat flour, and yeast together in bowl of stand mixer. Whisk 1¼ cups warm water, 2 tablespoons melted butter, and honey in 4-cup liquid measuring cup until honey has dissolved.

2 Using paddle on low speed, slowly add water mixture to flour mixture and mix until batter comes together, about 1 minute. Increase speed to medium and mix for 4 minutes, scraping down bowl and paddle as needed. Cover bowl tightly with plastic wrap and let batter rise until doubled in size, about 20 minutes.

3 Adjust oven rack to lower-middle position and heat oven to 375 degrees. Grease 8½ by 4½-inch loaf pan. Dissolve salt in remaining warm water, then add to batter and mix on low speed until water mixture is mostly incorporated, about 40 seconds. Increase speed to medium and mix until thoroughly combined, about 1 minute.

4 Transfer batter to prepared pan and smooth top. Cover tightly with plastic and let rise until batter reaches ½ inch below lip of pan, 15 to 20 minutes. Uncover and continue to let rise until center of batter is level with lip of pan, 5 to 10 minutes.

5 Gently brush loaf with egg mixture and bake until deep golden brown and loaf registers 205 to 210 degrees, 40 to 45 minutes, rotating pan halfway through baking.

6 Let loaf cool in pan for 15 minutes. Remove loaf from pan and transfer to wire rack. Brush top and sides with remaining melted butter. Let cool completely, about 3 hours, before serving.

troubleshooting

problem The dough seems very wet.

solution Don't worry; it should.

For adequate gluten development with minimal fuss, the dough for this sandwich bread is intentionally made to be more like a batter. You simply pour it straight from the mixer bowl into the loaf pan. Do not add any flour to yield a stiffer dough.

problem The loaf deflated while it was rising.

solution Keep the plastic wrap at a safe distance.

Avoid letting this delicate dough touch the plastic wrap as it rises. This could puncture the surface of the dough and allow valuable gas to escape.

problem The loaf is squat.

solution Knead with the paddle attachment.

Most yeasted breads call for extended kneading in a stand mixer with the dough hook. This dough, however, is made to be very wet and more like a batter, so the hook can't grasp it. To mix the dough properly and develop enough gluten, you need to use the paddle attachment, with its wider surface area. Just 4 minutes of mixing with the paddle is enough to develop the gluten needed to allow this loaf to rise tall and develop a soft crumb.

fluffy dinner rolls

makes 15 rolls
rising time 2½ to 3½ hours
baking time 25 minutes
total time 4½ to 5 hours
key equipment 13 by 9-inch baking dish, pastry brush

why this recipe works When it's time to prepare for a dinner party or holiday meal, the rolls typically get the last thought. That's too bad, because soft homemade dinner rolls beat plastic-wrapped store-bought versions any day. We wanted to develop a roll anyone could feel comfortable making—one with a fluffy crumb and a rich flavor. Before getting started, we assumed using all butter in the dough would give us the texture and flavor we desired. We were wrong. Instead, we found it best to use a duo of fats. Butter alone yielded flavorful rolls, but they were heavy (and greasy). Substituting vegetable shortening for a portion of the butter delivered a soft crumb. Why? It turns out that shortening coats the gluten strands in the flour more effectively than butter, creating tenderness. It also prevents the rolls from drying out. Whole milk provided our rolls with just the right level of moisture and richness, and one egg contributed structure and flavor. For a hint of sweetness, tasters preferred honey to sugar. When it came time to shape the rolls, we didn't need professional skills; forming the dough into balls and then cupping each ball and dragging it across the counter were all it took to form tight rounds. We lined the baking dish with a foil sling before adding the shaped dough so that it was easy to get the baked rolls out of the pan without flipping the pan over and damaging the tops. Finally, brushing the dough with an egg wash before baking gave the rolls a deep goldenbrown color. As a bonus, this dough can be refrigerated overnight after shaping into rolls, making it not only easy to serve rolls for a special meal but convenient too.

5 cups (25 ounces) all-purpose flour

2¼ teaspoons instant or rapid-rise yeast

2 teaspoons salt

1½ cups (12 ounces) whole milk, room temperature

⅓ cup (4 ounces) honey

1 large egg, room temperature

4 tablespoons (1⅔ ounces) vegetable shortening, melted

3 tablespoons unsalted butter, melted

1 large egg, lightly beaten with 1 tablespoon water and pinch salt

continued

fluffy dinner rolls, continued

1 Whisk flour, yeast, and salt together in bowl of stand mixer. Whisk milk, honey, egg, melted shortening, and melted butter in 4-cup liquid measuring cup until honey has dissolved.

2 Using dough hook on low speed, slowly add milk mixture to flour mixture and mix until cohesive dough starts to form and no dry flour remains, about 2 minutes, scraping down bowl as needed. Increase speed to medium-low and knead until dough is smooth and elastic and clears sides of bowl, about 8 minutes.

3 Transfer dough to lightly floured counter and knead by hand to form smooth, round ball, about 30 seconds. Place dough seam side down in lightly greased large bowl or container, cover tightly with plastic wrap, and let rise until doubled in size, 1½ to 2 hours.

4 Make foil sling for 13 by 9-inch baking dish by folding 2 long sheets of aluminum foil; first sheet should be 13 inches wide and second sheet should be 9 inches wide. Lay sheets of foil in dish perpendicular to each other, with extra foil hanging over edges of dish. Push foil into corners and up sides of dish, smoothing foil flush to dish, then spray foil with vegetable oil spray.

5 Press down on dough to deflate. Transfer dough to clean counter and stretch into even 15-inch log. Cut log into 15 equal pieces (about 3 ounces each) and cover loosely with greased plastic.

6 Working with 1 piece of dough at a time (keep remaining pieces covered), form into rough ball by stretching dough around your thumbs and pinching edges together so that top is smooth. Place ball seam side down on clean counter and, using your cupped hand, drag in small circles until dough feels taut and round.

7 Arrange dough balls seam side down into 5 rows of 3 in prepared dish, cover loosely with greased plastic, and let rise until nearly doubled in size and dough springs back minimally when poked gently with your knuckle, 1 to 1½ hours. (Unrisen rolls can be refrigerated for at least 8 hours or up to 16 hours; let rolls sit at room temperature for 1 hour before baking.)

8 Adjust oven rack to lower-middle position and heat oven to 350 degrees. Gently brush rolls with egg mixture and bake until golden brown, 25 to 30 minutes, rotating dish halfway through baking. Let rolls cool in dish for 15 minutes. Using foil overhang, transfer rolls to wire rack. Serve warm or at room temperature.

troubleshooting

problem The dough pieces are tough and hard to handle.

solution Keep the dough covered with plastic wrap.

If you work slowly after cutting the dough log into pieces, the individual portions of dough can form a skin and dry out as they wait on the counter for shaping. You can prevent this by covering the cut pieces of dough with plastic wrap so that air cannot get to them. Take them out from under the wrap one piece at a time when you form them into balls. This will keep the dough workable and make it easier to form into perfectly round, taut rolls.

butter fan rolls

makes 12 rolls
rising time 3 to 4 hours
baking time 20 minutes
total time 4½ to 5½ hours
key equipment 12-cup muffin tin, rolling pin, pastry brush

why this recipe works Butter fan rolls are fancy enough for a dinner party, but they're also great pulled apart and slathered with sweet jam for breakfast. The success of these rolls lies in the layers. But getting striking, fanned-out minibreads requires some serious countertop construction work. We kept the process easy with a roll, cut, butter, and stack technique. Once we'd built the stacks of dough, we placed them in a muffin tin, cut side up. In order to keep the tips of the fans from becoming crunchy, we baked the rolls on the upper-middle rack in the oven, which distanced them from the heat source. We used whole milk along with sugar and a liberal amount of butter to give these rolls plenty of richness.

3½ cups (17½ ounces) all-purpose flour

1 tablespoon instant or rapid-rise yeast

2 teaspoons salt

¾ cup (6 ounces) whole milk, room temperature

12 tablespoons (6 ounces) unsalted butter, melted

¼ cup (1¾ ounces) sugar

1 large egg plus 1 large yolk, room temperature

1 Whisk flour, yeast, and salt together in bowl of stand mixer. Whisk milk, 8 tablespoons melted butter, sugar, and egg and yolk in 4-cup liquid measuring cup until sugar has dissolved. Using dough hook on low speed, slowly add milk mixture to flour mixture and mix until cohesive dough starts to form and no dry flour remains,

about 2 minutes. Increase speed to medium-low and knead until dough is smooth and clears sides of bowl, about 6 minutes, scraping down bowl as needed.

2 Transfer dough to lightly floured counter and knead by hand to form smooth, round ball, about 30 seconds. Place dough seam side down in lightly greased large bowl or container, cover tightly with plastic wrap, and let rise until doubled in size, 1½ to 2 hours.

3 Grease 12-cup muffin tin. Press down on dough to deflate. Transfer dough to lightly floured counter, divide in half, and cover loosely with greased plastic. Press and roll 1 piece of dough (keep remaining piece covered) into 15 by 12-inch rectangle, with long side parallel to counter edge.

4 Using pizza cutter or chef's knife, square off edges of rectangle, then cut dough vertically into 6 (2½ by 12-inch) strips. Brush tops of 5 strips evenly with 1 tablespoon melted butter, leaving 1 strip unbuttered. Stack strips on top of each other, buttered to unbuttered side, finishing with unbuttered strip on top; cut into 6 stacks.

5 Place stacks cut side up in muffin cups. Repeat with remaining dough and 1 tablespoon melted butter. Cover muffin tin loosely with greased plastic and let dough rise until nearly doubled in size, 1½ to 2 hours. (Unrisen rolls can be refrigerated for at least 8 hours or up to 16 hours; let sit at room temperature for 1 hour before baking.)

6 Adjust oven rack to upper-middle position and heat oven to 350 degrees. Bake rolls until golden brown, 20 to 25 minutes, rotating muffin tin halfway through baking. Let rolls cool in muffin tin for 5 minutes, brush with remaining melted butter, and serve warm.

flour tortillas

makes twelve 8-inch tortillas
resting time 30 minutes
cooking time 24 minutes
total time 1½ hours
key equipment rolling pin, 12-inch nonstick skillet

2¾ cups (13¾ ounces) all-purpose flour

1½ teaspoons salt

6 tablespoons (2½ ounces) vegetable shortening, cut into 6 pieces

¾ cup plus 2 tablespoons (7 ounces) warm tap water

1 teaspoon vegetable oil

why this recipe works Supple and flavorful, home-made flour tortillas far surpass store-bought versions, and the dough requires just a few ingredients (flour, salt, fat, and water) that are in most pantries. Traditionally, you'd need a tortilla press, but we wanted to develop a dough that didn't require any special equipment—just a rolling pin and a skillet. We learned that too little fat produced brittle results that made rolling with a pin impossible; a generous 6 tablespoons of fat was just right. While tortillas are often made with lard, we preferred vegetable shortening as it's already a pantry staple for many cooks. As we continued our testing, we found that too little salt yielded tasteless tortillas, so we upped the amount; baking powder, which is used in some recipes, made tortillas that were doughy and thick, so we omitted it. All-purpose flour performed better than bread flour or cake flour, which produced tortillas that were tough and crumbly, respectively. Most important, though, how we combined the ingredients turned out to be the secret to truly great flour tortillas. Adding warm water to the dough melted the shortening, which then coated the flour and prevented it from absorbing excess moisture. This resulted in less gluten development and yielded more tender tortillas. The tortillas cooked quickly—just 1 minute per side in a preheated skillet. To make ten 10-inch tortillas, double the recipe, divide the dough evenly into 10 pieces, and roll each into a 10-inch round; cook as directed. Cooled tortillas can be layered between sheets of parchment paper, wrapped in plastic wrap, and refrigerated for up to 3 days. To reheat, place the tortillas on a plate, invert a second plate on top, and microwave until warm and soft, 60 to 90 seconds.

1 Whisk flour and salt together in large bowl. Using your hands, rub shortening into flour mixture until mixture resembles coarse meal.

2 Stir warm water into flour mixture with wooden spoon until incorporated and dough comes together. Transfer dough to clean counter and knead by hand to form smooth, cohesive ball, about 30 seconds.

3 Divide dough into quarters and cut each quarter into 3 equal pieces (about 2 ounces each). Roll each piece into ball and transfer to plate. Cover with plastic wrap and refrigerate for at least 30 minutes or up to 3 days.

4 Working with 1 piece of dough at a time (keep remaining pieces covered), roll into 8-inch-round tortilla between two 12-inch squares of greased parchment paper.

5 Heat oil in 12-inch nonstick skillet over medium-high heat until shimmering. Meanwhile, remove top parchment from 1 tortilla and gently reshape edges. Using paper towels, carefully wipe out skillet, leaving thin film of oil on bottom. Flip tortilla onto your palm, then remove second piece of parchment and lay tortilla in skillet.

6 Cook until surface begins to bubble, about 1 minute. Flip tortilla and cook until puffed and bottom is spotty brown, about 1 minute. Transfer to plate and cover with dish towel. Repeat with remaining tortillas. Serve.

pan-grilled flatbread

makes four 9-inch flatbreads
rising time 1½ to 2 hours
resting time 10 minutes
cooking time 16 minutes
total time 3 to 3½ hours
key equipment 12-inch cast-iron skillet with lid, rolling pin, water-filled spray bottle, pastry brush

2½ cups (13¾ ounces) bread flour

¼ cup (1⅓ ounces) whole-wheat flour

2¼ teaspoons instant or rapid-rise yeast

1½ teaspoons salt

1 cup (8 ounces) water, room temperature

¼ cup (2 ounces) plain whole-milk yogurt, room temperature

2 tablespoons extra-virgin olive oil

2 teaspoons sugar

1½ tablespoons unsalted butter, melted

coarse sea salt

why this recipe works Flatbreads are eaten all over the world, often accompanying stewed meals—they're perfect for mopping up aromatic braising liquids and curries. We set out to make flavorful, rustic flatbreads that were tender yet chewy, and easy enough to cook while dinner was on the stove. We knew we wanted a hearty wheat flavor without compromising the flatbread's texture, so we added a small amount of whole-wheat flour—just ¼ cup—to the high-protein bread flour. Taking a cue from the Indian flatbread naan, we enriched the dough with yogurt and oil, which tenderized it. A little sugar and salt improved the flavor of the bread. For the cooking vessel, we turned to a cast-iron skillet, which mimicked the tandoor or brick oven often used to bake similar breads around the world. The cast iron's great heat retention helped create the signature spotty brown flecks covering these breads. But our flatbreads were developing a tough crust. We found that softening the crust and prolonging the optimal tender texture of the bread required a two-tiered approach. First, we misted the dough with water before cooking it to moisten the flour that coated it. Then we covered the pan during the bread's brief cooking time, which trapped steam and moisture. Brushing the finished breads with melted butter and sprinkling them with sea salt added a final layer of flavor to these easy-to-make flatbreads. We prefer a cast-iron skillet here, but any 12-inch nonstick skillet will work fine. For efficiency, stretch the next ball of dough while each flatbread is cooking.

continued

pan-grilled flatbread, continued

1 Whisk bread flour, whole-wheat flour, yeast, and salt together in bowl of stand mixer. Whisk water, yogurt, 1 tablespoon oil, and sugar in 4-cup liquid measuring cup until sugar has dissolved. Using dough hook on low speed, slowly add water mixture to flour mixture and mix until cohesive dough starts to form and no dry flour remains, about 2 minutes, scraping down bowl as needed. Increase speed to medium-low and knead until dough is smooth and elastic and clears sides of bowl but sticks to bottom, about 8 minutes.

2 Transfer dough to lightly floured counter and knead by hand to form smooth, round ball, about 30 seconds. Place dough seam side down in lightly greased large bowl or container, cover tightly with plastic wrap, and let rise until doubled in size, 1½ to 2 hours.

3 Adjust oven rack to middle position and heat oven to 200 degrees. Transfer dough to clean counter, divide into quarters, and cover loosely with greased plastic. Working with 1 piece of dough at a time (keep remaining pieces covered), form into rough ball by stretching dough around your thumbs and pinching edges together so that top is smooth. Place ball seam side down on clean counter, and using your cupped hand, drag in small circles until dough feels taut and round. Let balls rest, covered, for 10 minutes.

4 Grease 12-inch cast-iron skillet with remaining 1 tablespoon oil and heat over medium heat for 5 minutes. Meanwhile, press and roll 1 dough ball into 9-inch round of even thickness, sprinkling dough and counter with flour as needed to prevent sticking. Using fork, poke entire surface of round 20 to 25 times.

5 Using paper towels, carefully wipe out skillet, leaving thin film of oil on bottom and sides. Mist top of dough with water. Place dough moistened side down in skillet, then mist top of dough with water. Cover and cook until flatbread is lightly puffed and bottom is spotty brown, 2 to 4 minutes. Flip flatbread, cover, and continue to cook until spotty brown on second side, 2 to 4 minutes. (If large air pockets form, gently poke with fork to deflate.)

6 Brush 1 side of flatbread with about 1 teaspoon melted butter and sprinkle with sea salt. Serve immediately or transfer to ovensafe plate, cover loosely with aluminum foil, and keep warm in oven. Repeat with remaining dough balls, melted butter, and sea salt. Serve.

troubleshooting

problem The flatbreads have a floury crust.

solution **Mist the dough with water and cover the skillet.**

Flatbreads should have a browned, blistered exterior, but they should also be uniformly soft and tender. To prevent a floury crust from forming, spray the raw dough lightly with water before cooking it to moisten the flour that coats it. In addition, cook the flatbread covered to trap steam around the bread as it bakes. This not only softens the crust but also allows the flatbreads to stay moist and tender for longer after cooking.

problem The flatbreads are tough.

solution **Use whole-milk yogurt.**

Although it may be tempting to reach for any plain yogurt you have on hand for this recipe, you must use whole-milk yogurt. Using low-fat yogurt will yield tough bread. The extra fat in whole-milk yogurt coats the flour proteins, weakening gluten formation by preventing the proteins from binding to each other too tightly. The higher-fat yogurt also holds in more moisture for a tender bread.

skillet pizza

makes two 11-inch pizzas
resting time 2 minutes
rising time 1½ to 2 hours
cooking time 20 minutes
total time 2¾ to 3¼ hours
key equipment food processor, rolling pin, 12-inch ovensafe skillet

why this recipe works Making pizza at home is gratifying, and it almost always tastes better than what you can get from delivery. But achieving a pizza with a crisp crust in the home oven can also be a real challenge. You need to stretch the dough carefully, preheat a heavy baking stone, and then swiftly slide the topped dough round into a hot oven, making sure the pizza maintains its shape. In searching for a foolproof method for cooking pizza whenever the mood struck, we found that making truly great pizza is a breeze in a skillet. Our dough came together quickly in the food processor; after we let it rise, we rolled it thin and then transferred it to a cool oiled skillet, where we topped it with a fast no-cook sauce and slices of fresh mozzarella cheese. We placed the skillet over a hot burner to get it good and hot and to set the bottom of the crust. Once the crust began to brown, we simply slid the skillet into a 500-degree oven. In the oven, the hot skillet functioned like a pizza stone, crisping up our crust in just minutes and melting the cheese. We've featured a Margherita pizza topping here, adorning the sauce and cheese with just a sprinkle of basil. But if you'd like a more substantial topping for your pizza, feel free to sprinkle pepperoni, sautéed mushrooms, or browned sausage over the cheese before baking; just be sure to keep the toppings light or they may weigh down the thin crust and make it soggy. The sauce will yield more than is needed in the recipe; extra sauce can be refrigerated for up to one week or frozen for up to one month.

dough

2 cups (11 ounces) plus 2 tablespoons bread flour

1⅛ teaspoons instant or rapid-rise yeast

¾ teaspoon salt

1 tablespoon extra-virgin olive oil

¾ cup (6 ounces) ice water

sauce and toppings

1 (28-ounce) can whole peeled tomatoes, drained with juice reserved

5 tablespoons extra-virgin olive oil

2 garlic cloves, minced

1 teaspoon red wine vinegar

1 teaspoon dried oregano

½ teaspoon salt

¼ teaspoon pepper

8 ounces fresh mozzarella cheese, sliced ¼ inch thick and patted dry with paper towels

2 tablespoons chopped fresh basil

continued

1 **For the dough** Pulse flour, yeast, and salt in food processor until combined, about 5 pulses. With processor running, add oil, then water, and process until rough ball forms, 30 to 40 seconds. Let dough rest for 2 minutes, then process for 30 seconds longer.

2 Transfer dough to lightly floured counter and knead by hand to form smooth, round ball, about 30 seconds. Place dough seam side down in lightly greased large bowl or container, cover tightly with plastic wrap, and let rise until doubled in size, 1½ to 2 hours. (Unrisen dough can be refrigerated for at least 8 hours or up to 16 hours; let sit at room temperature for 30 minutes before shaping in step 5.)

3 **For the sauce and toppings** Process tomatoes, 1 tablespoon oil, garlic, vinegar, oregano, salt, and pepper in clean, dry workbowl until smooth, about 30 seconds. Transfer mixture to 2-cup liquid measuring cup and add reserved tomato juice until sauce measures 2 cups. Reserve 1 cup sauce; set aside remaining sauce for another use.

4 Adjust oven rack to upper-middle position and heat oven to 500 degrees. Grease 12-inch ovensafe skillet with 2 tablespoons oil.

5 Transfer dough to lightly floured counter, divide in half, and cover loosely with greased plastic. Press and roll 1 piece of dough (keep remaining piece covered) into 11-inch round of even thickness.

6 Transfer dough to prepared skillet and reshape as needed. Spread ½ cup sauce over dough, leaving ½-inch border around edge. Top with half of mozzarella.

7 Set skillet over high heat and cook until outside edge of dough is set, pizza is lightly puffed, and bottom of crust looks spotty brown when gently lifted with spatula, about 3 minutes.

8 Transfer skillet to oven and bake pizza until edges are brown and cheese is melted and spotty brown, 7 to 10 minutes. Using potholders, remove skillet from oven and slide pizza onto wire rack; let cool slightly. Sprinkle with 1 tablespoon basil, cut into wedges, and serve. Being careful of hot skillet, repeat with remaining oil, dough, ½ cup sauce, remaining mozzarella, and basil.

troubleshooting

problem The crust is soggy.

solution Use a light hand when adding the tomato sauce.

This recipe yields more tomato sauce than you need to make the two pizzas. Do not be tempted to top each pizza with more than the ½ cup of sauce called for in the recipe. An overload of sauce will create a heavy pizza and weigh down the crust, and the excess moisture will make for a crust that is soft and soggy rather than light and crisp. This versatile tomato sauce can be refrigerated for up to one week or frozen for up to one month for use in future pizza making or in other dishes that require tomato sauce.

monkey bread

makes 1 loaf
rising time 3 to 4 hours
baking time 30 minutes
total time 5 to 6 hours
key equipment 12-cup nonstick Bundt pan

why this recipe works Monkey bread is a knotty-looking loaf made from rich balls of dough coated in cinnamon, sugar, and melted butter and baked in a Bundt pan. It's traditionally served warm so that the sticky baked pieces can be pulled apart. The older recipes we found produced a delicious bread, but they were two-day affairs; newer versions favored convenience, calling for store-bought biscuit dough and yielding lean, dry, bland bread that simply wasn't worth the time saved. We wanted a faster recipe for monkey bread that didn't compromise on its delicious flavor and sticky, sweet appeal. To expedite the rising and proofing in this recipe we used a generous amount of instant yeast and added sugar to the dough, which jump-started the yeast. Butter and milk helped keep the dough tender and flavorful. Before assembling the bread, we rolled the balls of dough in melted butter and sugar to give them a thick, caramel-like coating. White sugar was good, but light brown sugar, with its molasses notes, made a coating that was even better. Mixing multiple spices with the sugar muddied the flavor, but a generous amount of cinnamon alone added warm character to the coating. Once the bread had cooled slightly, we finished by drizzling a simple confectioners' sugar glaze over the top.

dough
3¼ cups (16¼ ounces) all-purpose flour
2¼ teaspoons instant or rapid-rise yeast
2 teaspoons salt
1 cup (8 ounces) whole milk, room temperature
⅓ cup (2⅔ ounces) water, room temperature
¼ cup (1¾ ounces) granulated sugar
2 tablespoons unsalted butter, melted

brown sugar coating
1 cup packed (7 ounces) light brown sugar
2 teaspoons ground cinnamon
8 tablespoons (4 ounces) unsalted butter, melted and cooled

glaze
1 cup (4 ounces) confectioners' sugar
2 tablespoons whole milk

continued

1 For the dough Whisk flour, yeast, and salt together in bowl of stand mixer. Whisk milk, water, sugar, and melted butter in 4-cup liquid measuring cup until sugar has dissolved. Using dough hook on low speed, slowly add milk mixture to flour mixture and mix until cohesive dough starts to form and no dry flour remains, about 2 minutes, scraping down bowl as needed. Increase speed to medium-low and knead until dough is smooth and elastic and clears sides of bowl but sticks to bottom, 8 to 10 minutes.

2 Transfer dough to lightly floured counter and knead by hand to form smooth, round ball, about 30 seconds. Place dough seam side down in lightly greased large bowl or container, cover tightly with plastic wrap, and let rise until doubled in size, 1½ to 2 hours. (Unrisen dough can be refrigerated for at least 8 hours or up to 16 hours; let sit at room temperature for 1 hour before shaping in step 4.)

3 For the brown sugar coating Thoroughly grease 12-cup nonstick Bundt pan. Combine sugar and cinnamon in medium bowl. Place melted butter in second bowl.

4 Transfer dough to lightly floured counter and press into rough 8-inch square. Using pizza cutter or chef's knife, cut dough into 8 even strips. Cut each strip into 8 pieces (64 pieces total). Cover loosely with greased plastic.

5 Working with a few pieces of dough at a time (keep remaining pieces covered), place on clean counter and, using your cupped hand, drag in small circles until dough feels taut and round. Dip balls in melted butter, then roll in sugar mixture to coat. Place balls in prepared pan, staggering seams where dough balls meet as you build layers.

6 Cover pan tightly with plastic and let rise until dough balls reach 1 to 2 inches below lip of pan, 1½ to 2 hours.

7 Adjust oven rack to middle position and heat oven to 350 degrees. Bake until top is deep golden brown and caramel begins to bubble around edges, 30 to 35 minutes. Let bread cool in pan for 5 minutes, then invert onto serving platter and let cool for 10 minutes.

8 For the glaze Meanwhile, whisk sugar and milk in bowl until smooth. Drizzle glaze over bread, letting it run down sides. Serve warm.

troubleshooting

problem The bread won't release from the pan.

solution Let the bread rest in the pan for no longer than 5 minutes.

The bread needs to rest in the Bundt pan for 5 minutes before you invert it onto a serving platter. This ensures that it can solidify into a cohesive mass. However, if you leave the bread in the pan any longer, the thin caramel-like coating on the dough balls will cool and thicken, cementing the bread to the pan and making it difficult to remove in one piece. For an easy release, be sure to remove the bread from the pan immediately after it has rested for the required 5 minutes. That said, if you do accidentally leave the bread in the pan for too long, you can return the bread to a 350-degree oven for 5 minutes to remelt the sugar.

sandwich
breads
everyday
loaves,
modern
and classic

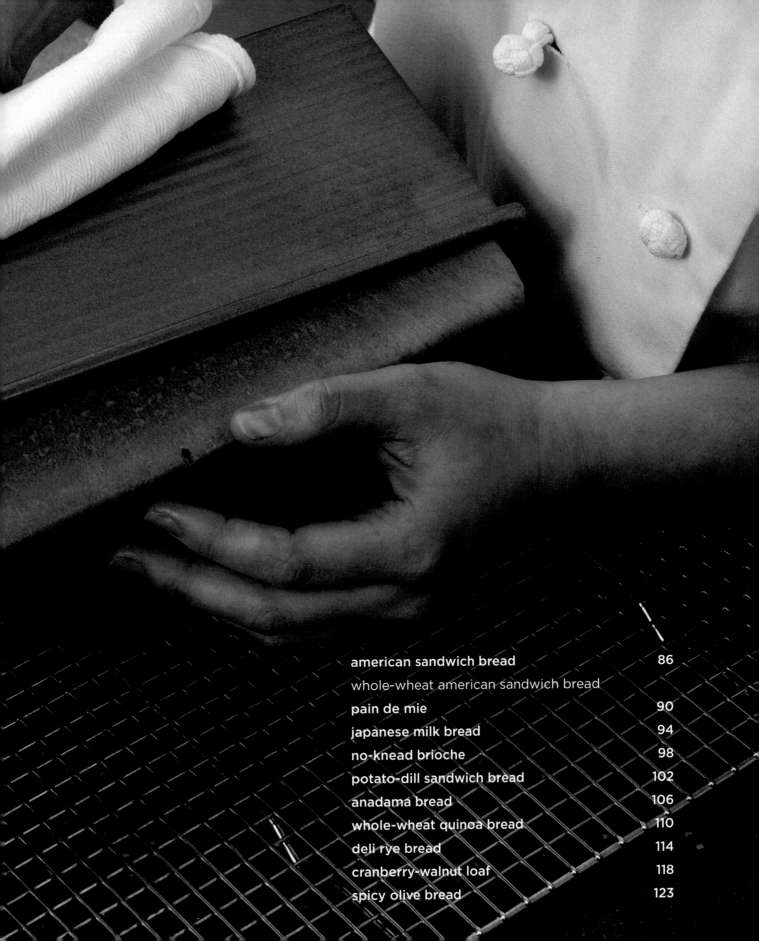

american sandwich bread

makes 1 loaf
rising time 2½ to 3½ hours
baking time 35 minutes
total time 4 to 5 hours, plus 3 hours cooling time
key equipment 8½ by 4½-inch loaf pan, water-filled spray bottle, instant-read thermometer

2½ cups (13¾ ounces) bread flour

2 teaspoons instant or rapid-rise yeast

1½ teaspoons salt

¾ cup (6 ounces) whole milk, room temperature

⅓ cup (2⅔ ounces) water, room temperature

2 tablespoons unsalted butter, melted

2 tablespoons honey

why this recipe works The quintessential American sandwich loaf—tall and domed, with a fine, snowy-white crumb and a light brown crust—is a supermarket staple. Since it's eaten so often, we wanted to develop a recipe that wasn't just better than bouncy plastic-wrapped bread, but the best—an impressive loaf that was a worthy base for sandwiches. For this bread's soft crumb we needed to include a fair amount of fat; we used whole milk for a majority of the liquid and then enriched the dough further with 2 tablespoons of melted butter. These amounts were enough to tenderize the bread without making it too rich. A couple spoonfuls of honey gave the bread the faint sweetness we'd expect. But because our dough contained milk, butter, and honey, the crust was prone to browning before the inside was done. We tested oven temperatures of 350, 375, and 400 degrees and found that the lowest temperature gave us the soft crust we wanted and avoided a doughy interior. Still, we felt that our loaf was a bit dense. We experimented with letting the loaf proof longer, until it reached a full inch above the lip of the pan; the increased rise produced an airy crumb and a bigger loaf. This additional rise also meant we could eliminate slashing the loaf because it wouldn't expand much more in the oven. Nixing the slashing gave our finished loaf the smooth top of supermarket bread. The test kitchen's preferred loaf pan measures 8½ by 4½ inches; if you use a 9 by 5-inch loaf pan, increase the shaped rising time by 20 to 30 minutes and start checking for doneness 10 minutes earlier than advised in the recipe.

continued

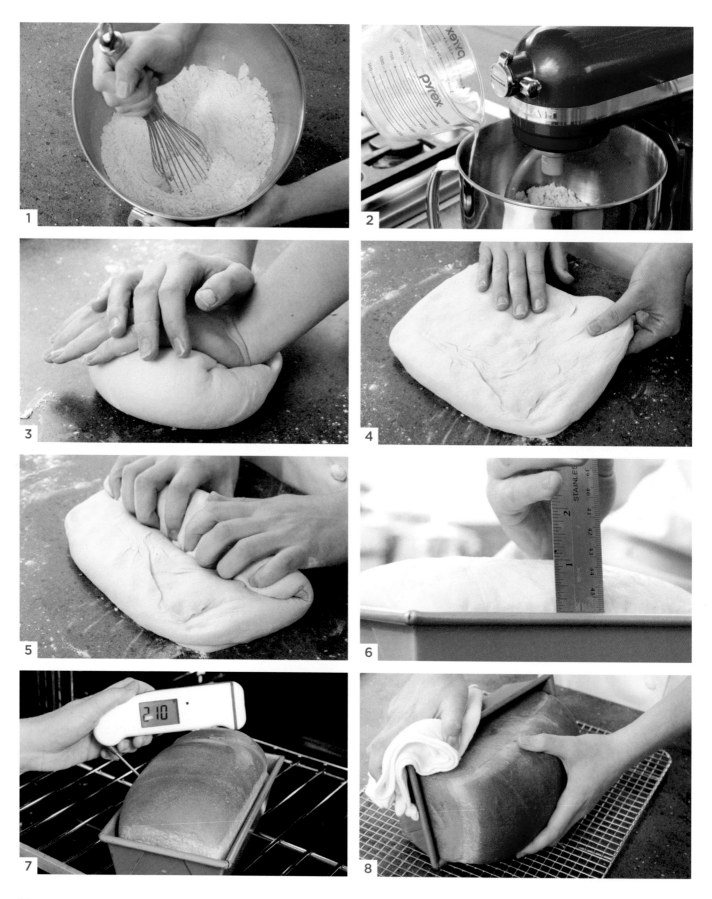

1 Whisk flour, yeast, and salt together in bowl of stand mixer. Whisk milk, water, melted butter, and honey in 4-cup liquid measuring cup until honey has dissolved.

2 Using dough hook on low speed, slowly add milk mixture to flour mixture and mix until cohesive dough starts to form and no dry flour remains, about 2 minutes, scraping down bowl as needed. Increase speed to medium-low and knead until dough is smooth and elastic and clears sides of bowl, about 8 minutes.

3 Transfer dough to lightly floured counter and knead by hand to form smooth, round ball, about 30 seconds. Place dough seam side down in lightly greased large bowl or container, cover tightly with plastic wrap, and let rise until doubled in size, 1½ to 2 hours.

4 Grease 8½ by 4½-inch loaf pan. Press down on dough to deflate. Turn dough out onto lightly floured counter (side of dough that was against bowl should now be facing up). Press and stretch dough into 8 by 6-inch rectangle, with long side parallel to counter edge.

5 Roll dough away from you into firm cylinder, keeping roll taut by tucking it under itself as you go. Pinch seam closed and place loaf seam side down in prepared pan, pressing dough gently into corners.

6 Cover loosely with greased plastic and let rise until loaf reaches 1 inch above lip of pan and dough springs back minimally when poked gently with your knuckle, 1 to 1½ hours.

7 Adjust oven rack to lower-middle position and heat oven to 350 degrees. Mist loaf with water and bake until deep golden brown and loaf registers 205 to 210 degrees, 35 to 40 minutes, rotating pan halfway through baking.

8 Let loaf cool in pan for 15 minutes. Remove loaf from pan and let cool completely on wire rack, about 3 hours, before serving.

variation **whole-wheat american sandwich bread**
Reduce bread flour to 1½ cups (8¼ ounces) and add 1 cup (5½ ounces) whole-wheat flour and 3 tablespoons toasted wheat germ in step 1. Increase honey to 3 tablespoons.

troubleshooting

problem The loaf is uneven.	*problem* The loaf is dense.	*problem* The loaf tears on the sides.
solution Roll the dough neatly.	*solution* Roll the dough into a tight cylinder.	*solution* Let the loaf rise for the proper amount of time.

Proper shaping of the dough determines the appearance of the baked loaf. If the dough is rolled unevenly, it will rise and bake unevenly too. Make sure to tuck the loaf under itself as you roll it, and pinch the seams so that they don't open while the loaf is proofing or baking.

Rolling sandwich bread dough into a taut cylinder creates a tight skin on the shaped loaf. This skin ensures that the gases don't escape and the loaf rises properly to create an airy crumb.

If the shaped loaf is underproofed, the gluten doesn't get a chance to relax before the loaf hits the oven, and the network of gluten tears. This causes the gases to escape at random, weak points along the sides of the loaf. Let the loaf rise a full inch above the lip of the pan.

pain
de
mie

makes 1 loaf
rising time 2 to 3 hours
baking time 35 minutes
total time 3½ to 4½ hours, plus 3 hours cooling time
key equipment 13 by 4-inch Pullman loaf pan, instant-read thermometer

4 cups (20 ounces) all-purpose flour

1 tablespoon instant or rapid-rise yeast

2 teaspoons salt

1 cup plus 2 tablespoons (9 ounces) whole milk, room temperature

¼ cup (2 ounces) water, room temperature

4 tablespoons (2 ounces) unsalted butter, melted

2 tablespoons honey

why this recipe works *Pain de mie* (*mie* means "crumb" in French) is a loaf of bread with straight edges, a tender, velvety crumb, and a minimal crust—excellent for making a standout peanut butter and jelly or grilled cheese sandwich. This bread gets its perfectly square corners from being baked in a straight-sided Pullman loaf pan, which has a cover that slides over the bread. These pans were famously used in the small kitchens of Pullman railway cars because the bakers could stack the squared-off loaves. In the early 18th century, long before the pans were used on trains, European bread makers started using squared pans in an effort to minimize crust. We wanted to do just that: create a straight-edged, airy loaf with crust so thin that no child would ask to remove it. For the flour, we landed on all-purpose instead of bread flour because it produced an airier interior and a softer crust. Curiously, many pain de mie recipes we researched included dry milk powder, so we thought it might soften the crumb even further. Not so. Loaves made with a combination of liquid whole milk and water had a much fluffier, more tender crumb. Four tablespoons of butter, melted and combined with the milk and water, enriched the bread's flavor without making it greasy. Finally, for a hint of sweetness, we preferred the addition of honey to sugar because it increased the moisture of our bread enough so that we wouldn't have to add an excessive amount of milk or water, which would make the dough difficult to work with. To obtain even browning, we removed the lid of the Pullman loaf pan and rotated the loaf halfway through baking.

continued

1 Whisk flour, yeast, and salt together in bowl of stand mixer. Whisk milk, water, melted butter, and honey in 4-cup liquid measuring cup until honey has dissolved.

2 Using dough hook on low speed, slowly add milk mixture to flour mixture and mix until cohesive dough starts to form and no dry flour remains, about 2 minutes, scraping down bowl as needed. Increase speed to medium-low and knead until dough is smooth and elastic and clears sides of bowl, about 8 minutes.

3 Transfer dough to lightly floured counter and knead by hand to form smooth, round ball, about 30 seconds. Place dough seam side down in lightly greased large bowl or container, cover tightly with plastic wrap, and let rise until doubled in size, 1 to 1½ hours.

4 Grease lid, bottom, and sides of 13 by 4-inch Pullman loaf pan. Press down on dough to deflate. Turn dough out onto lightly floured counter (side of dough that was against bowl should now be facing up). Press and stretch dough into 12 by 10-inch rectangle, with long side parallel to counter edge.

5 Roll dough away from you into firm cylinder, keeping roll taut by tucking it under itself as you go. Pinch seam closed and place loaf seam side down in prepared pan, pressing dough gently into corners.

6 Slide lid onto pan, leaving 2-inch opening at end. Cover opening tightly with greased plastic and let dough rise until loaf is level with lip of pan and dough springs back minimally when poked gently with your knuckle, 1 to 1½ hours.

7 Adjust oven rack to lower-middle position and heat oven to 350 degrees. Slide lid completely onto pan and bake until loaf is light golden brown and registers 205 to 210 degrees, 35 to 40 minutes, removing lid and rotating pan halfway through baking.

8 Let loaf cool in pan for 15 minutes. Remove loaf from pan and let cool completely on wire rack, about 3 hours, before serving.

troubleshooting

problem The sides of the loaf collapse.

solution Let the loaf cool in the pan for 15 minutes.

Many pain de mie recipes call for removing the bread from the pan just 5 to 10 minutes after baking, but we found that this amount of time is not sufficient. If you don't let this airy bread cool for a full 15 minutes before removing it from the pan, it will not have a chance to set up and the sides will collapse, making for a loaf that lacks clean lines.

problem The top of the loaf is pale.

solution Remove the lid halfway through baking.

Covering the loaf pan ensures that the bread emerges straight and squared. However, if you keep the cover on for the full baking time, the bread will have a pale crust with a steamed texture. Be sure to remove the lid halfway through baking, at which point the bread will be done rising and the crust won't overbrown and toughen.

japanese milk bread

makes 1 loaf
resting time 15 minutes
rising time 1½ to 2½ hours
baking time 30 minutes
total time 3½ to 4½ hours, plus 3 hours cooling time
key equipment stand mixer, 8½ by 4½-inch loaf pan, rolling pin, instant-read thermometer, pastry brush

2 cups (11 ounces) plus 3 tablespoons bread flour

½ cup (4 ounces) water

½ cup (4 ounces) cold whole milk

1 large egg

1½ teaspoons instant or rapid-rise yeast

2 tablespoons sugar

1½ teaspoons salt

3 tablespoons unsalted butter, softened, plus 1 tablespoon melted

why this recipe works Japanese milk bread, or Hokkaido milk bread, may look like any white loaf. But this plush bread is distinctly different from American sandwich bread; it boasts a superlatively fluffy texture and a unique shaping method. A staple in Asian bakeries, the loaf is composed of portions of dough rolled thin and formed into tight spirals. This shaping organizes the gluten strands into coils, which bake into feathery sheets. Here's why: When dough is kneaded, the proteins link up in a random way. Standard shaping organizes the proteins into a matrix on the exterior of the dough, but they remain random in the interior. Shaping the dough instead into two spirals before placing in the pan builds an orderly structure throughout, creating this bread's gossamer-thin layers. The bread also employs a special technique called *tangzhong* to yield its delicate crumb. This method incorporates extra moisture into the dough in the form of a flour-and-water paste. Typically, a well-hydrated dough like this one is hard to shape. The paste avoids this. We microwaved a portion of the flour with the water and then mixed the paste into the dough; flour can absorb twice as much hot water as cold, so heating the two together allowed us to pack in moisture for a pillowy crumb without making the dough too slack to work with. The test kitchen's preferred loaf pan measures 8½ by 4½ inches; if you use a 9 by 5-inch loaf pan, increase the shaped rising time by 20 to 30 minutes and start checking for doneness 10 minutes earlier than advised in the recipe. We do not recommend mixing this dough by hand.

continued

1 Whisk 3 tablespoons flour and water in small bowl until no lumps remain. Microwave, whisking every 20 seconds, until mixture thickens to stiff, smooth, pudding-like consistency that forms mound when dropped from end of whisk into bowl, 40 to 80 seconds.

2 Whisk milk, egg, and flour paste in bowl of stand mixer until smooth. Add yeast and remaining 2 cups flour. Using dough hook on low speed, mix until cohesive dough starts to form and no dry flour remains, about 2 minutes, scraping down bowl as needed. Cover bowl tightly with plastic wrap and let dough rest for 15 minutes.

3 Add sugar and salt to dough and mix on low speed, about 5 minutes. With mixer running, add softened butter, 1 tablespoon at a time, and mix until butter is fully incorporated, about 2 minutes. Increase speed to medium-low and knead until dough is smooth and elastic and clears sides of bowl but sticks to bottom, about 5 minutes.

4 Transfer dough to lightly floured counter and knead by hand to form smooth, round ball, about 30 seconds. Place dough seam side down in lightly greased large bowl or container, cover tightly with plastic, and let rise until doubled in size, 1 to 1½ hours.

5 Grease 8½ by 4½-inch loaf pan. Press down on dough to deflate. Turn dough out onto lightly floured counter (side of dough that was against bowl should now be facing up). Gently press and roll into 24 by 4-inch rectangle, with short side parallel to counter edge. Using pizza cutter or chef's knife, cut rectangle lengthwise into 2 equal strips.

6 Roll 1 strip of dough into snug cylinder, pinch seam closed, and place seam side down in prepared pan, with spiral against long side of pan. Repeat with remaining strip of dough, placing it adjacent to other in pan.

7 Cover loosely with greased plastic and let rise until loaf is level with lip of pan and dough springs back minimally when poked gently with your knuckle, 30 minutes to 1 hour.

8 Adjust oven rack to lowest position and heat oven to 375 degrees. Bake until deep golden brown and loaf registers 205 to 210 degrees, 30 to 35 minutes, rotating pan halfway through baking. Let loaf cool in pan for 15 minutes. Remove loaf from pan and transfer to wire rack. Brush top and sides with melted butter. Let cool completely, about 3 hours, before serving.

troubleshooting

problem The loaf is dense.

solution Don't overwork the dough while rolling it.

This loaf requires more shaping than the average sandwich bread to create its trademark feathery interior. When pressing the dough into a rectangle and then rolling the cut dough strips into cylinders, be sure to be gentle and avoid overworking the dough. Handling the dough too much will toughen it and result in a squat, dense loaf.

no-knead brioche

makes 1 loaf
resting time 15 minutes
rising time 17½ to 18 hours
baking time 35 minutes
total time 21 to 23 hours, plus 3 hours cooling time
key equipment 8½ by 4½-inch loaf pan, pastry brush, instant-read thermometer

1⅔ cups (9⅛ ounces) bread flour

1¼ teaspoons instant or rapid-rise yeast

¾ teaspoon salt

3 large eggs, room temperature

8 tablespoons (4 ounces) unsalted butter, melted

¼ cup (2 ounces) water, room temperature

3 tablespoons sugar

1 large egg, lightly beaten with 1 tablespoon water and pinch salt

why this recipe works Classic brioche has a tender crumb, an appealing golden color, and a buttery flavor that's richer than that of any other sandwich bread. But achieving these sumptuous results can cause a butter-induced headache. Typically, the process is laborious: Butter, softened to just the right temperature, is kneaded into the dough in increments. And patience is crucial: Only after one portion is fully incorporated is the next added to ensure that the butter is completely combined and doesn't cause the dough to separate. We wondered if we could avoid this process and use melted butter. Simply streaming melted butter into the stand mixer gave us a greasy, separated dough that lacked structure. That's when we thought of the technique we used for our Almost No-Knead Bread (page 52), in which we combine all the ingredients and let the mixture sit for hours. This allows the dough to stitch itself together into a loaf with only a bit of stirring and a couple of folds or turns. Happily, this method worked with our rich dough, allowing us to simplify the conventional brioche method dramatically. But the bread did need more structure. Switching from the all-purpose flour that's used in many recipes to bread flour was a big help. In addition, instead of shaping the dough into a single long loaf, we found that we could add even more strength to the dough by dividing it in two and shaping each half into a ball. Placed side by side in the pan, the two balls merged to form a single strong loaf. The test kitchen's preferred loaf pan measures 8½ by 4½ inches; if you use a 9 by 5-inch loaf pan, increase the shaped rising time by 20 to 30 minutes and start checking for doneness 10 minutes earlier than advised in the recipe.

continued

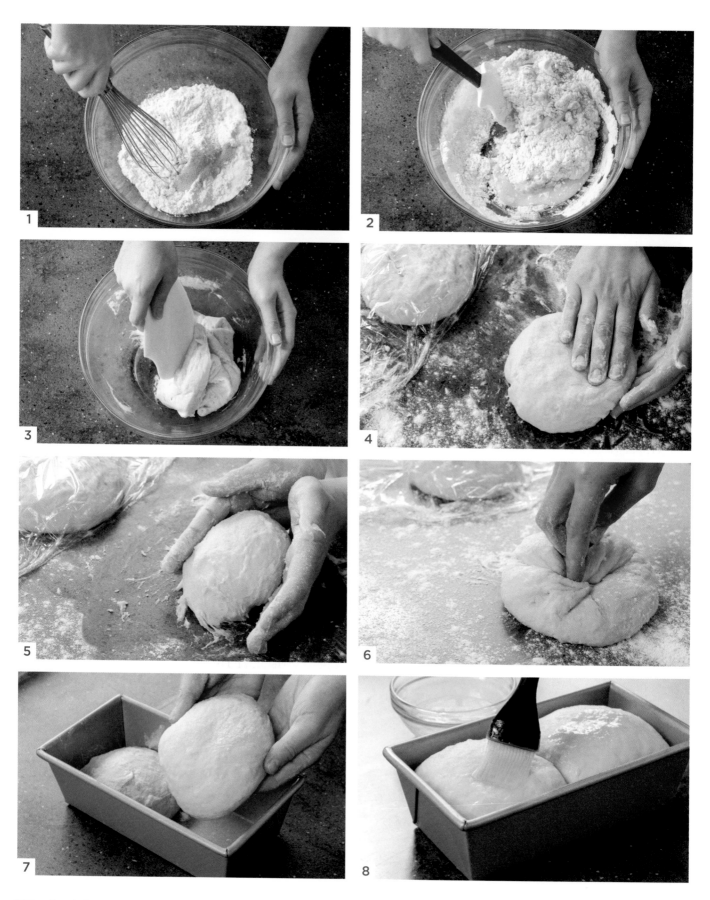

no-knead brioche, continued

1 Whisk flour, yeast, and salt together in large bowl. Whisk eggs, melted butter, water, and sugar in second bowl until sugar has dissolved.

2 Using rubber spatula, gently fold egg mixture into flour mixture, scraping up dry flour from bottom of bowl, until cohesive dough starts to form and no dry flour remains. Cover bowl tightly with plastic wrap and let dough rest for 10 minutes.

3 Using greased bowl scraper (or your fingertips), fold dough over itself by gently lifting and folding edge of dough toward middle. Turn bowl 90 degrees and fold dough again; repeat turning bowl and folding dough 2 more times (total of 4 folds). Cover tightly with plastic and let rise for 30 minutes. Repeat folding and rising every 30 minutes, 3 more times. After fourth set of folds, cover bowl tightly with plastic and refrigerate for at least 16 hours or up to 48 hours.

4 Transfer dough to well-floured counter, divide in half, and cover loosely with greased plastic. Using your well-floured hands, press 1 piece of dough into 4-inch round (keep remaining piece covered). Working around circumference of dough, fold edges toward center until ball forms. Repeat with remaining piece of dough.

5 Flip each dough ball seam side down and, using your cupped hands, drag in small circles on counter until dough feels taut and round and all seams are secured on underside. (If dough sticks to your hands, lightly dust top of dough with flour.) Cover dough rounds loosely with greased plastic and let rest for 5 minutes.

6 Grease 8½ by 4½-inch loaf pan. Flip each dough ball seam side up, press into 4-inch disk, and repeat folding and rounding steps.

7 Place rounds seam side down, side by side, into prepared pan. Press dough gently into corners. Cover loosely with greased plastic and let rise until loaf reaches ½ inch below lip of pan and dough springs back minimally when poked gently with your knuckle, 1½ to 2 hours.

8 Adjust oven rack to middle position and heat oven to 350 degrees. Gently brush loaf with egg mixture and bake until deep golden brown and loaf registers 190 to 195 degrees, 35 to 40 minutes, rotating pan halfway through baking. Let loaf cool in pan for 15 minutes. Remove loaf from pan and let cool completely on wire rack, about 3 hours, before serving.

troubleshooting

problem The loaf lacks an airy interior.

solution **Don't forget to fold the dough.**

During this dough's long refrigerator stay, the enzymes present in the flour untangle the proteins without kneading to encourage the gluten network to stitch itself together. But the dough still requires some manual manipulation to build the strength necessary for an airy crumb. Folding encourages the gluten to form and ensures that the no-knead method is successful.

problem The loaf lacks structure.

solution **Shape the dough balls twice.**

To build strength in this dough, instead of placing a single loaf in the pan we divide the dough in half and shape the halves into tight, round balls that we place side by side in the pan to encourage structure. But this still isn't quite enough. Let the dough balls rest and then flatten and re-form them; even this little bit of extra manipulation yields a crumb that is much more fine and uniform.

potato-dill sandwich bread

makes 1 loaf
rising time 1 hour 20 minutes to 2 hours
baking time 45 minutes
total time 3½ to 4 hours, plus 3 hours cooling time
key equipment medium saucepan, potato ricer, 8½ by 4½-inch loaf pan, pastry brush, instant-read thermometer

1 large russet potato (10 ounces), peeled and cut into 1-inch pieces

3 tablespoons unsalted butter, cut into 6 pieces

2⅔ cups (14⅔ ounces) bread flour

1½ teaspoons instant or rapid-rise yeast

1½ teaspoons salt

2 tablespoons minced fresh dill

1 large egg, lightly beaten with 1 tablespoon water and pinch salt

why this recipe works This earthy-tasting bread is a sturdy sandwich loaf that's packed with potato, and yet it has a wonderfully light, moist crumb. But if mashed potatoes are hefty and substantial, how do they contribute to a downy bread? As it turns out, the starches in potatoes work to dilute gluten-forming proteins, thereby weakening bread's structural network and making it much more tender. We found that 8 ounces of mashed russet potatoes were the right amount to add to our dough for light slices that were still stable enough to hold sandwich fixings. After boiling and mashing the potatoes, we dried them out on the stovetop. This gave us control over how much liquid we were incorporating and ensured that we were not over- hydrating the dough. We thought we'd boost the flavor of our bread with complementary dill; adding minced fresh dill during the last 1 minute of kneading lent the loaf a distinctive herbal flavor. In our testing, we had noticed that our loaves were tearing on the sides. This bread experiences a lot of oven spring (the rapid rising of bread after it's placed in a hot oven), so we found that letting the loaf rise ½ inch above the lip of the pan ensured that its rise in the oven wouldn't be so dramatic. Slashing the loaf before placing it in the oven was another foolproof way to eliminate tears by helping the loaf expand before its crust set. Don't salt the water in which you boil the potatoes. The test kitchen's preferred loaf pan measures 8½ by 4½ inches; if you use a 9 by 5-inch loaf pan, increase the shaped rising time by 20 to 30 minutes and start checking for doneness 10 minutes earlier than advised in the recipe.

continued

1 Place potato in medium saucepan and cover with 1 inch cold water. Bring to boil over high heat, then reduce to simmer and cook until potato is just tender (paring knife slipped in and out of potato meets little resistance), 8 to 10 minutes.

2 Transfer ¾ cup (6 ounces) potato cooking water to liquid measuring cup and let cool completely; drain potatoes. Return potatoes to now-empty saucepan and place over low heat. Cook, shaking saucepan occasionally, until any surface moisture has evaporated, about 30 seconds. Off heat, process potatoes through ricer or food mill or mash well with potato masher. Measure 1 cup very firmly packed potatoes (8 ounces) and transfer to separate bowl. Stir in butter until melted and let mixture cool completely before using. Discard remaining mashed potatoes or save for another use.

3 Whisk flour, yeast, and salt together in bowl of stand mixer. Add mashed potato mixture to flour mixture and mix with your hands until combined (some large lumps are OK). Using dough hook on low speed, slowly add potato cooking water and mix until cohesive dough starts to form and no dry flour remains, about 2 minutes, scraping down bowl as needed. Increase speed to medium-low and knead until dough is smooth and elastic and clears sides of bowl, about 8 minutes. Reduce speed to low, add dill, and mix until incorporated, about 1 minute.

4 Transfer dough to lightly floured counter and knead by hand to form smooth, round ball, about 30 seconds. Place dough seam side down in lightly greased large bowl or container, cover tightly with plastic wrap, and let rise until doubled in size, 1 to 1½ hours.

5 Grease 8½ by 4½-inch loaf pan. Press down on dough to deflate. Turn dough out onto lightly floured counter (side of dough that was against bowl should now be facing up). Press and stretch dough into 8 by 6-inch rectangle, with long side parallel to counter edge.

6 Roll dough away from you into firm cylinder, keeping roll taut by tucking it under itself as you go. Pinch seam closed and place loaf seam side down in prepared pan, pressing dough gently into corners. Cover loosely with greased plastic and let rise until loaf reaches ½ inch above lip of pan and dough springs back minimally when poked gently with your knuckle, 20 to 30 minutes.

7 Adjust oven rack to lower-middle position and heat oven to 350 degrees. Using sharp paring knife or single-edge razor blade, make one ½-inch-deep slash with swift, fluid motion lengthwise along top of loaf, starting and stopping about ½ inch from ends.

8 Gently brush loaf with egg mixture and bake until golden brown and loaf registers 205 to 210 degrees, 45 to 50 minutes, rotating pan halfway through baking. Let loaf cool in pan for 15 minutes. Remove loaf from pan and let cool completely on wire rack, about 3 hours, before serving.

anadama bread

makes 1 loaf
rising time 2 to 3 hours
baking time 40 minutes
total time 3¾ to 4¾ hours, plus 3 hours cooling time
key equipment 8½ by 4½-inch loaf pan, water-filled spray bottle, instant-read thermometer

2¾ cups (13¾ ounces) all-purpose flour

½ cup (2½ ounces) cornmeal

1½ teaspoons instant or rapid-rise yeast

1¼ teaspoons salt

1 cup (8 ounces) water, room temperature

¼ cup (2 ounces) mild or robust molasses

3 tablespoons unsalted butter, melted

why this recipe works Anadama bread is a New England classic, with two defining ingredients that have a centuries-old association with the region: molasses and cornmeal. We wanted a sandwich loaf that was moist and chewy, sturdy yet tender, faintly bitter yet sweet, and ever so slightly gritty. And we wanted the two star ingredients to have real presence. We found mild and robust varieties of molasses all worked well in this bread, while blackstrap molasses imparted too much bitter flavor. We increased the amount of molasses called for in most recipes until we landed on a full ¼ cup—enough to impart a decidedly bittersweet flavor and a beautiful golden color. We found that ½ cup of cornmeal was necessary to achieve the heartiness and pleasant grit we were after, but that meant cutting down on the flour and therefore the gluten, leaving us with a dense loaf. The fix was surprisingly easy: Adding a bit more yeast than is found in traditional recipes helped keep the texture light. Some recipes call for softening the cornmeal in water before mixing the dough, but we found this step unnecessary. For the liquid, milk made a softer bread but we preferred the heartier chew of the bread made with water. For extra moisture and tenderness, we added butter instead of oil for the fat, as this seemed truer to the bread's colonial past. Do not use coarse-ground cornmeal. The test kitchen's preferred loaf pan measures 8½ by 4½ inches; if you use a 9 by 5-inch loaf pan, increase the shaped rising time by 20 to 30 minutes and start checking for doneness 10 minutes earlier than advised in the recipe.

continued

1 Whisk flour, cornmeal, yeast, and salt together in bowl of stand mixer. Whisk water, molasses, and melted butter in 4-cup liquid measuring cup until molasses has dissolved.

2 Using dough hook on low speed, slowly add water mixture to flour mixture and mix until cohesive dough starts to form and no dry flour remains, about 2 minutes, scraping down bowl as needed. Increase speed to medium-low and knead until dough is smooth and elastic and clears sides of bowl, about 8 minutes.

3 Transfer dough to lightly floured counter and knead by hand to form smooth, round ball, about 30 seconds. Place dough seam side down in lightly greased large bowl or container, cover tightly with plastic wrap, and let rise until doubled in size, 1½ to 2 hours.

4 Grease 8½ by 4½-inch loaf pan and dust with cornmeal. Press down on dough to deflate. Turn dough out onto lightly floured counter (side of dough that was against bowl should now be facing up) and press into 8 by 6-inch rectangle, with long side parallel to counter edge.

5 Roll dough away from you into firm cylinder, keeping roll taut by tucking it under itself as you go. Pinch seam closed and place loaf seam side down in prepared pan, pressing dough gently into corners.

6 Cover loosely with greased plastic and let rise until loaf reaches 1 inch above lip of pan and dough springs back minimally when poked gently with your knuckle, 30 minutes to 1 hour.

7 Adjust oven rack to lower-middle position and heat oven to 350 degrees. Mist loaf with water and bake until deep golden brown and loaf registers 205 to 210 degrees, 40 to 45 minutes, rotating pan halfway through baking.

8 Let loaf cool in pan for 15 minutes. Remove loaf from pan and let cool completely on wire rack, about 3 hours, before serving.

troubleshooting

problem The bread tastes bitter.

solution Use the right molasses.

Molasses comes in many varieties, and because the recipe calls for just ¼ cup it's tempting to use whatever you have on hand. Happily, we found in our testing that the bread turns out nicely with both mild and robust, or full, molasses varieties. However, blackstrap molasses will not work in this recipe. Good for gingerbread, this strong sweetener will result in a bitter, burnt-tasting bread.

problem The loaf is too dense.

solution Use the right cornmeal.

This loaf packs in ½ cup of cornmeal for the right hearty texture and grit. Both fine and stone-ground yellow cornmeal work well. However, coarse-ground cornmeal, though flavorful, will throw off the delicate balance of ingredients, yielding a loaf that is too heavy and gritty.

whole-wheat quinoa bread

makes 1 loaf
rising time 2½ to 3½ hours
baking time 45 minutes
total time 4½ to 5½ hours, plus 3 hours cooling time
key equipment stand mixer, 8½ by 4½-inch loaf pan, pastry brush, instant-read thermometer

why this recipe works White sandwich breads are a lunchbox classic, but we also like having whole-wheat options for our sandwiches. We set out to create a loaf that was high in protein and packed with nutrients, and thought that hearty quinoa and a bit of nutty-tasting flaxseeds would be great additions to a whole-wheat loaf. We started with a combination of bread flour and whole-wheat flour. Using bread flour allowed us to pack a good amount of cooked quinoa into the dough; its high protein content gave us a sturdy crumb. We tested various methods of preparing the quinoa before incorporating it into the loaf, from toasting the raw kernels to softening them in liquid. Simply cooking the quinoa in the microwave with a measured amount of water until all the liquid was absorbed gave the bread just the right texture. Incorporating a small amount of oil helped coat the protein strands, making the loaf more moist and tender, and adding 3 full tablespoons of honey balanced the earthiness of the quinoa. Sprinkling 1 teaspoon of raw flaxseeds and 1 teaspoon of raw quinoa atop the loaf just before baking gave each slice pleasant textural contrast and crunch. The test kitchen's preferred loaf pan measures 8½ by 4½ inches; if you use a 9 by 5-inch loaf pan, increase the shaped rising time by 20 to 30 minutes and start checking for doneness 10 minutes earlier than advised in the recipe. We do not recommend mixing this dough by hand.

1 cup (8 ounces) water, room temperature
⅓ cup (1¾ ounces) plus 1 teaspoon prewashed white quinoa

1½ cups (8¼ ounces) bread flour

1 cup (5½ ounces) whole-wheat flour

2 tablespoons plus 1 teaspoon flaxseeds

2 teaspoons instant or rapid-rise yeast

1½ teaspoons salt

¾ cup (6 ounces) whole milk, room temperature

3 tablespoons honey

1 tablespoon vegetable oil

1 large egg, lightly beaten with 1 tablespoon water and pinch salt

continued

whole-wheat quinoa bread, continued

1 Microwave ¾ cup water and ⅓ cup quinoa in covered bowl at 50 percent power until water is almost completely absorbed, about 10 minutes, stirring halfway through microwaving. Uncover quinoa and let sit until cooled slightly and water is completely absorbed, about 10 minutes.

2 Whisk bread flour, whole-wheat flour, 2 tablespoons flaxseeds, yeast, and salt together in bowl of stand mixer. Whisk milk, honey, oil, and remaining water in 4-cup liquid measuring cup until honey has dissolved. Using dough hook on low speed, slowly add milk mixture to flour mixture and mix until cohesive dough starts to form and no dry flour remains, about 2 minutes, scraping down bowl as needed.

3 Increase speed to medium-low and knead until dough is smooth, elastic, and slightly sticky, about 6 minutes. Reduce speed to low, slowly add cooked quinoa, ¼ cup at a time, and mix until mostly incorporated, about 3 minutes.

4 Transfer dough to lightly floured counter. Using your lightly floured hands, knead dough until quinoa is evenly distributed and dough forms smooth, round ball, about 30 seconds. Place dough seam side down in lightly greased large bowl or container, cover tightly with plastic wrap, and let rise until doubled in size, 1½ to 2 hours.

5 Grease 8½ by 4½-inch loaf pan. Press down on dough to deflate. Turn dough out onto lightly floured counter (side of dough that was against bowl should now be facing up) and press into 8 by 6-inch rectangle, with long side parallel to counter edge.

6 Roll dough away from you into firm cylinder, keeping roll taut by tucking it under itself as you go. Pinch seam closed and place loaf seam side down in prepared pan, pressing dough gently into corners.

7 Cover loosely with greased plastic and let rise until loaf reaches 1 inch above lip of pan and dough springs back minimally when poked gently with your knuckle, 1 to 1½ hours.

8 Adjust oven rack to lower-middle position and heat oven to 350 degrees. Combine remaining 1 teaspoon quinoa and 1 teaspoon flaxseeds in bowl. Gently brush loaf with egg mixture and sprinkle with quinoa mixture. Bake until golden brown and loaf registers 205 to 210 degrees, 45 to 50 minutes, rotating pan halfway through baking. Let loaf cool in pan for 15 minutes. Remove loaf from pan and let cool completely on wire rack, about 3 hours, before serving.

deli rye bread

makes 1 loaf
resting time 20 minutes
rising time 2 to 3 hours
baking time 35 minutes
total time 4 to 5 hours, plus 3 hours cooling time
key equipment 2 rimmed baking sheets, pastry brush, instant-read thermometer

why this recipe works Genuine rye bread—the kind that delis pile high with rosy pastrami—should be slightly moist and chewy but not too dense, and it should have a noticeably tangy flavor. Developing a rye bread recipe isn't a simple proposition because rye flour doesn't contain enough gluten-forming proteins to make the bread rise, so it can turn out heavy. To lighten our loaf, we used twice as much high-protein bread flour as rye flour. Still, the gluten-developing kneading process didn't build enough structure for our rye bread, so we let the mixed dough rest for a 20-minute autolyse to jump-start gluten development. Deli rye almost always contains caraway seeds; 2 teaspoons gave us tangy flavor. Use light or medium rye flour in this bread; dark rye flour is overpowering. Be sure to reduce the temperature immediately after putting the loaf in the oven.

2 cups (11 ounces) bread flour

1 cup (5½ ounces) light or medium rye flour

2 teaspoons caraway seeds

2 teaspoons salt

1½ teaspoons instant or rapid-rise yeast

1¼ cups (10 ounces) water, room temperature

2 teaspoons honey

2 teaspoons vegetable oil

1 large egg, lightly beaten with 1 tablespoon water and pinch salt

1 Whisk bread flour, rye flour, caraway seeds, salt, and yeast together in bowl of stand mixer. Whisk water, honey, and oil in 4-cup liquid measuring cup until honey has dissolved.

2 Using dough hook on low speed, slowly add water mixture to flour mixture and mix until cohesive dough starts to form and no dry flour remains, about 2 minutes, scraping down bowl as needed. Cover bowl tightly with plastic wrap and let dough rest for 20 minutes.

3 Knead dough on medium-low speed until smooth and elastic and clears sides of bowl, about 8 minutes.

4 Transfer dough to lightly floured counter and knead by hand to form smooth, round ball, about 30 seconds. Place dough seam side down in lightly greased large bowl or container, cover tightly with plastic, and let rise until doubled in size, 1½ to 2 hours.

5 Stack 2 rimmed baking sheets and line with aluminum foil. Press down on dough to deflate. Turn dough out onto lightly floured counter (side of dough that was against bowl should now be facing up). Press and stretch dough into 6-inch square.

6 Fold top corners of dough diagonally into center of square and press gently to seal. Stretch and fold upper third of dough toward center and press seam gently to seal.

continued

deli rye bread, continued

7 Stretch and fold dough in half toward you to form rough 8 by 4-inch loaf and pinch seam closed. Roll loaf seam side down. Gently slide your hands underneath each end of loaf and transfer seam side down to prepared sheet. Reshape loaf as needed, tucking edges under to form taut torpedo shape.

8 Cover loosely with greased plastic and let rise until loaf increases in size by about half and dough springs back minimally when poked gently with your knuckle, 30 minutes to 1 hour.

9 Adjust oven rack to lower-middle position and heat oven to 450 degrees. Using sharp paring knife or single edge razor blade, make three 4-inch-long, ½-inch-deep slashes with swift, fluid motion across width of loaf, spacing slashes about 2 inches apart.

10 Gently brush loaf with egg mixture and place in oven. Reduce oven temperature to 375 degrees and bake until deep golden brown and loaf registers 205 to 210 degrees, 35 to 40 minutes, rotating sheet halfway through baking. Transfer loaf to wire rack and let cool completely, about 3 hours, before serving.

cranberry-walnut loaf

makes 1 loaf
rising time 2 to 3 hours
baking time 45 minutes
total time 3¾ to 4¾ hours, plus 3 hours cooling time
key equipment 2 rimmed baking sheets, pastry brush, instant-read thermometer

why this recipe works Baked goods studded with tart dried cranberries and rich walnuts often grace the table during the fall and winter holidays. We wanted to bring these seasonal flavors to a sturdy yet moist sandwich bread that we could top with the previous day's leftovers—or just bake whenever we wished to dress up lunch. We cut the bread flour for our loaf with some whole-wheat flour; since whole-wheat flour doesn't form a strong gluten network as readily as does bread flour, it helped yield the density we were looking for. The whole-wheat flour also complemented the earthy flavor of the walnuts in our bread. We noticed that the bottom of our loaf consistently emerged from the oven dark and bitter, so we baked it on a stacked set of two baking sheets for added insulation, and we raised the oven rack to the middle position for even heat distribution around the loaf. This browned the entire exterior evenly.

2¼ cups (12⅓ ounces) bread flour

10 tablespoons (3½ ounces) whole-wheat flour

¾ cup dried cranberries

¾ cup walnuts, toasted and chopped

2 teaspoons instant or rapid-rise yeast

2 teaspoons salt

1¼ cups (10 ounces) water, room temperature

2 tablespoons packed light brown sugar

1 tablespoon vegetable oil

1 large egg, lightly beaten with 1 tablespoon water and pinch salt

1 Whisk bread flour, whole-wheat flour, cranberries, walnuts, yeast, and salt together in bowl of stand mixer. Whisk water, sugar, and oil in 4-cup liquid measuring cup until sugar has dissolved.

2 Using dough hook on low speed, slowly add water mixture to flour mixture and mix until cohesive dough starts to form and no dry flour remains, about 2 minutes, scraping down bowl as needed.

3 Increase speed to medium-low and knead until dough is smooth and elastic and clears sides of bowl, about 8 minutes.

4 Transfer dough to lightly floured counter and knead by hand to form smooth, round ball, about 30 seconds. Place dough seam side down in lightly greased large bowl or container, cover tightly with plastic wrap, and let rise until doubled in size, 1½ to 2 hours.

5 Stack 2 rimmed baking sheets and line with aluminum foil. Press down on dough to deflate. Turn dough out onto lightly floured counter (side of dough that was against bowl should now be facing up). Press and stretch dough into 6-inch square.

6 Fold top corners of dough diagonally into center of square and press gently to seal. Stretch and fold upper third of dough toward center and press seam gently to seal.

continued

cranberry-walnut loaf, continued

7 Stretch and fold dough in half toward you to form rough 8 by 4-inch loaf and pinch seam closed. Roll loaf seam side down. Gently slide your hands underneath each end of loaf and transfer to prepared sheet. Reshape loaf as needed, tucking edges under to form taut torpedo shape.

8 Cover loosely with greased plastic and let rise until loaf increases in size by about half and dough springs back minimally when poked gently with your knuckle, 30 minutes to 1 hour.

9 Adjust oven rack to middle position and heat oven to 450 degrees. Using sharp paring knife or single-edge razor blade, make one ½-inch-deep slash with swift, fluid motion lengthwise along top of loaf, starting and stopping about ½ inch from ends.

10 Gently brush loaf with egg mixture and bake for 15 minutes. Reduce oven temperature to 375 degrees and continue to bake until dark brown and loaf registers 205 to 210 degrees, 30 to 35 minutes, rotating sheet halfway through baking. Transfer loaf to wire rack and let cool completely, about 3 hours, before serving.

spicy olive bread

makes 1 loaf
rising time 2 to 3 hours
baking time 50 minutes
total time 3¾ to 4¾ hours, plus 3 hours cooling time
key equipment stand mixer, Dutch oven with lid, instant-read thermometer

why this recipe works In pursuit of the ideal artisanal sandwich bread, perfect for a piquant Italian salumi sandwich, we turned to olives, garlic, and red pepper flakes. Many olive bread recipes go to great lengths to incorporate the olives without bruising them and staining the dough. We tried many of these techniques and found all of the frustrating shaping to be unnecessary. We simply kneaded our dough as normal and then reduced the mixer speed to low and slowly added the olives. The low-speed mixing was gentle enough that it didn't beat up the olives' flesh. We wanted a crust for our olive bread that was crisp and flavorful yet not tough. Baking the bread in the steamy environment of a Dutch oven created an artisan bakery–style crust. Almost any variety of brined or oil-cured olive works in this recipe, although we preferred a mix of green and black. We do not recommend mixing this dough by hand.

¾ cup pitted olives, rinsed, patted dry, and chopped coarse

2 garlic cloves, minced

3 cups (16½ ounces) bread flour

2 teaspoons instant or rapid-rise yeast

2 teaspoons salt

2 teaspoons red pepper flakes

1⅓ cups (10⅔ ounces) water, room temperature

2 tablespoons sugar

1 tablespoon extra-virgin olive oil

1 Combine olives and garlic in bowl. Whisk flour, yeast, salt, and pepper flakes together in bowl of stand mixer. Whisk water, sugar, and oil in 4-cup liquid measuring cup until sugar has dissolved. Using dough hook on low speed, slowly add water mixture to flour mixture and mix until cohesive dough starts to form and no dry flour remains, about 2 minutes, scraping down bowl as needed.

2 Increase speed to medium-low and knead until dough is smooth and elastic and clears sides of bowl, about 8 minutes. Reduce speed to low, slowly add olive mixture, ¼ cup at a time, and mix until mostly incorporated, about 1 minute.

3 Transfer dough and any loose olives to lightly floured counter and knead by hand to form smooth, round ball, about 30 seconds. Place dough seam side down in lightly greased large bowl or container, cover tightly with plastic wrap, and let rise until doubled in size, 1½ to 2 hours.

4 Press down on dough to deflate. Turn dough out onto lightly floured counter (side of dough that was against bowl should now be facing up). Press and stretch dough into 10-inch round.

5 Working around circumference of dough, fold edges toward center until ball forms.

6 Flip dough ball seam side down and, using your cupped hands, drag in small circles on counter until dough feels taut and round and all seams are secured on underside of loaf.

continued

spicy olive bread, continued

7 Lay 16 by 12-inch sheet of parchment paper on counter and lightly spray with vegetable oil spray. Transfer loaf seam side down to center of prepared parchment. Using parchment as sling, gently lower dough into Dutch oven. Cover tightly with plastic and let rise until loaf increases in size by about half and dough springs back minimally when poked gently with your knuckle, 30 minutes to 1 hour.

8 Adjust oven rack to middle position and heat oven to 450 degrees. Using sharp paring knife or single-edge razor blade, make two 5-inch-long, ½-inch-deep slashes with swift, fluid motion along top of loaf to form cross.

9 Cover pot, place in oven, and bake loaf for 30 minutes. Remove lid, reduce oven temperature to 375 degrees, and continue to bake until deep golden brown and loaf registers 205 to 210 degrees, 20 to 25 minutes.

10 Using parchment sling, remove loaf from pot and transfer to wire rack; discard parchment. Let cool completely, about 3 hours, before serving.

mastering
size and
shape
dinner
rolls and
more

rustic dinner rolls

makes 16 rolls
resting time 30 minutes
rising time 2½ to 3 hours
baking time 20 minutes
total time 4½ to 5 hours, plus 1 hour cooling time
key equipment stand mixer, two 9-inch round cake pans, water-filled spray bottle, rimmed baking sheet

3 cups (16½ ounces) bread flour

3 tablespoons whole-wheat flour

1½ teaspoons instant or rapid-rise yeast

1½ cups (12 ounces) plus 1 tablespoon water, room temperature

2 teaspoons honey

1½ teaspoons salt

why this recipe works European-style dinner rolls are different from their rich, tender American cousins. The dough for these rustic rolls is lean and the crumb is open, with a yeasty, savory flavor. But the best part might be their crust—so crisp it practically shatters when you bite into it, yet chewy enough to offer satisfying resistance. It is this crust that keeps European-style dinner rolls in the domain of professionals, who use steam-injected ovens to expose the developing crust to moisture. We wanted a reliable recipe for rolls as good as any from a European bakery. Unfortunately, when we tasted our first batch, we found a dense, bland crumb beneath a leathery crust. The flavor was easy enough to improve: We added whole-wheat flour for earthiness (just 3 tablespoons did the trick) and honey for sweetness. Extra yeast opened the crumb slightly, but it wasn't enough. The crumb structure of artisan-style loaves is achieved with a wet dough, so we ultimately found success when we upped the hydration of our roll dough. The water created steam during baking, opening up the crumb and making it airier. For an ultracrisp crust, we came up with a two-step process that mimicked a steam-injected oven: First, we misted the rolls with water before starting them in a cake pan at a high temperature to help set their shape (since the dough was soft, individually baked rolls turned out squat). Next, we lowered the temperature, pulled the rolls apart, and returned them to the oven on a baking sheet until they were golden on all sides. We do not recommend mixing this dough by hand.

continued

1 Whisk bread flour, whole-wheat flour, and yeast together in bowl of stand mixer. Whisk water and honey in 4-cup liquid measuring cup until honey has dissolved.

2 Using dough hook on low speed, slowly add water mixture to flour mixture and mix until cohesive dough starts to form and no dry flour remains, about 2 minutes, scraping down bowl and hook as needed. Cover bowl tightly with plastic wrap and let dough rest for 30 minutes.

3 Add salt to dough and mix on low speed for 5 minutes. Increase speed to medium and knead until dough is smooth and slightly sticky, about 1 minute. Transfer dough to lightly greased large bowl or container, cover tightly with plastic, and let rise until doubled in size, 1 to 1½ hours.

4 Using greased bowl scraper (or your fingertips), fold dough over itself by gently lifting and folding edge of dough toward middle. Turn bowl 90 degrees and fold dough again; repeat turning bowl and folding dough 2 more times (total of 4 folds). Cover tightly with plastic and let rise for 30 minutes. Repeat folding, then cover bowl tightly with plastic and let dough rise until doubled in size, about 30 minutes.

5 Grease two 9-inch round cake pans. Press down on dough to deflate. Transfer dough to well-floured counter, sprinkle lightly with flour, and divide in half. Stretch each half into even 16-inch log and cut into 8 equal pieces (about 2 ounces each). Using your well-floured hands, gently pick up each piece and roll in your palms to coat with flour, shaking off excess.

6 Arrange rolls in prepared pans, placing 1 in center and 7 around edges, with cut side facing up and long side of each piece running from center to edge of pan. Cover loosely with greased plastic and let rolls rise until nearly doubled in size and dough springs back minimally when poked gently with your knuckle, about 30 minutes. (Unrisen rolls can be refrigerated for at least 8 hours or up to 16 hours; let rolls sit at room temperature for 1½ hours before baking.)

7 Adjust oven rack to middle position and heat oven to 500 degrees. Mist rolls with water and bake until tops are brown, about 10 minutes. Remove rolls from oven and reduce oven temperature to 400 degrees.

8 Carefully invert rolls out of pans onto baking sheet and let cool slightly. Turn rolls right side up, pull apart, and arrange evenly on sheet. Continue to bake until deep golden brown, 10 to 15 minutes, rotating sheet halfway through baking. Transfer rolls to wire rack and let cool completely, about 1 hour, before serving.

troubleshooting

problem The dough is too sticky to work with.

solution Flour your hands.

This dough is wet; a high-hydration dough gives the rolls an airy crumb. We skip shaping these rolls into rounds, but the dough can still stick to your hands when you're handling it. Be sure to flour the counter well before stretching the dough into a log and to quickly roll the individual pieces between your floured palms to coat them.

problem The rolls are pale around the sides.

solution Remember to remove the rolls from the cake pan halfway through baking.

Baking the rolls in a pan ensures that the wet dough doesn't spread and bake into a squat shape. But crowding the rolls steams the sides and prevents them from browning. Once the tops are brown, remove the rolls from the oven, reduce the oven temperature, separate the rolls, and finish baking on a baking sheet.

honey-wheat dinner rolls

makes 15 rolls
rising time 2½ to 3½ hours
baking time 25 minutes
total time 4¼ to 5¼ hours
key equipment 13 by 9-inch baking dish, pastry brush

why this recipe works Good honey-wheat dinner rolls have the softness of white rolls, with satisfying heft and a nutty whole-wheat flavor that's complemented by a touch of floral sweetness. That said, these appealing rolls rarely hit the mark: Commercial versions are soft but taste artificially sweet, while homemade rolls have good flavor but can be as dense as wet sand. We wanted a flavorful alternative to white rolls that was tender and fluffy and that actually tasted like its namesake ingredients. What makes achieving great whole-wheat breads so difficult is the presence of the bran. This part of the grain, which is removed from white flour, gives whole-wheat flour its distinct hearty flavor. But the bran is sharp—so sharp that it cuts through the bread's gluten structure, leaving you with a dense product. To produce a light, fluffy whole-wheat roll, we'd have to incorporate some all-purpose flour—but not so much that we'd lose the roll's earthy, nutty whole-wheat flavor. We also had success when we made a very wet dough. The excess liquid softened the bran's edges, ensuring that it didn't wreak havoc on the dough's structure. To boost the honey flavor, we used 6 tablespoons instead of the 2 tablespoons that many recipes call for. As a bonus, the liquid honey hydrated the dough further and contributed softness. And to make sure the flavor came through loud and clear, we brushed the warm baked rolls with honey butter. With this finishing touch, our fluffy, pleasantly sweet, nutty-tasting rolls really earned their honey-wheat title.

2½ cups (13¾ ounces) whole-wheat flour

1¾ cups (8¾ ounces) all-purpose flour

2¼ teaspoons instant or rapid-rise yeast

2¼ teaspoons salt

1¾ cups (14 ounces) whole milk, room temperature

6 tablespoons (4½ ounces) plus 1 teaspoon honey

5 tablespoons (2½ ounces) unsalted butter, melted

1 large egg, room temperature

1 large egg, lightly beaten with 1 tablespoon water and pinch salt

continued

1 Whisk whole-wheat flour, all-purpose flour, yeast, and salt together in bowl of stand mixer. Whisk milk, 6 tablespoons honey, 4 tablespoons melted butter, and egg in 4-cup liquid measuring cup until honey has dissolved.

2 Using dough hook on low speed, slowly add milk mixture to flour mixture and mix until cohesive dough starts to form and no dry flour remains, about 2 minutes, scraping down bowl as needed. Increase speed to medium-low and knead until dough is smooth and elastic and clears sides of bowl but sticks to bottom, about 8 minutes.

3 Transfer dough to lightly floured counter and knead by hand to form smooth, round ball, about 30 seconds. Place dough seam side down in lightly greased large bowl or container, cover tightly with plastic wrap, and let rise until doubled in size, 1½ to 2 hours.

4 Make foil sling for 13 by 9-inch baking dish by folding 2 long sheets of aluminum foil; first sheet should be 13 inches wide and second sheet should be 9 inches wide. Lay sheets of foil in dish perpendicular to each other, with extra foil hanging over edges of dish. Push foil into corners and up sides of dish, smoothing foil flush to dish, then spray foil with vegetable oil spray.

5 Press down on dough to deflate. Transfer dough to clean counter and stretch into even 15-inch log. Cut log into 15 equal pieces (about 2½ ounces each) and cover loosely with greased plastic. Working with 1 piece of dough at a time (keep remaining pieces covered), form into rough ball by stretching dough around your thumbs and pinching edges together so that top is smooth. Place ball seam side down on clean counter and, using your cupped hand, drag in small circles until dough feels taut and round.

6 Arrange dough balls seam side down into 5 rows of 3 in prepared dish, cover loosely with greased plastic, and let rise until nearly doubled in size and dough springs back minimally when poked gently with your knuckle, 1 to 1½ hours. (Unrisen rolls can be refrigerated for at least 8 hours or up to 16 hours; let rolls sit at room temperature for 1 hour before baking.)

7 Adjust oven rack to lower-middle position and heat oven to 350 degrees. Gently brush rolls with egg mixture and bake until golden brown, 25 to 30 minutes, rotating dish halfway through baking.

8 Combine remaining honey and melted butter in bowl. Let rolls cool in dish for 15 minutes. Using foil overhang, transfer rolls to wire rack and brush with honey mixture. Serve warm or at room temperature.

troubleshooting

problem The rolls have visible seams.

solution Stretch the dough around your thumbs.

It is important when shaping the dough pieces to stretch them around your thumbs and pinch the ends before rolling them on the counter. This will ensure the seams are hidden and the final roll is smooth.

problem The rolls aren't perfectly round.

solution Don't flour the counter for shaping.

Shaping the rolls on a clean counter may seem wrong, but you want to create friction between the dough and the counter, which forces the dough into its desired round shape.

potato dinner rolls

makes 12 rolls
rising time 1 to 2 hours
baking time 12 minutes
total time 2½ to 3½ hours, plus 15 minutes cooling time
key equipment medium saucepan, potato ricer, rimmed baking sheet, pastry brush

why this recipe works While the decadently buttery white dinner rolls associated with holiday dinners are delicious, sometimes we crave something similarly soft and tender but a little leaner. Old-fashioned potato rolls, with their light, moist crumb, fit the bill. Potato roll recipes abound, but almost none specify what type of potato to use, and some turn out heavy, rather than feathery-light, rolls. We wanted to nail down a foolproof recipe for these tender rolls. We learned when we developed our Potato-Dill Sandwich Bread recipe (page 102) that more starch is better, so we chose high-starch russets. Potato starch granules are about five times larger than wheat granules, so they can absorb at least five times as much water, resulting in a moister crumb. As we made batch after batch of rolls with different amounts of mashed russets, we discovered something interesting: The more potato we used, the less time the dough needed to rise. As it turns out, the potassium in potatoes activates yeast; the more of it there is, the quicker and more vigorous the rise. This led us to consider the cooking water. When potatoes are boiled, they leach almost half of their potassium into the water, which helped explain why so many recipes called for adding it to the dough. We found that when we switched from using 5 tablespoons of milk to using the same amount of potato cooking water, the rising times dropped still more. These rolls weren't just light, moist, and satisfying; they needed significantly less rising time than many standard dinner rolls. Don't salt the water in which you boil the potatoes.

1 large russet potato (10 ounces), peeled and cut into 1-inch pieces

2 tablespoons unsalted butter, cut into 4 pieces

2¼ cups (12⅓ ounces) bread flour

2 teaspoons instant or rapid-rise yeast

1 teaspoon salt

1 large egg, room temperature

1 tablespoon sugar

1 large egg, lightly beaten with 1 tablespoon water and pinch salt

continued

1 Place potato in medium saucepan and cover with 1 inch cold water. Bring to boil over high heat, then reduce to simmer and cook until potato is just tender (paring knife can be slipped in and out of potato with little resistance), 8 to 10 minutes.

2 Transfer 5 tablespoons (2½ ounces) potato cooking water to 4-cup liquid measuring cup and let cool completely; drain potatoes. Return potatoes to now-empty saucepan and place over low heat. Cook, shaking saucepan occasionally, until any surface moisture has evaporated, about 30 seconds. Off heat, process potatoes through ricer or food mill or mash well with potato masher. Measure 1 cup very firmly packed potatoes (8 ounces) and transfer to separate bowl. Stir in butter until melted and let mixture cool completely before using. Discard remaining mashed potatoes or save for another use.

3 Whisk flour, yeast, and salt together in bowl of stand mixer. Whisk egg and sugar into potato cooking water until sugar has dissolved. Add mashed potato mixture to flour mixture and mix with your hands until combined (some large lumps are OK). Using dough hook on low speed, slowly add cooking water mixture and mix until cohesive dough starts to form and no dry flour remains, about 2 minutes, scraping down bowl as needed. Increase speed to medium-low and knead until dough is smooth and elastic and clears sides of bowl but sticks to bottom, about 8 minutes.

4 Transfer dough to lightly floured counter and knead by hand to form smooth, round ball, about 30 seconds. Place dough seam side down in lightly greased large bowl or container, cover tightly with plastic wrap, and let rise until doubled in size, 30 minutes to 1 hour.

5 Line rimmed baking sheet with parchment paper. Press down on dough to deflate. Transfer dough to clean counter and stretch into even 12-inch log. Cut log into 12 equal pieces (about 2 ounces each) and cover loosely with greased plastic.

6 Working with 1 piece of dough at a time (keep remaining pieces covered), form into rough ball by stretching dough around your thumbs and pinching edges together so that top is smooth. Place ball seam side down on clean counter and, using your cupped hand, drag in small circles until dough feels taut and round.

7 Arrange dough balls seam side down on prepared sheet, spaced about 1½ inches apart. Cover loosely with greased plastic and let rise until nearly doubled in size and dough springs back minimally when poked gently with your knuckle, 30 minutes to 1 hour. (Unrisen rolls can be refrigerated for at least 8 hours or up to 16 hours; let rolls sit at room temperature for 1 hour before baking.)

8 Adjust oven rack to upper-middle position and heat oven to 425 degrees. Gently brush rolls with egg mixture and bake until golden brown, 12 to 14 minutes, rotating sheet halfway through baking. Transfer rolls to wire rack and let cool for 15 minutes. Serve warm or at room temperature.

variations **potato dinner rolls with cheddar and mustard**
Stir ½ cup shredded cheddar cheese and 1 teaspoon dry mustard into flour mixture in step 3. Sprinkle each roll with 1 teaspoon shredded cheddar (¼ cup total) before baking.

potato burger buns
Divide dough into 9 pieces (about 2¾ ounces each) and shape into smooth, taut rounds as directed in step 6. Let rounds rest for 15 minutes, then press into 3½-inch disks of even thickness. Arrange disks on 2 parchment paper–lined rimmed baking sheets and let rise as directed in step 7. Sprinkle rolls with 1 tablespoon sesame seeds, if desired, and bake on upper-middle and middle racks until rolls are deep golden brown, 15 to 18 minutes, switching and rotating sheets halfway through baking. Makes 9 burger buns.

parker house rolls

makes 24 rolls
resting time 15 minutes
rising time 2 to 3 hours
baking time 20 minutes
total time 4 to 5 hours, plus 15 minutes cooling time
key equipment 2 rimmed baking sheets, pastry brush,
water-filled spray bottle

4 cups (20 ounces) all-purpose flour

2¼ teaspoons instant or rapid-rise yeast

1½ teaspoons salt

1¼ cups (10 ounces) whole milk,
room temperature

14 tablespoons (7 ounces) unsalted butter,
melted

1 large egg, room temperature

2 tablespoons sugar

why this recipe works Parker House rolls are the fully loaded Cadillac of dinner rolls. These thin-crusted, fluffy-crumbed, glossy American rolls are pillowy-soft, a little sweet, and packed with butter. They owe their name to Boston's famed Parker House, a hotel that has been a bastion of Brahmin hospitality since the middle of the 19th century. Luxurious as the dough is, the folded shape and buttery shellac are the hallmarks of these rolls. We found the best way to shape the dough was to first roll each piece into a ball (like with standard dinner rolls) to redistribute the yeast and sugars and expunge the carbon dioxide. Then we lightly flattened each piece of dough into a round shape. Once the rounds were formed, we created a crease in the middle with the handle of a wooden spoon. Keeping the edges of the dough thicker than the center so that they adhered to each other when the dough was folded ensured that the rolls didn't puff open during baking. Many recipes for Parker House rolls call for baking them in a dish. While we liked the height of the rolls baked together in a baking dish, the rolls situated in the middle were still gummy and raw long after the outer rolls were perfectly baked, and the sides of the rolls lacked browning. Instead, we arranged the rolls on a baking sheet; the rolls baked evenly from crust to crumb since they were all exposed to the same amount of heat. For buttery flavor and sheen, we brushed the rolls with melted butter before folding them and again before baking.

continued

1 Whisk flour, yeast, and salt together in bowl of stand mixer. Whisk milk, 8 tablespoons melted butter, egg, and sugar in 4-cup liquid measuring cup until sugar has dissolved.

2 Using dough hook on low speed, slowly add milk mixture to flour mixture and mix until cohesive dough starts to form and no dry flour remains, about 2 minutes, scraping down bowl as needed. Increase speed to medium-low and knead until dough is smooth and elastic and clears sides of bowl but sticks to bottom, about 8 minutes.

3 Transfer dough to lightly floured counter and knead by hand to form smooth, round ball, about 30 seconds. Place dough seam side down in lightly greased large bowl or container, cover tightly with plastic wrap, and let rise until doubled in size, 1 to 1½ hours.

4 Line 2 rimmed baking sheets with parchment paper. Press down on dough to deflate. Transfer dough to clean counter and divide in half. Stretch each half into even 12-inch log, cut each log into 12 equal pieces (about 1½ ounces each), and cover loosely with greased plastic. Working with 1 piece of dough at a time (keep remaining pieces covered), form into rough ball by stretching dough around your thumbs and pinching edges together so that top is smooth. Place ball seam side down on clean counter and, using your cupped hand, drag in small circles until dough feels taut and round. Cover balls loosely with greased plastic and let rest for 15 minutes.

5 Working with few dough balls at a time, press balls into ¼-inch-thick rounds. Using thin handle of wooden spoon or dowel, firmly press down across width of rounds to create crease in center.

6 Brush tops of rounds with 3 tablespoons melted butter, then fold in half along creases and gently press edges to seal.

7 Arrange rolls on prepared sheets, spaced about 2 inches apart. Cover loosely with greased plastic and let rise until nearly doubled in size and dough springs back minimally when poked gently with your knuckle, 1 to 1½ hours. (Unrisen rolls can be refrigerated for at least 8 hours or up to 16 hours; let rolls sit at room temperature for 1 hour before baking.)

8 Adjust oven racks to upper-middle and lower-middle positions and heat oven to 350 degrees. Gently brush rolls with remaining melted butter, then mist with water. Bake until golden brown, 20 to 25 minutes, switching and rotating sheets halfway through baking. Transfer rolls to wire rack and let cool for 15 minutes. Serve warm or at room temperature.

troubleshooting

problem The rolls pop open during baking.

solution **Keep the edges thicker than the center.**

After pressing the dough pieces into rounds, it is important to make the crease in the middle with the handle of a wooden spoon or a dowel. The edges of the dough need to be thicker than the center; if you skip this step and the oval is even, the edges of the dough will not adhere and they'll open up when they're exposed to the heat of the oven.

crescent rolls

makes 12 rolls
rising time 2 to 3 hours
baking time 20 minutes
total time 3¼ to 4¼ hours, plus 15 minutes cooling time
key equipment rimmed baking sheet, rolling pin, pastry brush

why this recipe works Most recipes for buttery, flaky crescent rolls require laborious repeated rolling and folding to layer softened butter into the dough. At the same time, we wouldn't think of settling for the artificial-tasting, dry canned versions from the supermarket. After dozens of tests, we found a way to avoid either extreme: You can make rolls that are only a modicum less flaky and just as tender as labor-intensive versions by simply kneading all the ingredients together. We determined that a precise 7 tablespoons of melted butter in the dough delivered great flavor without making the dough too sticky to work with. To enhance the richness of our rolls, without weighing them down, we used half-and-half instead of milk, resulting in extra-tender rolls with big buttery taste.

2½ cups (12½ ounces) all-purpose flour

1 teaspoon instant or rapid-rise yeast

1 teaspoon salt

½ cup (4 ounces) half-and-half, room temperature

8 tablespoons (4 ounces) unsalted butter, melted

¼ cup (1¾ ounces) sugar

1 large egg plus 1 large yolk, room temperature

1 large egg, lightly beaten with 1 tablespoon water and pinch salt

1 Whisk flour, yeast, and salt together in bowl of stand mixer. Whisk half-and-half, 7 tablespoons melted butter, sugar, and egg and yolk in 4-cup liquid measuring cup until sugar has dissolved.

2 Using dough hook on low speed, slowly add half-and-half mixture to flour mixture and mix until cohesive dough starts to form and no dry flour remains, about 2 minutes, scraping down bowl as needed. Increase speed to medium-low and knead until dough is smooth and elastic and clears sides of bowl but sticks to bottom, about 8 minutes.

3 Transfer dough to lightly floured counter and knead by hand to form smooth, round ball, about 30 seconds. Place dough seam side down in lightly greased large bowl or container, cover tightly with plastic wrap, and let rise until doubled in size, 1 to 1½ hours.

4 Line rimmed baking sheet with parchment paper. Press down on dough to deflate, then transfer to lightly floured counter. Press and roll dough into 12-inch round.

5 Brush top of dough with remaining melted butter and cut into 12 wedges.

6 Starting at wide end, gently roll up each dough wedge, ending with pointed tip on bottom. Push ends toward each other to form crescent shape.

7 Arrange rolls on prepared sheet, spaced about 2 inches apart, with tip of dough underneath each roll. Cover loosely with greased plastic and let rise until nearly doubled in size and dough springs back minimally when poked gently with your knuckle, 1 to 1½ hours. (Unrisen rolls can be refrigerated for at least 8 hours or up to 16 hours; let rolls sit at room temperature for 1 hour before baking.)

8 Adjust oven rack to middle position and heat oven to 350 degrees. Gently brush rolls with egg mixture and bake until golden brown, 20 to 25 minutes, rotating sheet halfway through baking. Transfer rolls to wire rack and let cool for 15 minutes. Serve warm.

popovers

makes 6 popovers
resting time 1 hour
baking time 65 minutes
total time 2½ hours, plus 2 minutes cooling time
key equipment 6-cup popover pan.

why this recipe works The perfect popover soars to towering heights without the addition of whipped egg whites or leavener for lift—but only if you get the baking magic just right. Skip a step or alter the timing slightly and you'll have squat, tough, or sunken popovers. Do they have to be this finicky? We aimed to develop a foolproof recipe that would produce tall popovers with a crisp exterior and an airy, custardy interior every time. Since many recipes turned out skimpy popovers, our first move was to double the ingredient amounts found in most recipes so we could fill the cups of the popover pan almost completely. We tested cake flour, all-purpose flour, and bread flour; because bread flour has the highest protein content of the three, it gave the popovers the strongest structure, and thus the highest rise and crispest crust. The downside was that it sometimes caused the batter to set up too quickly, which impeded rise. Resting the batter for an hour before baking relaxed the proteins and prevented the popovers from setting up too quickly. Whole milk is traditional, but the fat weighed down our popovers; low-fat milk fixed the problem. Popovers can collapse as they cool, so we poked a hole in the top of each toward the end of baking and then again once they were out of the oven. The small holes enabled the popovers to release the steam slowly and maintain their crispness. Greasing the popover pan with shortening ensures the best release, but vegetable oil spray may be substituted; do not use butter. To monitor the popovers' progress without opening the oven door, use the oven light. Popovers can be stored in a zipper-lock bag at room temperature for up to 2 days. To serve, heat the popovers on a rimmed baking sheet and bake in a 400-degree oven for 5 to 8 minutes.

shortening

3 large eggs, room temperature

2 cups (16 ounces) warm 1 or 2 percent low-fat milk (110 degrees)

3 tablespoons unsalted butter, melted

1 teaspoon sugar

2 cups (11 ounces) bread flour, plus extra for pan

1 teaspoon salt

1 Grease 6-cup popover pan with shortening, then flour pan lightly. Whisk eggs in medium bowl until light and foamy. Slowly whisk in warm milk, melted butter, and sugar until incorporated.

2 Whisk flour and salt together in large bowl. Whisk three-quarters of milk mixture into flour mixture until no lumps remain, then whisk in remaining milk mixture.

3 Transfer batter to 4-cup liquid measuring cup, cover tightly with plastic wrap, and let rest for 1 hour. (Batter can be refrigerated for up to 1 day; let sit at room temperature for 1 hour before portioning.)

4 Adjust oven rack to lower-middle position and heat oven to 450 degrees. Whisk batter to recombine, then pour into prepared pan (batter will not reach top of cups). Bake until just beginning to brown, about 20 minutes.

5 Without opening oven door, reduce oven temperature to 300 degrees and continue to bake until popovers are golden brown, 35 to 40 minutes.

6 Poke small hole in top of each popover with skewer and continue to bake until deep golden brown, about 10 minutes. Transfer pan to wire rack, poke popovers again with skewer, and let cool for 2 minutes. Remove popovers from pan and serve warm.

kaiser rolls

makes 12 rolls
rising time 1½ to 2½ hours
baking time 30 minutes
total time 3¼ to 4¼ hours, plus 1 hour cooling time
key equipment 2 rimmed baking sheets, pastry brush

why this recipe works Originally from Austria, these crusty deli-style rolls are perfect for overstuffed sandwiches or for dipping into soup. Consistently disappointed by pale, dry, store-bought versions, we set out to re-create the thin, crisp, golden exterior; moist, sturdy crumb; and signature rosette shape of the real thing. To start, we chose higher-protein bread flour to achieve a roll that was tender yet could support mounds of deli meat. One egg and a bit of vegetable oil reinforced the tenderness and added richness. Many traditional recipes call for malt syrup to add a layer of sweetness and to boost browning, but tasters preferred the subtle flavor of white sugar. To achieve a deep golden sheen without the malt, we brushed on an egg wash before baking. While many delis imprint their rolls with a special stamp, we opted for the traditional rosette shaping method, which was easy with our supple dough, and it didn't require us to purchase extra equipment.

5 cups (27½ ounces) bread flour

4 teaspoons instant or rapid-rise yeast

1 tablespoon salt

2 cups (16 ounces) water, room temperature

3 tablespoons vegetable oil

1 large egg, room temperature

4 teaspoons sugar

1 large egg, lightly beaten with 1 tablespoon water and pinch salt

1 tablespoon poppy seeds (optional)

1 Whisk flour, yeast, and salt together in bowl of stand mixer. Whisk water, oil, egg, and sugar in 4-cup liquid measuring cup until sugar has dissolved.

2 Using dough hook on low speed, slowly add water mixture to flour mixture and mix until cohesive dough starts to form and no dry flour remains, about 2 minutes, scraping down bowl as needed. Increase speed to medium-low and knead until dough is smooth and elastic and clears sides of bowl but sticks to bottom, about 8 minutes.

3 Transfer dough to lightly floured counter and knead by hand to form smooth, round ball, about 30 seconds. Place dough seam side down in lightly greased large bowl or container, cover tightly with plastic wrap, and let rise until doubled in size, 1 to 1½ hours.

4 Line 2 rimmed baking sheets with parchment paper. Press down on dough to deflate. Transfer dough to clean counter. Press and stretch dough into 12 by 6-inch rectangle, with long side parallel to counter edge.

5 Using pizza cutter or chef's knife, cut dough vertically into 12 (6 by 1-inch) strips and cover loosely with greased plastic.

6 Working with 1 piece of dough at a time (keep remaining pieces covered), stretch and roll into 14-inch rope.

7 Shape rope into U with 2-inch-wide bottom curve and ends facing away from you.

8 Tie ends into single overhand knot, with 1½-inch open loop at bottom.

continued

kaiser rolls, continued

9 Wrap 1 tail over loop and press through opening from top. Wrap other tail under loop and pinch ends together to seal.

10 Arrange rolls pinched side down on prepared sheets, spaced about 3 inches apart. Cover loosely with greased plastic and let rise until nearly doubled in size and dough springs back minimally when poked gently with your knuckle, 30 minutes to 1 hour.

11 Adjust oven racks to upper-middle and lower-middle positions and heat oven to 350 degrees. Gently brush rolls with egg mixture and sprinkle with poppy seeds, if using. Bake until golden brown, 30 to 35 minutes, switching and rotating sheets halfway through baking.

12 Transfer rolls to wire racks and let cool completely, about 1 hour, before serving.

hoagie rolls

makes 8 rolls
rising time 1½ to 2½ hours
baking time 30 minutes
total time 3¼ to 4¼ hours, plus 1 hour cooling time
key equipment 2 rimmed baking sheets

why this recipe works Sandwich lovers get into battles over the name of the long white rolls that are stuffed with meats, cheeses, and relishes at corner delis. Whether you call them hoagie, hero, grinder, or submarine rolls, they make for one delicious sandwich bread. We wanted to create a version big enough to hold tons of hearty fillings and soft enough to sink our teeth into. Nailing down the dough was simple: The formula for our Kaiser Rolls (page 151) delivered the desirable chew, tenderness, and hint of richness that are appropriate for hoagie rolls. With the dough ready, we needed to find a way to shape it into evenly sized buns. To create smooth, uniform long rolls, we treated each portion as a small baguette and used a baguette shaping technique that included folding the dough multiple times before forming it into a taut roll. This ensured a roll with no visible seams and a consistent shape. Scoring the rolls ¼ inch deep allowed them to expand evenly while baking and created an attractive appearance.

5 cups (27½ ounces) bread flour

4 teaspoons instant or rapid-rise yeast

1 tablespoon salt

2 cups (16 ounces) water, room temperature

3 tablespoons vegetable oil

1 large egg, room temperature

4 teaspoons sugar

1 Whisk flour, yeast, and salt together in bowl of stand mixer. Whisk water, oil, egg, and sugar in 4-cup liquid measuring cup until sugar has dissolved.

2 Using dough hook on low speed, slowly add water mixture to flour mixture and mix until cohesive dough starts to form and no dry flour remains, about 2 minutes, scraping down bowl as needed. Increase speed to medium-low and knead until dough is smooth and elastic and clears sides of bowl but sticks to bottom, about 8 minutes.

3 Transfer dough to lightly floured counter and knead by hand to form smooth, round ball, about 30 seconds. Place dough seam side down in lightly greased large bowl or container, cover tightly with plastic wrap, and let rise until doubled in size, 1 to 1½ hours.

4 Line 2 rimmed baking sheets with parchment paper. Press down on dough to deflate. Transfer dough to clean counter and divide into quarters, then cut each quarter into halves (about 5½ ounces each); cover loosely with greased plastic.

5 Working with 1 piece of dough at a time (keep remaining pieces covered), press into 4-inch square.

6 Fold upper quarter of dough toward center and press gently to seal. Rotate dough 180 degrees and repeat folding step to form 5 by 3-inch rectangle.

7 Fold dough in half toward you, using your thumb of 1 hand to create crease along center of dough, sealing with heel of your other hand as you work your way along roll.

8 Cup your hand over center of dough and, without pressing down, roll dough back and forth to reinforce seal.

continued

hoagie rolls, continued

9 Stretch and roll dough into 8-inch cylinder. Moving your hands in opposite directions, use back and forth motion to roll ends of cylinder under your palms to form rounded points.

10 Arrange rolls seam side down on prepared sheets, spaced about 3 inches apart. Cover loosely with greased plastic and let rise until nearly doubled in size and dough springs back minimally when poked gently with your knuckle, 30 minutes to 1 hour.

11 Adjust oven racks to upper-middle and lower-middle positions and heat oven to 350 degrees. Using sharp paring knife or single-edge razor blade, make one ¼-inch-deep slash with swift, fluid motion lengthwise along top of rolls, starting and stopping about ½ inch from ends.

12 Bake rolls until golden brown, 30 to 35 minutes, switching and rotating sheets halfway through baking. Transfer rolls to wire racks and let cool completely, about 1 hour, before serving.

english muffins

makes 12 muffins
resting time 1½ hours
rising time 13 to 13½ hours
cooking time 42 minutes
total time 16¼ to 16¾ hours, plus 15 minutes cooling time
key equipment 2 rimmed baking sheets, 12-inch skillet, instant-read thermometer

why this recipe works For the ultimate English muffin—one that's chock-full of butter-thirsty nooks and crannies—we found that we needed a high-hydration dough. Drier doughs produced muffins with a compressed, even crumb. To enhance the bubbly crumb, we incorporated a series of folds into our recipe to encourage the yeast to produce more gases and to build the structure necessary to trap them. English muffins have a distinct yeasty character, so we allowed the shaped dough to proof slowly in the refrigerator so it would develop more flavor. After you brown the muffins, group the batches in different spots on the baking sheet to help you keep track of their cooking times. Split muffins can be stored in a zipper-lock bag at room temperature for up to 3 days. Wrapped in aluminum foil before being placed in the bag, the muffins can be frozen for up to 1 month. We do not recommend mixing this dough by hand.

3¼ cups (16¼ ounces) all-purpose flour

1 tablespoon instant or rapid-rise yeast

2 teaspoons salt

1 cup (8 ounces) whole milk, room temperature

½ cup (4 ounces) water, room temperature

2 tablespoons unsalted butter, melted

1 tablespoon sugar

6 tablespoons (1¾ ounces) cornmeal

1 Whisk flour, yeast, and salt together in bowl of stand mixer. Whisk milk, water, melted butter, and sugar in 4-cup liquid measuring cup until sugar has dissolved. Using dough hook on low speed, slowly add milk mixture to flour mixture and mix until cohesive dough starts to form and no dry flour remains, about 2 minutes, scraping down bowl as needed.

2 Increase speed to medium-low and knead until dough is smooth and elastic and clears sides of bowl but sticks to bottom, about 8 minutes. Transfer dough to lightly greased large bowl or container, cover tightly with plastic wrap, and let rise for 30 minutes.

3 Using greased bowl scraper (or your fingertips), fold dough over itself by gently lifting and folding edge of dough toward middle. Turn bowl 90 degrees and fold dough again; repeat turning bowl and folding dough 2 more times (total of 4 folds). Cover tightly with plastic and let dough rise until doubled in size, 30 minutes to 1 hour.

4 Sprinkle half of cornmeal over rimmed baking sheet. Press down on dough to deflate; transfer to well-floured counter, divide into quarters, and cut each quarter into thirds (2½ ounces each). Cover loosely with greased plastic.

5 Working with 1 piece of dough at a time (keep remaining pieces covered), form into rough ball by stretching dough around your thumbs and pinching edges together so that top is smooth. Place ball seam side down on clean counter and, using your cupped hand, drag in small circles until dough feels taut and round.

6 Arrange dough balls seam side down on prepared sheet, spaced about 2 inches apart. Cover loosely with greased plastic, then gently place second baking sheet on top.

continued

english muffins, continued

7 Let dough balls rest for 30 minutes, then refrigerate for at least 12 hours or up to 24 hours. Remove top sheet and loosen plastic covering muffins. Let muffins sit at room temperature for 1 hour. Sprinkle muffins with remaining cornmeal and press gently to adhere.

8 Adjust oven rack to lower-middle position and heat oven to 350 degrees. Heat 12-inch skillet over medium heat for 2 minutes. Using metal spatula, carefully place 4 muffins in skillet and cook until puffed and well browned, 3 to 6 minutes per side. Do not press down on muffins.

9 Transfer muffins to clean baking sheet and bake until sides are firm and muffins register 205 to 210 degrees, about 10 minutes. Repeat with remaining muffins in 2 batches, adjusting burner temperature as needed to prevent burning.

10 Transfer muffins to wire rack and let cool for 15 minutes. Split muffins open with fork and toast before serving.

classic bialys

makes 12 bialys
resting time 30 minutes
rising time 3 to 3½ hours
baking time 15 minutes
total time 2½ to 3 hours, plus 15 minutes cooling time
key equipment 12-inch skillet, 2 rimmed baking sheets

why this recipe works Kissing cousin to the bagel, the bialy was first brought to the United States by Jewish immigrants from Poland who settled in lower Manhattan in the early 20th century. Downtown bakeries producing the golden, chewy, onion-and poppy seed–filled rolls eventually became so prevalent that the Lower East Side was once referred to as Bialytown. These salty-savory yeasted rolls boast puffed edges that are at once soft and chewy, and they feature a generous dimple in the middle to hold filling. We wanted to bring Bialytown to our town, but the "authentic" recipes we tried produced bland bialys that were heavy and dense. To really highlight the requisite salty flavor, we used a generous 2 tablespoons of kosher salt in our dough. And to address the texture problems, we tried using all-purpose flour rather than the bread flour that most recipes call for, thinking that its lower gluten content would help tenderize the dough. This brought us closer to our goal, but the rolls were still too tough, so we incorporated two resting periods, one after portioning the dough and forming it into balls, and another after shaping the balls into disks. Resting the dough gave the gluten a chance to relax and the yeast an opportunity to create bigger air pockets within the dough, ultimately producing more tender bialys. Bialys can be stored in a zipper-lock bag at room temperature for up to 2 days. Wrapped in aluminum foil before being placed in the bag, bialys can be frozen in for up to 1 month. To reheat, wrap the bialys (thawed if frozen) in aluminum foil, place them on a baking sheet, and bake in a 350-degree oven for 10 minutes.

dough
4¾ cups (23¾ ounces) all-purpose flour

2 tablespoons kosher salt

2 teaspoons instant or rapid-rise yeast

2 cups (16 ounces) water, room temperature

1 tablespoon sugar

filling
3 tablespoons extra-virgin olive oil

3 onions, chopped fine

1 teaspoon kosher salt

1 tablespoon poppy seeds

continued

classic bialys, continued

1 **For the dough** Whisk flour, salt, and yeast together in bowl of stand mixer. Whisk water and sugar in 4-cup liquid measuring cup until sugar has dissolved. Using dough hook on low speed, slowly add water mixture to flour mixture and mix until cohesive dough starts to form and no dry flour remains, about 2 minutes, scraping down bowl as needed. Increase speed to medium-low and knead until dough is smooth and elastic and clears sides of bowl but sticks to bottom, about 8 minutes.

2 Transfer dough to well-floured counter. Using your well-floured hands, knead dough to form smooth, round ball, about 30 seconds. Place dough seam side down in lightly greased large bowl or container, cover tightly with plastic wrap, and let rise until doubled in size, 1 to 1½ hours. (Unrisen dough can be refrigerated for at least 8 hours or up to 16 hours; let dough sit at room temperature for 1 hour before shaping.)

3 Press down on dough to deflate. Transfer dough to lightly floured counter and stretch into even 12-inch log. Cut log into 12 equal pieces (about 3 ounces each) and cover loosely with greased plastic.

4 Working with 1 piece of dough at a time (keep remaining pieces covered), form into rough ball by stretching dough around your thumbs and pinching edges together so that top is smooth. Place ball seam side down on clean counter and, using your cupped hand, drag in small circles until dough feels taut and round. Cover balls loosely with greased plastic and let rest for 30 minutes.

5 **For the filling** Heat oil in 12-inch skillet over medium heat until shimmering. Add onions and salt and cook until softened and golden brown, about 10 minutes. Off heat, stir in poppy seeds.

6 Line 2 rimmed baking sheets with parchment paper and lightly flour parchment. Press each dough ball into 5-inch round of even thickness and arrange on prepared sheets, spaced about 1 inch apart. Cover loosely with greased plastic and let rise until puffy, 15 to 20 minutes.

7 Adjust oven racks to upper-middle and lower-middle positions and heat oven to 475 degrees. Grease and flour bottom of round 1-cup dry measuring cup (or 3-inch-diameter drinking glass). Press cup firmly into center of each dough round until cup touches sheet to make indentation for filling. (Reflour cup as needed to prevent sticking.)

8 Divide filling evenly among bialys (about 1 heaping tablespoon each) and smooth with back of spoon. Bake until light golden brown, 15 to 20 minutes, switching and rotating sheets halfway through baking. Transfer bialys to wire rack and let cool for 15 minutes. Serve warm or at room temperature.

garlic knots

makes 12 knots
rising time 2 to 3 hours
baking time 10 minutes
total time 3¼ to 4¼ hours, plus 15 minutes cooling time
key equipment 8-inch skillet, rimmed baking sheet, pastry brush

why this recipe works Made from leftover pizza dough, buttery, supremely garlicky garlic knots are a pizzeria classic. Could we bring them home without the help of a pizza delivery driver? The pizza dough recipes we tried made knots that were too dry or too hard. We wanted something fluffier than pizza crust but chewier than dinner rolls. Substituting all-purpose flour for bread flour softened the knots, and kneading for about 8 minutes provided the right elasticity. To give our knots potent flavor, we first tried dousing them in garlic powder, which tasted artificial, and then in raw garlic, which was too harsh. So we sautéed minced garlic—nine cloves of it—in butter, which we brushed over the knots. We also stirred some of the butter and the reserved toasty garlic solids into the dough. Finally, brushing the knots with garlic butter during baking and again just after taking them out of the oven satisfied our garlic cravings. Knots can be stored in a zipper-lock bag at room temperature for up to 3 days. Wrapped in aluminum foil before being placed in the bag, the knots can be frozen for up to 1 month. To reheat, wrap the knots (thawed if frozen) in foil, place them on a baking sheet, and bake in a 350-degree oven for 10 minutes.

9 garlic cloves, minced (2 tablespoons)

6 tablespoons (3 ounces) unsalted butter

¾ cup (6 ounces) plus 1 teaspoon water

2 cups (10 ounces) all-purpose flour

1½ teaspoons instant or rapid-rise yeast

1 teaspoon salt

coarse sea salt

1 Cook garlic, 1 tablespoon butter, and 1 teaspoon water in 8-inch skillet over low heat, stirring occasionally, until garlic is straw-colored, 8 to 10 minutes. Stir in remaining butter until melted. Strain into bowl; reserve garlic solids.

2 Whisk flour, yeast, and salt together in bowl of stand mixer. Whisk remaining ¾ cup water, 1 tablespoon garlic butter, and garlic solids together in 4-cup liquid measuring cup. Using dough hook on low speed, slowly add water mixture to flour mixture and mix until cohesive dough starts to form and no dry flour remains, about 2 minutes, scraping down bowl as needed. Increase speed to medium-low and knead until dough is smooth and elastic and clears sides of bowl but sticks to bottom, about 8 minutes.

3 Transfer dough to lightly floured counter and knead by hand to form smooth, round ball, about 30 seconds. Place dough seam side down in lightly greased large bowl or container, cover tightly with plastic wrap, and let rise until doubled in size, 1 to 1½ hours.

4 Line rimmed baking sheet with parchment paper. Press down on dough to deflate. Transfer dough to clean counter. Press and stretch dough into 12 by 6-inch rectangle, with long side parallel to counter edge.

5 Using pizza cutter or chef's knife, cut dough vertically into 12 (6 by 1-inch) strips; cover loosely with greased plastic.

6 Working with 1 piece of dough at a time (keep remaining pieces covered), stretch and roll into 14-inch rope.

7 Shape rope into U with 2-inch-wide bottom curve.

8 Tie ends into single overhand knot, with 1½-inch open loop at bottom.

continued

garlic knots, continued

9 Wrap 1 tail over loop and press through opening from top. Wrap other tail under loop and through opening from bottom. Pinch ends together to seal.

10 Arrange knots pinched side down on prepared sheet, spaced about 1 inch apart. Cover loosely with greased plastic and let rise until nearly doubled in size and dough springs back minimally when poked gently with your knuckle, 1 to 1½ hours. (Unrisen garlic knots can be refrigerated for at least 8 hours or up to 16 hours; let garlic knots sit at room temperature for 1 hour before baking.)

11 Adjust oven rack to middle position and heat oven to 500 degrees. Bake knots until set, about 5 minutes. Brush with 2 tablespoons garlic butter, rotate sheet, and bake until knots are golden brown, about 5 minutes.

12 Transfer knots to wire rack. Brush with remaining garlic butter, sprinkle with sea salt, and let cool for 15 minutes. Serve warm.

parmesan breadsticks

makes 18 breadsticks
rising time 1½ to 2 hours
baking time 12 minutes
total time 3 to 3½ hours, plus 15 minutes cooling time
key equipment 2 rimmed baking sheets, pastry brush

4 cups (20 ounces) all-purpose flour

1 tablespoon instant or rapid-rise yeast

1 tablespoon salt

2 teaspoons onion powder

1½ cups (12 ounces) water, room temperature

¼ cup (1¾ ounces) extra-virgin olive oil

3 ounces Parmesan cheese, grated (1½ cups)

1 large egg, lightly beaten with 2 tablespoons extra-virgin olive oil and pinch salt

why this recipe works The best part about going to an Italian American restaurant might be the Parmesan breadsticks. Our goal was to re-create these flavorful, golden breadsticks—and serve them warm and fresh at home. First, we wanted to ensure that the flavor of our breadsticks' namesake really came through. In addition to sprinkling Parmesan on top, we mixed some into the dough for a rich cheese taste that wasn't just an afterthought. Adding a small amount of onion powder to our dough enhanced the nutty taste of the cheese and further boosted the savory appeal. Nailing down the perfect texture proved more complex. We wanted chewy yet soft-crumbed breadsticks, so we used all-purpose flour rather than higher-protein bread flour. But we found that our sticks were still too tough and dry inside. Our first thought, adding more water to the dough, left us with a sticky mess that was too difficult to shape. Doubling the amount of extra-virgin olive oil in the dough from 2 tablespoons to ¼ cup was the perfect solution. The oil acted as a tenderizer and coated the gluten strands, preventing them from sticking to one another and forming a strong gluten network. This created an easy-to-shape dough that baked up with a soft crumb. We set our oven to 500 degrees to ensure that our breadsticks took on a nice golden hue in the short time required to cook them through. Brushing our breadsticks with an egg-and-oil wash enhanced browning and flavor, while making the exterior chewy, not crunchy. Breadsticks can be stored in a zipper-lock bag at room temperature for up to 3 days. Wrapped in aluminum foil before being placed in the bag, the breadsticks can be frozen for up to 1 month. To reheat, wrap the breadsticks (thawed if frozen) in foil, place them on baking sheet, and bake in a 350-degree oven for 10 minutes.

continued

1 Whisk flour, yeast, salt, and onion powder together in bowl of stand mixer. Combine water and oil in 4-cup liquid measuring cup.

2 Using dough hook on low speed, slowly add water mixture to flour mixture and mix until cohesive dough starts to form and no dry flour remains, about 2 minutes, scraping down bowl as needed. Increase speed to medium-low and knead until dough is smooth and elastic and clears sides of bowl but sticks to bottom, about 8 minutes. Reduce speed to low, slowly add 1 cup Parmesan, ¼ cup at a time, and mix until mostly incorporated, about 2 minutes.

3 Transfer dough to lightly floured counter and knead by hand until Parmesan is evenly distributed and dough forms smooth, round ball, about 30 seconds. Place dough seam side down in lightly greased large bowl or container, cover tightly with plastic wrap, and let rise until doubled in size, 1 to 1½ hours. (Unrisen dough can be refrigerated for at least 8 hours or up to 16 hours; let sit at room temperature for 1 hour before shaping.)

4 Press down on dough to deflate. Transfer dough to clean counter and divide in half. Stretch each half into 9-inch log, cut log into 9 equal pieces (about 2 ounces each), and cover loosely with greased plastic.

5 Working with 1 piece of dough at a time (keep remaining pieces covered), form into rough ball by stretching dough around your thumbs and pinching edges together so that top is smooth. Place ball seam side down on clean counter and, using your cupped hand, drag in small circles until dough feels taut and round. Cover balls loosely with greased plastic and let rest for 30 minutes.

6 Line 2 rimmed baking sheets with greased parchment paper. Stretch and roll each dough ball into 8-inch-long cylinder. Moving your hands in opposite directions, use back and forth motion to roll ends of cylinder under your palms to form rounded points.

7 Arrange breadsticks on prepared sheets, spaced about 1½-inches apart. Cover loosely with greased plastic and let rise until nearly doubled in size and dough springs back minimally when poked gently with your knuckle, about 30 minutes.

8 Adjust oven racks to upper-middle and lower-middle positions and heat oven to 500 degrees. Gently brush breadsticks with egg mixture and sprinkle with remaining Parmesan. Bake until golden brown, 12 to 14 minutes, switching and rotating sheets halfway through baking. Transfer breadsticks to wire rack and let cool for 15 minutes. Serve warm.

variations **asiago and black pepper breadsticks**
Use the small holes of a box grater to shred the Asiago.

Add 1 tablespoon coarsely ground pepper to flour mixture in step 1. Substitute 1 cup shredded Asiago cheese for Parmesan; add ½ cup cheese to dough in step 2 and sprinkle breadsticks with remaining ½ cup cheese before baking in step 8.

pecorino and mixed herb breadsticks
Substitute 1½ cups grated Pecorino Romano for Parmesan. Combine 1 cup Pecorino, 2 tablespoons finely chopped fresh basil, 2 tablespoons minced fresh parsley, and 2 tablespoons minced fresh oregano in bowl before adding to dough in step 2.

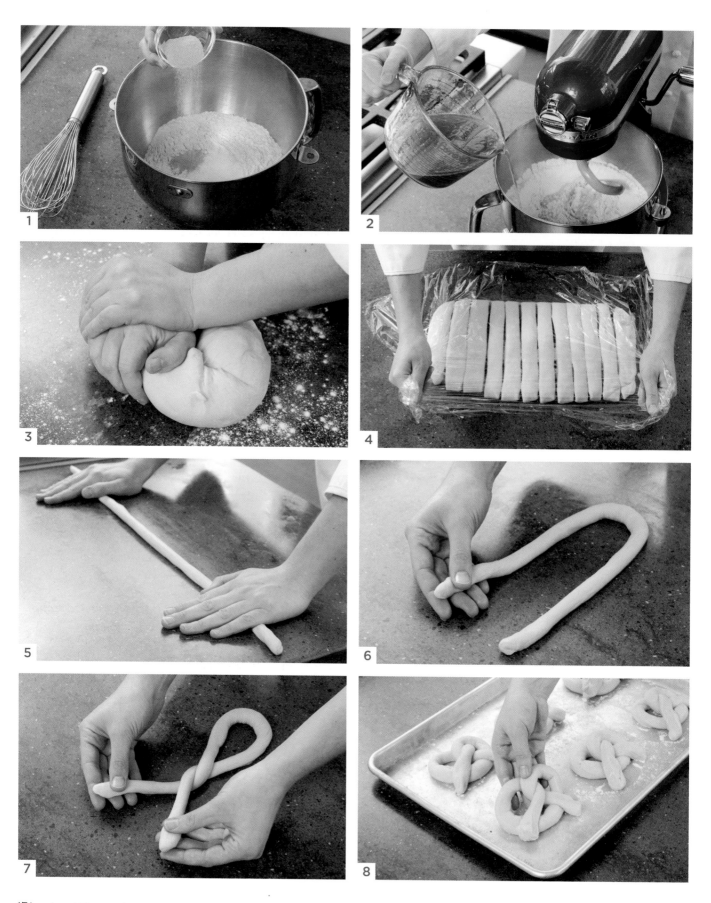

ballpark
pretzels

makes 12 pretzels
resting time 5 minutes
rising time 1¼ to 1¾ hours
baking time 15 minutes
total time 3 to 3½ hours, plus 15 minutes cooling time
key equipment 2 rimmed baking sheets, Dutch oven

why this recipe works With their mahogany-brown crusts, tender insides, and salty bite, soft pretzels are the ultimate snack—and hard to come by, unless you are at a ballpark or live in an urban area. We wanted to bring these treats to the home kitchen. The challenge? Cracking that dark, distinctly flavored exterior. We knew that professional bakers treat the dough with an alkaline solution called lye, which helps a small piece of dough achieve a rich brown exterior before its center overcooks. Of course, most home cooks don't have lye—it's abrasive and caustic. But every home cook has worked with a more subdued alkali: baking soda. We gave the pretzels a quick dip in a boiling water and baking soda mixture. After letting the pretzels dry, we baked them and watched them turn a beautiful mahogany. We use kosher salt for our pretzels, but coarse pretzel salt may be substituted (do not use pretzel salt in the dough). Pretzels can be stored in a zipper-lock bag at room temperature for up to 2 days. Wrapped in aluminum foil before being placed in the bag, the pretzels can be frozen for up to 1 month. To reheat, place the pretzels (thawed if frozen) on a baking sheet, mist lightly with water, sprinkle with salt, and bake in a 300-degree oven for 5 minutes.

3¾ cups (20⅔ ounces) bread flour

Kosher salt

2 teaspoons instant or rapid-rise yeast

1½ cups (12 ounces) water, room temperature

3 tablespoons vegetable oil

2 tablespoons packed dark brown sugar

¼ cup baking soda

1 Whisk flour, 4 teaspoons salt, and yeast together in bowl of stand mixer. Whisk water, 2 tablespoons oil, and sugar in 4-cup liquid measuring cup until sugar has dissolved.

2 Using dough hook on low speed, slowly add water mixture to flour mixture and mix until cohesive dough starts to form and no dry flour remains, about 2 minutes, scraping down bowl as needed. Increase speed to medium-low and knead until dough is smooth and elastic and clears sides of bowl, about 8 minutes.

3 Transfer dough to lightly floured counter and knead by hand to form smooth, round ball, about 30 seconds. Place dough seam side down in lightly greased large bowl or container, cover tightly with plastic wrap, and let rise until doubled in size, 1 to 1½ hours.

4 Lightly flour 2 rimmed baking sheets. Press down on dough to deflate. Transfer dough to clean counter. Press and stretch dough into 12 by 6-inch rectangle, with long side parallel to counter edge. Using pizza cutter or chef's knife, cut dough vertically into 12 (6 by 1-inch) strips; cover loosely with greased plastic.

5 Working with 1 piece of dough at a time (keep remaining pieces covered), stretch and roll into 22-inch rope.

6 Shape rope into U with 2-inch-wide bottom curve and ends facing away from you.

7 Crisscross ropes in middle. Fold ends toward bottom of U, spaced 1 inch apart; firmly press into bottom curve.

8 Arrange pretzels knot side up on prepared sheets, spaced about 2 inches apart. Cover loosely with greased plastic and let rise until puffy, about 15 minutes.

continued

ballpark pretzels, continued

9 Adjust oven racks to upper-middle and lower-middle positions and heat oven to 425 degrees. Dissolve baking soda in 4 cups water in Dutch oven and bring to boil over medium-high heat.

10 Using slotted spatula, transfer 4 pretzels knot side down to boiling water and cook for 30 seconds, flipping pretzels halfway through cooking. Transfer pretzels knot side up to wire rack and repeat with remaining 8 pretzels in 2 batches. Let pretzels rest for 5 minutes.

11 Wipe flour from now-empty sheets and grease with remaining oil. Sprinkle each sheet with ½ teaspoon salt. Transfer 6 pretzels knot side up to each prepared sheet and sprinkle with 1 teaspoon salt.

12 Bake pretzels until mahogany brown and any yellowish color around seams has faded, 15 to 20 minutes, switching and rotating sheets halfway through baking. Transfer pretzels to wire rack and let cool for 15 minutes. Serve warm.

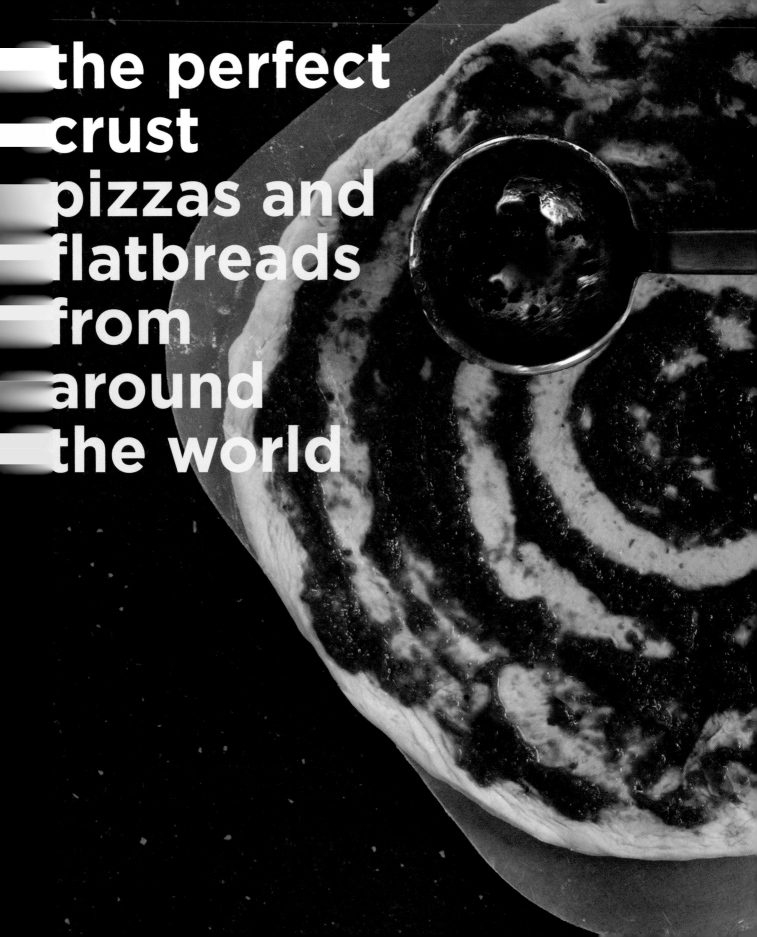

the perfect crust
pizzas and flatbreads from around the world

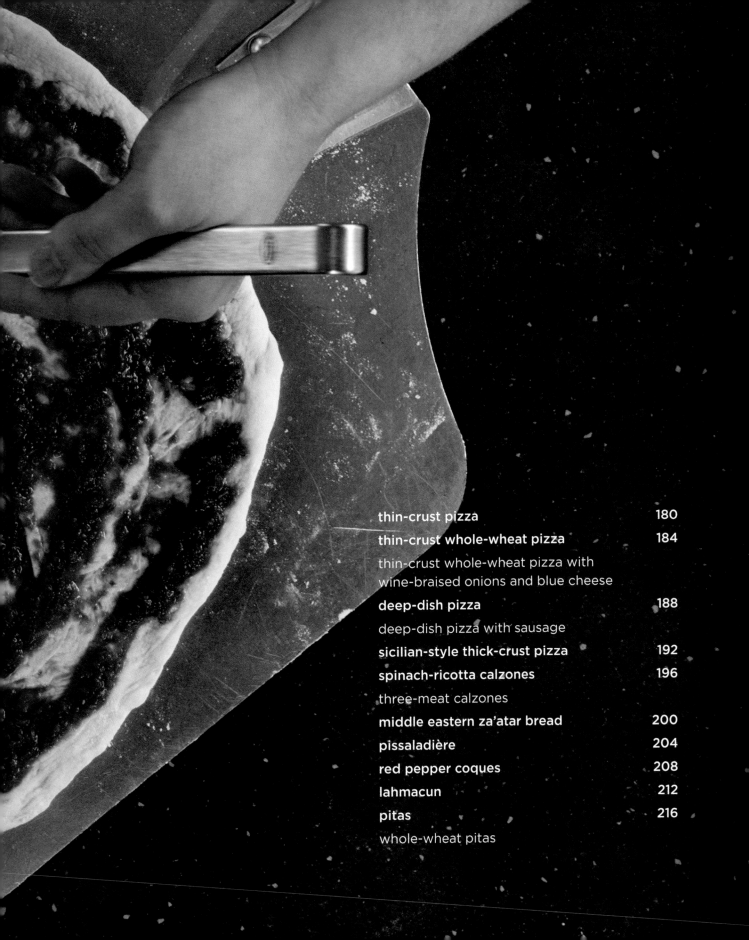

thin-crust pizza

makes two 13-inch pizzas
resting time 1 hour 10 minutes
rising time 24 hours
baking time 16 minutes
total time 26½ hours, plus 5 minutes cooling time
key equipment food processor, baking stone, pizza peel

why this recipe works New York–style pizza is
something special: It has a thin, crisp, and spottily charred
exterior, and it's tender yet chewy within. But with home
ovens that reach only 500 degrees and dough that's
impossible to stretch thin, the savviest cooks struggle to
produce parlor-quality pies. In pursuit of the perfect crust
at home, we made the dough fairly wet so it was easy to
stretch. This also allowed it to retain moisture. This dough
was the perfect candidate to knead in the food processor—
wet but not too loose. The blade's rapid action turned the
dough elastic in just about a minute (after a brief rest).
This dough was easy to stretch, but it puffed in the oven
and was a little bland. The solution was to employ a slow,
cold fermentation by chilling the dough in the refrigerator
for a day or so instead of letting it rise on the counter. This
kept the bubbles in the dough tighter, and it created more
flavor via the prolonged production of sugar, alcohol,
and acids. Adding oil and sugar to the dough encouraged
more crunch and color, but the oven rack placement really
gave us the crust we were looking for. Most recipes call for
placing the pizza on the bottom rack, close to the heating
element. That browns the bottom but dries out the crust.
Situating the baking stone on the highest rack mimicked the
shallow chamber of a commercial pizza oven, in which
heat rises, radiates off the top of the oven, and browns the
pizza before the interior dries out. Shape the second dough
ball while the first pizza bakes, but don't top the pizza until
right before you bake it. If you add more toppings, keep
them light or they may weigh down the thin crust. The sauce
will yield more than is needed in the recipe; extra
sauce can be refrigerated for up to one week or frozen
for up to one month.

dough

3 cups (16½ ounces) bread flour

2 teaspoons sugar

½ teaspoon instant or rapid-rise yeast

1⅓ cups (10⅔ ounces) ice water

1 tablespoon vegetable oil

1½ teaspoons salt

sauce and toppings

1 (28-ounce) can whole peeled tomatoes,
drained with juice reserved

1 tablespoon extra-virgin olive oil

2 garlic cloves, minced

1 teaspoon red wine vinegar

1 teaspoon dried oregano

½ teaspoon salt

¼ teaspoon pepper

1 ounce Parmesan cheese, grated fine (½ cup)

8 ounces whole-milk mozzarella cheese,
shredded (2 cups)

continued

1 ***For the dough*** Pulse flour, sugar, and yeast in food processor until combined, about 5 pulses. With processor running, slowly add ice water and process until dough is just combined and no dry flour remains, about 10 seconds. Let dough rest for 10 minutes.

2 Add oil and salt to dough and process until dough forms satiny, sticky ball that clears sides of bowl, 30 to 60 seconds. Transfer dough to lightly oiled counter and knead by hand to form smooth, round ball, about 30 seconds. Place dough seam side down in lightly greased large bowl or container, cover tightly with plastic wrap, and refrigerate for at least 24 hours or up to 3 days.

3 ***For the sauce and toppings*** Process tomatoes, oil, garlic, vinegar, oregano, salt, and pepper in clean, dry workbowl until smooth, about 30 seconds. Transfer mixture to 2-cup liquid measuring cup and add reserved tomato juice until sauce measures 2 cups. Reserve 1 cup sauce; set aside remaining sauce for another use.

4 One hour before baking, adjust oven rack 4 inches from broiler element, set baking stone on rack, and heat oven to 500 degrees. Press down on dough to deflate. Transfer dough to clean counter, divide in half, and cover loosely with greased plastic. Pat 1 piece of dough (keep remaining piece covered) into 4-inch round. Working around circumference of dough, fold edges toward center until ball forms.

5 Flip ball seam side down and, using your cupped hands, drag in small circles on counter until dough feels taut and round and all seams are secured on underside. (If dough sticks to your hands, lightly dust top of dough with flour.) Repeat with remaining piece of dough. Space dough balls 3 inches apart, cover loosely with greased plastic, and let rest for 1 hour.

6 Heat broiler for 10 minutes. Meanwhile, coat 1 dough ball generously with flour and place on well-floured counter. Using your fingertips, gently flatten into 8-inch round, leaving 1 inch of outer edge slightly thicker than center. Using your hands, gently stretch dough into 12-inch round, working along edge and giving disk quarter turns.

7 Transfer dough to well-floured pizza peel and stretch into 13-inch round. Using back of spoon or ladle, spread ½ cup tomato sauce in even layer over surface of dough, leaving ¼-inch border around edge. Sprinkle ¼ cup Parmesan evenly over sauce, followed by 1 cup mozzarella.

8 Slide pizza carefully onto baking stone and return oven to 500 degrees. Bake until crust is well browned and cheese is bubbly and partially browned, 8 to 10 minutes, rotating pizza halfway through baking. Transfer pizza to wire rack and let cool for 5 minutes before slicing and serving. Heat broiler for 10 minutes. Repeat with remaining dough, sauce, and toppings, returning oven to 500 degrees when pizza is placed on stone.

troubleshooting

problem The crust lacks flavor.

solution **Let the dough rise for a full day.**

For crust as good as that found in New York City, we employ a cold fermentation and let the dough rise in the refrigerator instead of on the counter. Don't take shortcuts; let the dough chill for a minimum of 24 hours or up to 3 days. This slow fermentation is essential for flavor development; it is during this time that more complex sugars, alcohols, and acids develop. It also keeps the air bubbles uniform.

thin-crust whole-wheat pizza

makes two 13-inch pizzas
resting time 1 hour 10 minutes
rising time 18 hours
baking time 16 minutes
total time 20¾ hours, plus 5 minutes cooling time
key equipment 8-inch skillet, baking stone, pizza peel

why this recipe works Whole-wheat pizza sounds like a great idea: A nutty, wheaty-tasting crust would be a satisfying and flavorful change of pace from the typical parlor pie. Unfortunately, it's nearly impossible to come by a whole-wheat dough that develops the same char and chew of traditional thin-crust pizzas; most are dry and dense. We wanted to find a way to make a flavorful whole-wheat crust with the same great texture as our Thin-Crust Pizza (page 180). Using whole-wheat flour alone would give us a dense crust, so we incorporated just enough structure-building white bread flour. To help strengthen the gluten network, a highly hydrated dough was particularly important for this pie; the whole-wheat flour's mix of starch, bran, and germ absorbed more water than if we used white flour only. But because our dough was so wet, simply preheating the pizza stone in a 500-degree oven wasn't enough; we found we needed to heat the stone under the broiler's high heat so that the crust would brown before the toppings overcooked. After perfecting our thin, crisp, earthy-tasting crust, we realized that the sweet-tart flavors of the sauce and cheese clashed with it. Instead, we topped our crust with three cheeses (including creamy finishing dollops of ricotta), garlicky oil, and basil. This combination of flavors added richness and complexity without competing with the flavor of the crust. Shape the second dough ball while the first pizza bakes, but don't top the pizza until right before you bake it.

dough

1½ cups (8¼ ounces) whole-wheat flour

1 cup (5½ ounces) bread flour

2 teaspoons honey

¾ teaspoon instant or rapid-rise yeast

1¼ cups (10 ounces) ice water

2 tablespoons extra-virgin olive oil

1¾ teaspoons salt

garlic oil and toppings

¼ cup extra-virgin olive oil

2 garlic cloves, minced

2 anchovy fillets, rinsed, patted dry, and minced (optional)

½ teaspoon pepper

½ teaspoon dried oregano

⅛ teaspoon red pepper flakes

⅛ teaspoon salt

1 cup fresh basil leaves

1 ounce Pecorino Romano cheese, grated fine (½ cup)

8 ounces whole-milk mozzarella cheese, shredded (2 cups)

6 ounces (¾ cup) whole-milk ricotta cheese

continued

1 **For the dough** Pulse whole-wheat flour, bread flour, honey, and yeast in food processor until combined, about 5 pulses. With processor running, slowly add ice water and process until dough is just combined and no dry flour remains, about 10 seconds. Let dough rest for 10 minutes.

2 Add oil and salt to dough and process until dough forms satiny, sticky ball that clears sides of bowl, 45 to 60 seconds. Transfer dough to lightly oiled counter and knead by hand to form smooth, round ball, about 30 seconds. Place dough seam side down in lightly greased large bowl or container, cover tightly with plastic wrap, and refrigerate for at least 18 hours or up to 2 days.

3 **For the garlic oil and toppings** Heat oil in 8-inch skillet over medium-low heat until shimmering. Add garlic, anchovies, if using, pepper, oregano, pepper flakes, and salt. Cook, stirring constantly, until fragrant, about 30 seconds. Transfer to bowl and let cool completely before using.

4 One hour before baking, adjust oven rack 4 inches from broiler element, set baking stone on rack, and heat oven to 500 degrees. Press down on dough to deflate. Transfer dough to clean counter, divide in half, and cover loosely with greased plastic. Pat 1 piece of dough (keep remaining piece covered) into 4-inch round. Working around circumference of dough, fold edges toward center until ball forms.

5 Flip dough ball seam side down and, using your cupped hands, drag in small circles on counter until dough feels taut and round and all seams are secured on underside. (If dough sticks to your hands, lightly dust top of dough with flour.) Repeat with remaining piece of dough. Space dough balls 3 inches apart, cover loosely with greased plastic, and let rest for 1 hour.

6 Heat broiler for 10 minutes. Meanwhile, generously coat 1 dough ball with flour and place on well-floured counter. Using your fingertips, gently flatten into 8-inch round, leaving 1 inch of outer edge slightly thicker than center. Using your hands, gently stretch dough into 12-inch round, working along edge and giving disk quarter turns.

7 Transfer dough to well-floured pizza peel and stretch into 13-inch round. Using back of spoon, spread half of garlic oil in even layer over surface of dough, leaving ¼-inch border around edge. Layer ½ cup basil leaves over garlic oil. Sprinkle with ¼ cup Pecorino, followed by 1 cup mozzarella.

8 Slide pizza carefully onto baking stone and return oven to 500 degrees. Bake until crust is well browned and cheese is bubbly and partially browned, 8 to 10 minutes, rotating pizza halfway through baking. Transfer pizza to wire rack and dollop half of ricotta over surface. Let cool for 5 minutes before slicing and serving. Heat broiler for 10 minutes. Repeat with remaining dough, garlic oil, and toppings, returning oven to 500 degrees when pizza is placed on stone.

variation **thin-crust whole-wheat pizza with wine-braised onions and blue cheese**
Bring 1 onion, halved and sliced ⅛ inch thick, 1½ cups water, ¾ cup dry red wine, 3 tablespoons sugar, and ¼ teaspoon salt to simmer in 10-inch skillet over medium heat. Cook, stirring often, until liquid evaporates and onions are crisp-tender, about 30 minutes. Transfer mixture to bowl, stir in 2 teaspoons red wine vinegar, and let cool completely before using. Substitute onion mixture for garlic oil in step 7. Omit Pecorino Romano, mozzarella, ricotta, and basil. Before baking, spread ⅓ cup crème fraîche over surface of each dough round, leaving ¼-inch border around edge. Sprinkle half of onion mixture evenly over each pizza, followed by ½ cup coarsely chopped walnuts and ½ cup crumbled blue cheese. Let each pizza rest for 5 minutes, top each with 2 tablespoons shredded basil, slice, and serve.

deep-dish pizza

makes two 9-inch pizzas
rising time 1½ to 2½ hours
baking time 20 minutes
total time 3 to 4 hours
key equipment stand mixer, medium saucepan, rolling pin, two 9-inch round cake pans

why this recipe works If you're from the Northeast, or if you haven't been to Chicago, you may dismiss deep-dish pizza out of regional pride. That would be a mistake. Real Chicago-style pizza is certainly thick, but its texture and flavor are something special: Instead of being bread-like, the crust offers the contrast of a good biscuit—airy inside, lightly crisp outside, and flaky throughout—and boasts a rich taste that holds its own under any topping. We wanted to achieve such results at home. Deep-dish pizza crust includes a fair amount of fat. Some recipes rely on oil, but we thought the rich flavor of butter was unbeatable in this crust. We found cornmeal in just about every ingredient list we reviewed, and it indeed added good earthy flavor and crunch. To achieve maximum flakiness, after mixing the dough and letting it rise, we employed a technique called laminating, which involves layering butter and dough through a sequence of rolling and folding to create ultraflaky pastries. Adding melted butter to the pizza dough and spreading the rolled-out dough with softened butter before folding did the trick in our crust. Moving the dough into the refrigerator for its second rise ensured that the butter remained in distinct layers and didn't get too soft. For the finishing touch on our crust, we oiled our cake pans, which made the crust crisp and even more flavorful. Following Chicago tradition, we covered the dough with shredded mozzarella before topping it with a thick tomato sauce. The cheese formed a barrier between the crust and the sauce, which prevented sogginess. A sprinkle of nutty Parmesan over the sauce provided a second layer of cheesy bite. We do not recommend mixing this dough by hand. Use the large holes of a box grater to grate the onion.

dough
3¼ cups (16¼ ounces) all-purpose flour
½ cup (2½ ounces) cornmeal
2¼ teaspoons instant or rapid-rise yeast
1½ teaspoons salt
1¼ cups (10 ounces) water, room temperature
3 tablespoons unsalted butter, melted, plus 4 tablespoons (2 ounces) softened
2 teaspoons sugar
¼ cup (1¾ ounces) extra-virgin olive oil

sauce and toppings
3 tablespoons extra-virgin olive oil
¼ cup grated onion
¼ teaspoon dried oregano
Salt and pepper
2 garlic cloves, minced
1 (28-ounce) can crushed tomatoes
¼ teaspoon sugar
2 tablespoons chopped fresh basil
1 pound whole-milk mozzarella cheese, shredded (4 cups)
¼ cup finely grated Parmesan cheese

continued

1 **For the dough** Whisk flour, cornmeal, yeast, and salt together in bowl of stand mixer. Whisk water, melted butter, and sugar in 4-cup liquid measuring cup until sugar has dissolved. Using dough hook on low speed, slowly add water mixture to flour mixture and mix until cohesive dough starts to form and no dry flour remains, about 2 minutes, scraping down bowl as needed. Increase speed to medium-low and knead until dough is smooth and elastic and clears sides of bowl, about 8 minutes.

2 Transfer dough to lightly floured counter and knead by hand to form smooth, round ball, about 30 seconds. Place dough seam side down in lightly greased large bowl or container, cover tightly with plastic wrap, and let rise until doubled in size, 1 to 1½ hours. (Unrisen dough can be refrigerated for at least 8 hours or up to 16 hours; let sit at room temperature for 30 minutes before shaping in step 4.)

3 **For the sauce and toppings** Heat 2 tablespoons oil in medium saucepan over medium heat until shimmering. Add onion, oregano, and ½ teaspoon salt and cook until onion is softened and lightly browned, 5 to 7 minutes. Stir in garlic and cook until fragrant, about 30 seconds. Stir in tomatoes and sugar, bring to simmer, and cook until sauce measures 2½ cups, 25 to 30 minutes. Off heat, stir in basil and remaining oil. Season with salt and pepper to taste. Transfer to bowl and let cool completely before using.

4 Adjust oven rack to lowest position and heat oven to 425 degrees. Press down on dough to deflate and transfer to clean counter. Press and roll dough into 15 by 12-inch rectangle, with short side parallel to counter edge. Spread softened butter over dough, leaving ½-inch border along edges.

5 Roll dough away from you into firm cylinder, keeping roll taut by tucking it under itself as you go. With seam side down, flatten cylinder into 18 by 4-inch rectangle. Cut rectangle in half crosswise.

6 Working with 1 half at a time, fold dough into thirds like business letter, then pinch seams together to form rough ball. Return dough balls seam side down to greased bowl, cover tightly with plastic, and let rise in refrigerator until nearly doubled in size, 30 minutes to 1 hour.

7 Coat two 9-inch round cake pans with 2 tablespoons oil each. Press and roll 1 dough ball into 13-inch round of even thickness, sprinkling dough and counter with flour as needed to prevent sticking. Loosely roll dough around rolling pin and gently unroll it into prepared pan. Gently press dough into pan, working it into corners and 1 inch up sides. (If dough resists stretching, let it relax for 5 to 10 minutes before trying to stretch it again.) Repeat with remaining dough ball.

8 For each pizza, sprinkle 2 cups mozzarella evenly over surface of dough, spread 1¼ cups tomato sauce over cheese, and sprinkle 2 tablespoons Parmesan over sauce. Bake pizzas until crusts are golden brown, 20 to 30 minutes. Let pizzas cool in pans for 10 minutes, then transfer to cutting board with metal spatula. Slice and serve.

variation **deep-dish pizza with sausage**
Cook 1 pound hot or sweet Italian sausage, casings removed, in 12-inch nonstick skillet over medium-high heat, breaking it into ½-inch pieces with wooden spoon, until browned, about 5 minutes. Using slotted spoon, transfer sausage to paper towel–lined plate. Sprinkle half of cooked sausage over mozzarella in each pizza before continuing with additional toppings in step 8.

sicilian-style thick-crust pizza

serves 6 to 8
resting time 10 minutes
rising time 24 hours
baking time 20 minutes
total time 27 hours
key equipment food processor, medium saucepan, baking stone, 2 rimmed baking sheets, rolling pin

why this recipe works Sicilian-style pizza gets a bad rap: At many American pizzerias, these thick slabs baked in baking sheets are just larger masses of the same dough that's used for round thin-crust pies. That means the crust is bready and dense, lacks textural contrast, and offers little in the way of interesting flavor. But good Sicilian-style thick-crust pizza is something else entirely. It features a tight, even, cake-like crumb that's pale yellow, almost creamy. The underside is delicately crisp. Spread over the top is a concentrated layer of tomato sauce, followed by a blanket of cheese. In order to create our ideal Sicilian pie, we used a mixture of all-purpose flour and traditional semolina. The latter, a flour variety made from durum wheat, is the same type used to make many Italian pastas and breads and is the source of the crust's pale yellow color; slightly sweet, rich flavor; and fine crumb. We used a generous amount of olive oil in the dough to tenderize it, cold-fermented the dough to let flavors develop and prevent large bubbles from forming, and then rolled it out and weighed it down with another baking sheet during the second rise to keep the crumb even and tight. Finally, we topped it with a long-cooked tomato sauce and a combination of mozzarella and Parmesan, which stood up to the thick crust. Anchovies give the sauce depth without a discernible fishy taste; if you decide not to use them, add an additional ¼ teaspoon of salt.

dough

2¼ cups (11¼ ounces) all-purpose flour

2 cups (12 ounces) semolina flour

1 teaspoon instant or rapid-rise yeast

1⅔ cups (13⅓ ounces) water, room temperature

3 tablespoons extra-virgin olive oil

1 teaspoon sugar

2¼ teaspoons salt

sauce and toppings

1 (28-ounce) can whole peeled tomatoes, drained

2 teaspoons sugar

¼ teaspoon salt

½ cup extra-virgin olive oil

3 garlic cloves, minced

1 tablespoon tomato paste

3 anchovy fillets, rinsed, patted dry, and minced

1 teaspoon dried oregano

¼ teaspoon red pepper flakes

2 ounces Parmesan cheese, grated fine (1 cup)

12 ounces whole-milk mozzarella cheese, shredded (3 cups)

continued

1 **For the dough** Whisk all-purpose flour, semolina flour, and yeast together in bowl of stand mixer. Whisk water, oil, and sugar in 4-cup liquid measuring cup until sugar has dissolved. Using dough hook on low speed, slowly add water mixture to flour mixture and mix until cohesive dough starts to form and no dry flour remains, about 2 minutes, scraping down bowl as needed. Cover bowl tightly with plastic wrap and let dough rest for 10 minutes.

2 Add salt to dough and knead on medium-low speed until dough is smooth and elastic and clears sides of bowl, about 8 minutes. Transfer dough to lightly floured counter and knead by hand to form smooth, round ball, about 30 seconds. Place dough seam side down in lightly greased large bowl or container, cover tightly with plastic, and refrigerate for at least 24 hours or up to 2 days.

3 **For the sauce and toppings** Process tomatoes, sugar, and salt in food processor until smooth, about 30 seconds. Heat ¼ cup oil and garlic in medium saucepan over medium-low heat, stirring occasionally, until garlic is fragrant and just beginning to brown, about 2 minutes. Stir in tomato paste, anchovies, oregano, and pepper flakes and cook until fragrant, about 30 seconds. Add tomato mixture and cook, stirring occasionally, until sauce measures 2 cups, 25 to 30 minutes. Transfer to bowl and let cool completely before using.

4 One hour before baking, adjust oven rack to middle position, set baking stone on rack, and heat oven to 500 degrees. Spray rimmed baking sheet (including rim) with vegetable oil spray, then coat bottom of sheet with remaining oil.

5 Press down on dough to deflate. Transfer dough to lightly floured counter and dust with flour. Press and roll dough into 18 by 13-inch rectangle.

6 Loosely roll dough around rolling pin and gently unroll it onto prepared sheet, fitting dough into corners. Cover loosely with greased plastic, then place second rimmed baking sheet on top and let dough rise for 1 hour.

7 Remove top sheet and plastic. Using your fingertips, gently press dough into corners of sheet. Using back of spoon or ladle, spread sauce in even layer over surface of dough, leaving ½-inch border around edges. Sprinkle Parmesan evenly over sauce, followed by mozzarella.

8 Place pizza in oven and reduce oven temperature to 450 degrees. Bake until bottom crust is evenly browned and cheese is bubbly and partially browned, 20 to 25 minutes, rotating sheet halfway through baking. Let pizza cool in sheet on wire rack for 5 minutes, then transfer to cutting board with metal spatula. Cut into squares and serve.

spinach-ricotta calzones

serves 4
resting time 2 minutes
rising time 1½ to 2 hours
baking time 15 minutes
total time 2¾ to 3¼ hours, plus 10 minutes cooling time
key equipment rolling pin, pastry brush, rimmed baking sheet

why this recipe works What's not to love about calzones, with their cheesy filling encased in a crisp and chewy crust? Nothing, if this is always the reality. Unfortunately, bad calzones, with wet fillings and bready crusts, are found at most pizzerias. In our experience, the only calzone worth eating is one made at home. To develop our version, we started with the dough. Pizzerias use their pizza dough for the crust, but when we tried using the dough for our Thin-Crust Pizza (page 180), we got bloated, misshapen calzones with unacceptable air bubbles. Our Skillet Pizza (page 77) dough is less hydrated and was a much better choice; it was easy to shape around the filling, and it baked up chewy and crisp. For the flavorful filling, we used a base of spinach and creamy ricotta to which we added an egg yolk to thicken the mixture, a bit of oil for richness, and two more cheeses, easy-melting mozzarella and nutty-tasting Parmesan. We spread the filling onto the bottom halves of two rolled-out pizza dough rounds and then brushed egg wash over the edges before folding the top halves over and sealing the dough so they'd stay closed as they baked. Cutting vents in the tops allowed excess moisture in the filling to escape during baking so the crust didn't become soggy. After the calzones baked for just 15 minutes, we let them cool briefly on a wire rack to keep the bottoms crisp. Serve the calzones with your favorite marinara sauce.

dough

2 cups (11 ounces) plus 2 tablespoons bread flour

1⅛ teaspoons instant or rapid-rise yeast

¾ teaspoon salt

1 tablespoon extra-virgin olive oil

¾ cup (6 ounces) ice water

filling

10 ounces frozen chopped spinach, thawed and squeezed dry

8 ounces (1 cup) whole-milk ricotta cheese

4 ounces mozzarella cheese, shredded (1 cup)

1 ounce Parmesan cheese, grated (½ cup)

1 tablespoon extra-virgin olive oil

1 large egg yolk

2 garlic cloves, minced

1½ teaspoons minced fresh oregano

¼ teaspoon salt

⅛ teaspoon red pepper flakes

1 large egg, lightly beaten with 1 tablespoon water and pinch salt

continued

1 **For the dough** Pulse flour, yeast, and salt in food processor until combined, about 5 pulses. With processor running, add oil, then ice water, and process until rough ball forms, 30 to 40 seconds. Let dough rest for 2 minutes, then process for 30 seconds longer.

2 Transfer dough to lightly floured counter and knead by hand to form smooth, round ball, about 30 seconds. Place dough seam side down in lightly greased large bowl or container, cover tightly with plastic wrap, and let rise until doubled in size, 1½ to 2 hours. (Unrisen dough can be refrigerated for at least 8 hours or up to 16 hours; let sit at room temperature for 30 minutes before shaping in step 4.)

3 **For the filling** Adjust oven rack to lower-middle position and heat oven to 500 degrees. Cut two 9-inch square pieces of parchment paper. Combine spinach, ricotta, mozzarella, Parmesan, oil, egg yolk, garlic, oregano, salt, and pepper flakes in bowl.

4 Press down on dough to deflate. Transfer dough to lightly floured counter, divide in half, and cover loosely with greased plastic. Press and roll 1 piece of dough (keep remaining piece covered) into 9-inch round of even thickness. Transfer to parchment square and reshape as needed. Repeat with remaining piece of dough.

5 Spread half of spinach filling evenly over half of each dough round, leaving 1-inch border at edge.

6 Brush edges with egg mixture. Fold other half of dough over filling, leaving ½-inch border of bottom half uncovered.

7 Press edges of dough together, pressing out any air pockets in calzones. Starting at 1 end of calzone, place your index finger diagonally across edge and pull bottom layer of dough over tip of your finger and press to seal.

8 Using sharp knife or single-edge razor blade, cut 5 steam vents, about 1½ inches long, in top of calzones. Brush tops with remaining egg mixture. Transfer calzones (still on parchment) to rimmed baking sheet, trimming parchment as needed to fit. Bake until golden brown, about 15 minutes, rotating sheet halfway through baking. Transfer calzones to wire rack and discard parchment. Let cool for 10 minutes before serving.

variation **three-meat calzones**
Omit spinach, oregano, salt, and pepper flakes from filling. Toss 4 ounces sliced salami, 4 ounces sliced capicola, and 2 ounces sliced pepperoni, all quartered, together in bowl. Working in 3 batches, microwave meats between triple layers of paper towels on plate for 30 seconds to render some fat; use fresh paper towels for each batch. Let meats cool, then add to ricotta mixture.

middle eastern za'atar bread

serves 6 to 8
resting time 1 hour 10 minutes
rising time 24 hours
baking time 20 minutes
total time 26 hours
key equipment rimmed baking sheet

3½ cups (19¼ ounces) bread flour

2½ teaspoons instant or rapid-rise yeast

2½ teaspoons sugar

1⅓ cups (10⅔ ounces) ice water

½ cup plus 2 tablespoons (4⅓ ounces) extra-virgin olive oil

2 teaspoons salt

⅓ cup za'atar

coarse sea salt

why this recipe works Inspired by *mana'eesh*, a round Arabic flatbread covered with a thick coating of *za'atar* and olive oil, we set out to develop a recipe for a finger-licking-good snack bread, great for dipping in yogurt sauces or eating on its own. Za'atar, used frequently in Middle Eastern cuisine, is a blend of wild thyme, ground sumac (a tart, lemony red berry), and sesame seeds. To showcase this delicious blend, we started by kneading together a simple dough from all-purpose flour, salt, yeast, water, sugar, and olive oil, and stretching it across a baking sheet. The result was a spongy, cakey bread with a dense, cottony crumb—not what we were looking for. Swapping out the all-purpose flour for higher-protein bread flour helped us develop chew. And we let the dough rise overnight in the refrigerator, which made for uniformly sized air bubbles and created more flavor. Having achieved the ideal density, chew, and flavor, we turned to the texture on the bottom, which was blond, limp, and soft. Coating the bottom of the pan with a generous amount of olive oil essentially fried the bottom of the flatbread as it baked, and shifting the oven rack to the lower-middle position for baking created a crisp, golden base. You can find za'atar in the international foods section of your supermarket or at Middle Eastern markets. Different blends include varying salt amounts, so finish with sea salt to taste.

continued

middle eastern za'atar bread, continued

1 Pulse flour, yeast, and sugar in food processor until combined, about 5 pulses. With processor running, slowly add ice water and process until dough is just combined and no dry flour remains, about 10 seconds. Let dough rest for 10 minutes.

2 Add 2 tablespoons oil and salt to dough and process until dough forms satiny, sticky ball that clears sides of bowl, 30 to 60 seconds. Transfer dough to lightly floured counter and knead by hand to form smooth, round ball, about 30 seconds. Place dough seam side down in lightly greased large bowl or container, cover tightly with plastic wrap, and refrigerate for at least 24 hours or up to 3 days.

3 Remove dough from refrigerator and let sit at room temperature for 1 hour. Coat rimmed baking sheet with 2 tablespoons oil. Gently press down on dough to deflate any large gas pockets. Transfer dough to prepared sheet and, using your fingertips, press out to uniform thickness, taking care not to tear dough. (Dough may not fit snugly into corners.) Cover loosely with greased plastic and let dough rest for 1 hour.

4 Adjust oven rack to lower-middle position and heat oven to 375 degrees. Using your fingertips, gently press dough into corners of sheet and dimple entire surface.

5 Combine remaining oil and za'atar in bowl. Using back of spoon, spread oil mixture in even layer over entire surface of dough to edge.

6 Bake until bottom crust is evenly browned and edges are crisp, 20 to 25 minutes, rotating sheet halfway through baking. Let bread cool in sheet for 10 minutes, then transfer to cutting board with metal spatula. Sprinkle with sea salt, slice, and serve warm.

troubleshooting

problem The crust lacks chew.

solution Add the salt to the dough after resting.

Remember to hold back the salt from the dough until after *autolyse*—the 10-minute rest—is complete. Because salt inhibits the enzymatic action that occurs during autolyse, adding it just before kneading begins, rather than at the outset with the other ingredients, gives the gluten a better chance of forming a strong network, which produces a chewy texture in the baked crust.

pissaladière

serves 4 to 6
resting time 1 hour 10 minutes
rising time 24 hours
baking time 26 minutes
total time 27¼ hours
key equipment 12-inch nonstick skillet, baking stone, rolling pin, pizza peel, pastry brush

why this recipe works Pissaladière is the ultimate Provençal street food. This fragrant, pizza-like tart is prized for its contrast of salty black olives and anchovies against a backdrop of sweet caramelized onions and earthy thyme. Supporting this rustic flavor combination is a wheaty crust with a texture that is part chewy pizza and part crisp cracker. The tart is easy enough to prepare, but each ingredient must be handled carefully. We made the dough in a food processor and kneaded it just enough so that it had the structure to stand up to the heavy toppings. As with pizza, bread flour worked best because its higher protein content translated to a more substantial chew. To keep our crust thin and prevent it from bubbling, we poked (or docked) it all over with the tines of a fork. Using a combination of high and low heat to cook the onions left them perfectly browned and caramelized and prevented them from burning. We stirred in a bit of water when the onions were done caramelizing to keep them from clumping when we spread them on the crust. To protect the black olives and fresh thyme leaves from burning in the oven, we spread them over the dough first and then covered them with the onions. Finally, we chopped the anchovies to keep them from overpowering the other flavors, but die-hard fish lovers can add more whole fillets as a garnish.

dough
3 cups (16½ ounces) bread flour

2 teaspoons sugar

½ teaspoon instant or rapid-rise yeast

1⅓ cups (10⅔ ounces) ice water

1 tablespoon vegetable oil

1½ teaspoons salt

toppings
¼ cup extra-virgin olive oil

2 pounds onions, halved and sliced ¼ inch thick

1 teaspoon packed brown sugar

½ teaspoon salt

1 tablespoon water

½ cup pitted niçoise olives, chopped coarse

8 anchovy fillets, rinsed, patted dry, and chopped coarse, plus 12 fillets for garnish (optional)

2 teaspoons minced fresh thyme

1 teaspoon fennel seeds

½ teaspoon pepper

2 tablespoons minced fresh parsley

continued

1 **For the dough** Pulse flour, sugar, and yeast in food processor until combined, about 5 pulses. With processor running, slowly add ice water and process until dough is just combined and no dry flour remains, about 10 seconds. Let dough rest for 10 minutes.

2 Add oil and salt to dough and process until dough forms satiny, sticky ball that clears sides of bowl, 30 to 60 seconds. Transfer dough to lightly floured counter and knead by hand to form smooth, round ball, about 30 seconds. Place dough seam side down in lightly greased large bowl or container, cover tightly with plastic wrap, and refrigerate for at least 24 hours or up to 3 days.

3 **For the toppings** Heat 2 tablespoons oil in 12-inch nonstick skillet over medium heat until shimmering. Stir in onions, sugar, and salt. Cover and cook, stirring occasionally, until onions are softened and have released their juice, about 10 minutes. Remove lid and continue to cook, stirring often, until onions are golden brown, 10 to 15 minutes. Transfer onions to bowl, stir in water, and let cool completely before using.

4 One hour before baking, adjust oven rack 4 inches from broiler element, set baking stone on rack, and heat oven to 500 degrees. Press down on dough to deflate. Transfer dough to clean counter, divide in half, and cover loosely with greased plastic. Pat 1 piece of dough (keep remaining piece covered) into 4-inch round. Working around circumference of dough, fold edges toward center until ball forms.

5 Flip ball seam side down and, using your cupped hands, drag in small circles on counter until dough feels taut and round and all seams are secured on underside. (If dough sticks to your hands, lightly dust top of dough with flour.) Repeat with remaining piece of dough. Space dough balls 3 inches apart, cover loosely with greased plastic, and let rest for 1 hour.

6 Heat broiler for 10 minutes. Meanwhile, generously coat 1 dough ball with flour and place on well-floured counter. Press and roll into 14 by 8-inch oval. Transfer oval to well-floured pizza peel and reshape as needed. (If dough resists stretching, let it relax for 10 to 20 minutes before trying to stretch it again.) Using fork, poke entire surface of oval 10 to 15 times.

7 Brush dough oval with 1 tablespoon oil, then sprinkle evenly with ¼ cup olives, half of chopped anchovies, 1 teaspoon thyme, ½ teaspoon fennel seeds, and ¼ teaspoon pepper, leaving ½-inch border around edge. Arrange half of onions on top, followed by 6 whole anchovies, if using.

8 Slide flatbread carefully onto baking stone and return oven to 500 degrees. Bake until bottom crust is evenly browned and edges are crisp, 13 to 15 minutes, rotating flatbread halfway through baking. Transfer flatbread to wire rack and let cool for 5 minutes. Sprinkle with 1 tablespoon parsley, slice, and serve. Heat broiler for 10 minutes. Repeat with remaining dough, oil, and toppings, returning oven to 500 degrees when flatbread is placed on stone.

red pepper coques

serves 6 to 8
resting time 1 hour 10 minutes
rising time 24 hours
baking time 21 minutes
total time 27 hours
key equipment 12-inch nonstick skillet, 2 rimmed baking sheets, rolling pin, pastry brush

why this recipe works *Coques* are the Catalan version of the thin and crunchy flatbreads that can be found in any tapas bar along the Mediterranean. Some are sweet, featuring a topping of candied fruits and pine nuts. But we set our sights on an intensely savory version topped with bold Spanish flavors. To get the perfect crust for our coques, we started with our thin-crust pizza dough since it produced a thin, flavorful crust that's appropriate for this dish. But to set our *coca* crust apart from pizza and get an extra-crisp base, we increased the amount of oil in the dough from 1 to 3 tablespoons and switched to fruity olive oil, as well as brushed each coca with oil before baking. These olive oil applications helped both the bottom and the top crisp up and imparted an earthy flavor to the dough. We found that parbaking the dough before topping it helped eliminate a soggy crust and created the sturdy base we were looking for—this crust shouldn't bend like a New York slice. For our well-balanced savory topping, we turned to sweet onions and rich roasted red peppers. And to introduce depth, balanced heat, and rounded acidity, we added garlic, a generous amount of red pepper flakes, and sherry vinegar to the mix. We cooked the topping before spreading it over the parbaked dough to cut our baking time in half and intensify the flavors. Stirring in the vinegar at the end of cooking gave the topping the vibrant kick that we wanted for these savory coques. If you cannot fit two coques on a single baking sheet, bake them in 2 batches.

dough

3 cups (16½ ounces) bread flour

2 teaspoons sugar

½ teaspoon instant or rapid-rise yeast

1⅓ cups (10⅔ ounces) ice water

3 tablespoons extra-virgin olive oil

1½ teaspoons salt

topping

½ cup extra-virgin olive oil

2 large onions, halved and sliced thin

2 cups jarred roasted red peppers, patted dry, and sliced thin

3 tablespoons sugar

3 garlic cloves, minced

1½ teaspoons salt

¼ teaspoon red pepper flakes

2 bay leaves

3 tablespoons sherry vinegar

¼ cup pine nuts (optional)

1 tablespoon minced fresh parsley

continued

1 **For the dough** Pulse flour, sugar, and yeast in food processor until combined, about 5 pulses. With processor running, slowly add ice water and process until dough is just combined and no dry flour remains, about 10 seconds. Let dough rest for 10 minutes.

2 Add oil and salt to dough and process until dough forms satiny, sticky ball that clears sides of bowl, 30 to 60 seconds. Transfer dough to lightly floured counter and knead by hand to form smooth, round ball, about 30 seconds. Place dough seam side down in lightly greased large bowl or container, cover tightly with plastic wrap, and refrigerate for at least 24 hours or up to 3 days.

3 **For the topping** Heat 3 tablespoons oil in 12-inch nonstick skillet over medium heat until shimmering. Stir in onions, red peppers, sugar, garlic, salt, pepper flakes, and bay leaves. Cover and cook, stirring occasionally, until onions are softened and have released their juice, about 10 minutes. Remove lid and continue to cook, stirring often, until onions are golden brown, 10 to 15 minutes. Off heat, discard bay leaves. Transfer onion mixture to bowl, stir in vinegar, and let cool completely before using.

4 Press down on dough to deflate. Transfer dough to clean counter, divide into quarters, and cover loosely with greased plastic. Working with 1 piece of dough at a time (keep remaining pieces covered), form into rough ball by stretching dough around your thumbs and pinching edges together so that top is smooth.

5 Place ball seam side down on counter and, using your cupped hand, drag in small circles until dough feels taut and round. Space dough balls 3 inches apart, cover loosely with greased plastic, and let rest for 1 hour.

6 Adjust oven racks to upper-middle and lower-middle positions and heat oven to 500 degrees. Coat 2 rimmed baking sheets with 2 tablespoons oil each. Generously coat 1 dough ball with flour and place on well-floured counter. Press and roll into 14 by 5-inch oval. Arrange oval on prepared sheet, with long edge fit snugly against 1 long side of sheet, and reshape as needed. (If dough resists stretching, let it relax for 10 to 20 minutes before trying to stretch it again.) Repeat with remaining dough balls, arranging 2 ovals on each sheet, spaced ½ inch apart. Using fork, poke surface of dough 10 to 15 times.

7 Brush dough ovals with remaining oil and bake until puffed, 6 to 8 minutes, switching and rotating sheets halfway through baking.

8 Scatter onion mixture evenly over flatbreads, from edge to edge, then sprinkle with pine nuts, if using. Bake until topping is heated through and edges of flatbreads are deep golden brown and crisp, about 15 minutes, switching and rotating sheets halfway through baking. Let flatbreads cool on sheets for 10 minutes, then transfer to cutting board using metal spatula. Sprinkle with parsley, slice, and serve.

lahmacun

makes four 9-inch flatbreads
resting time 1 hour 10 minutes
rising time 24 hours
cooking time 14 minutes
total time 26½ hours, plus 5 minutes cooling time
key equipment food processor, 2 rimmed baking sheets, rolling pin

why this recipe works *Lahmacun* is a meat pie found in Armenian and Turkish cuisines and is unlike any other flatbread we've tasted. The base is very thin and delightfully doughy—it flops over when picked up—with a crisp, spottily charred edge; the topping features ground lamb (and sometimes beef), warm spices, hot pepper paste, and aromatics. Lahmacun is typically served alongside a yogurt soda that's popular across the Middle East and that's called *tan* in Armenia and *ayran* in Turkey, but we love it served with a dollop of Greek yogurt, pickled vegetables, and fresh herbs. You can cut the flatbreads into wedges and serve them as an appetizer or use them as the wrap for a grilled vegetable roll-up. Lahmacun is traditionally cooked on a *saj*, a metal domed cooking surface, which achieves the perfect harmony of a doughy middle and crisp edges, all while simultaneously cooking the meat topping. To replicate this, we started by cooking ours in a cast-iron skillet over low heat. The bottom of the dough cooked perfectly, but the meat topping remained raw and steamed the dough directly beneath it. Next we tried putting the flatbreads on a hot baking stone in a 500-degree oven. The resulting pies were crisp and crunchy from edge to center, rather than supple and malleable, so we ditched the stone, dropped the oven temperature to 350 degrees, and placed the flatbreads on baking sheets. Baked this way, the flatbreads remained soft while the lamb cooked 90 percent of the way through. To crisp the edges and finish cooking the topping, we ran the flatbreads under the broiler. You can find Turkish hot pepper paste in the international foods section of your supermarket or at Middle Eastern markets. If you cannot fit two flatbreads on a single baking sheet, bake and broil the flatbreads in batches.

dough
1¾ cups (9⅔ ounces) bread flour
1 teaspoon sugar
¾ teaspoon instant or rapid-rise yeast
¾ cup (6 ounces) ice water
2 tablespoons extra-virgin olive oil
1 teaspoon salt

topping
3 tablespoons Turkish hot pepper paste
1 tablespoon tomato paste
1 garlic clove, minced
¾ teaspoon smoked hot paprika
¾ teaspoon ground allspice
½ teaspoon salt
1 cup coarsely chopped red bell pepper
⅔ cup coarsely chopped onion
4 ounces ground lamb
¼ cup chopped fresh parsley

continued

1 **For the dough** Pulse flour, sugar, and yeast in food processor until combined, about 5 pulses. With processor running, slowly add ice water and process until dough is just combined and no dry flour remains, about 10 seconds. Let dough rest for 10 minutes.

2 Add oil and salt to dough and process until dough forms satiny, sticky ball that clears sides of bowl, 30 to 60 seconds. Transfer dough to lightly floured counter and knead by hand to form smooth, round ball, about 30 seconds. Place dough seam side down in lightly greased large bowl or container, cover tightly with plastic wrap, and refrigerate for at least 24 hours or up to 3 days.

3 Press down on dough to deflate. Transfer dough to lightly floured counter, divide into quarters, and cover loosely with greased plastic. Working with 1 piece of dough at a time (keep remaining pieces covered), form into rough ball by stretching dough around your thumbs and pinching edges together so that top is smooth. Space balls 3 inches apart, cover loosely with greased plastic, and let rest for 1 hour.

4 **For the topping** Process pepper paste, tomato paste, garlic, paprika, allspice, and salt in clean, dry workbowl until well combined, about 20 seconds, scraping down bowl as needed. Add bell pepper and onion and pulse until finely ground, about 10 pulses. Add lamb and parsley and pulse until well combined, about 8 pulses.

5 Adjust oven racks to upper-middle and lower-middle positions and heat oven to 350 degrees. Grease 2 rimmed baking sheets. Generously coat 1 dough ball with flour and place on well-floured counter. Press and roll into 9-inch round. Arrange round on prepared sheet, with edges fit snugly into 1 corner of sheet, and reshape as needed. (If dough resists stretching, let it relax for 10 to 20 minutes before trying to stretch it again.) Repeat with remaining dough balls, arranging 2 rounds on each sheet in opposite corners.

6 Using back of spoon, spread one-quarter of topping in thin layer over surface of each dough round, leaving ¼-inch border around edge.

7 Bake until edges of flatbreads are set but still pale, 10 to 12 minutes, switching and rotating sheets halfway through baking. Remove flatbreads from oven and heat broiler.

8 Return 1 sheet to upper rack and broil until edges of flatbreads are crisp and spotty brown and filling is set, 2 to 4 minutes. Transfer flatbreads to wire rack with metal spatula and let cool for 5 minutes before serving. Repeat broiling with remaining flatbreads.

troubleshooting

problem Turkish hot pepper paste isn't available.

solution Use common ingredients to make your own paste.

Turkish hot pepper paste is worth seeking out; it has an acidic heat that makes recipes distinctly Middle Eastern. But if you can't find the real thing, you can approximate a version for the flavorful lamb topping for lahmacun by using ingredients that are probably already in your pantry. This simply involves upping the amounts of some of the ingredients in the recipe: Increase the tomato paste to 3 tablespoons, the smoked hot paprika to 1 teaspoon, and the salt to ¾ teaspoon in the topping.

pitas

makes eight 8-inch pitas
resting time 20 minutes
rising time 1 to 1½ hours
baking time 8 minutes
total time 2¼ to 2¾ hours, plus 10 minutes cooling time
key equipment rolling pin, baking stone, pizza peel

3⅔ cups (20⅛ ounces) bread flour

2½ teaspoons instant or rapid-rise yeast

2 teaspoons salt

1⅓ cups (10⅔ ounces) water, room temperature

¼ cup (1¾ ounces) extra-virgin olive oil

2½ teaspoons sugar

why this recipe works Pita breads vary dramatically depending on the region of the world where they're made. The thin, wheaty versions, often called Arabic bread, hail from all over the Middle East. We're partial to Greek-style pita, with a pillowy interior ideal for sopping up sauces and dips, and a structure strong enough to support succulent gyro ingredients. But the pita bread that's sold in the supermarket—no matter the style—is dry and tough, its stiff pockets unable to support sandwich fillings without splitting at the seams. Pitas don't need to come in bags; we aimed to make a Greek-style pita at home. To create a light crumb with substantial chew we turned to bread flour. Even though our pita was light, it was also tough. Increasing the amount of olive oil in the dough from 1 tablespoon to a generous ¼ cup tenderized the crumb nicely. While traditional Greek pita doesn't always have a pocket meant for stuffing (it's often held like a taco and wrapped around sandwich fixings), we felt that our pita was lacking without it. The tricks to getting the dough to puff up during baking and create this open pocket were a well-hydrated dough and a hot oven: We preheated a baking stone in a 500-degree oven; as soon as the dough hit the hot stone, the top and bottom exteriors began to set. Meanwhile, all that water in the dough turned to a cloud of steam inside, creating pressure outward. The exterior maintained its shape without stretching, while the steam inflated the dough into a balloon, creating the perfect pocket. Our favorite baking stone measures 16½ by 14½ inches. If you have a smaller baking stone, you may need to bake the pitas individually. Pitas can be stored in a zipper-lock bag at room temperature for up to 5 days.

continued

1 Whisk flour, yeast, and salt together in bowl of stand mixer. Whisk water, oil, and sugar in 4-cup liquid measuring cup until sugar has dissolved.

2 Using dough hook on low speed, slowly add water mixture to flour mixture and mix until cohesive dough starts to form and no dry flour remains, about 2 minutes, scraping down bowl as needed. Increase speed to medium-low and knead until dough is smooth and elastic and clears sides of bowl, about 8 minutes.

3 Transfer dough to lightly floured counter and knead by hand to form smooth, round ball, about 30 seconds. Place dough seam side down in lightly greased large bowl or container, cover tightly with plastic wrap, and let rise until doubled in size, 1 to 1½ hours.

4 Press down on dough to deflate. Transfer dough to lightly floured counter and divide into quarters, then cut each quarter into halves (about 4 ounces each); cover loosely with greased plastic.

5 Working with 1 piece of dough at a time (keep remaining pieces covered), form into rough ball by stretching dough around your thumbs and pinching edges together so that top is smooth.

6 Generously coat 1 dough ball with flour and place on well-floured counter. Press and roll into 8-inch round of even thickness and cover loosely with greased plastic. (If dough resists stretching, let it relax for 10 to 20 minutes before trying to stretch it again.) Repeat with remaining balls. Let dough rounds rest for 20 minutes.

7 One hour before baking, adjust oven rack to lower-middle position, place baking stone on rack, and heat oven to 500 degrees. Gently transfer 2 dough rounds to well-floured pizza peel. Slide rounds onto stone and bake until single air pocket is just beginning to form, about 1 minute.

8 Working quickly, flip pitas using metal spatula and continue to bake until light golden brown, 1 to 2 minutes. Transfer pitas to plate and cover with dish towel. Repeat with remaining dough rounds in 3 batches, allowing oven to reheat for 5 minutes after each batch. Let pitas cool for 10 minutes before serving.

variation **whole-wheat pitas**
Reduce bread flour to 1¾ cups (9⅔ ounces) and combine with 1¾ cups (9⅔ ounces) whole-wheat flour in step 1.

troubleshooting

problem The pitas don't puff.

solution Roll the dough thin.

Pita bread puffs when it comes in contact with a scorching-hot baking stone. The stone immediately turns all the water in the dough to steam. However, if the dough isn't thin enough, that heat won't reach the dough from bottom to top quickly enough to initiate a dramatic puff.

problem The pitas are crunchy.

solution Flip the pitas quickly.

These thin dough rounds cook quickly on the 500-degree stone. Waiting a few seconds too long to flip the pitas on their second side means they'll overbrown and become crisp upon cooling. Be sure to flip the pitas as soon as you see a single air pocket form.

the sweeter side
enriched breads and other treats

ultimate cinnamon buns

makes 8 buns
rising time 3 to 3½ hours
baking time 35 minutes
total time 5 to 5½ hours
key equipment stand mixer, 13 by 9-inch baking pan,
rolling pin

why this recipe works Sweet, gooey, softball-size cinnamon buns are worth every calorie. We set our sights on a mammoth breed of cinnamon bun, distinguished from its leaner, more diminutive cousins by its size, yes, but also by the richness of the soft, buttery yeasted dough, the abundance of the filling, and the thickness of the tangy cream cheese glaze. We wanted a soft, tender, brioche-like dough for the base of our buns. We began our testing using all-purpose flour but wondered whether swapping in cake flour might bring us closer to our ideal. Buns made with cake flour, however, just didn't have enough structure; they came out heavy and squat. A common substitute for cake flour is all-purpose flour cut with cornstarch, so we tried adding a small amount of cornstarch to the all-purpose flour—but not as much as we would use to approximate cake flour. This new blend, with a protein content somewhere between that of all-purpose flour and cake flour, gave us a soft dough that held its shape once baked. For a filling with deep caramel flavor, we combined a generous amount of cinnamon with brown sugar rather than flatter-tasting white sugar. Spreading softened butter over the dough before sprinkling it with the cinnamon sugar and rolling it up kept the sugar mixture from spilling out. Baked together, the butter and cinnamon sugar turned into a rich, gooey filling. Finally, no cinnamon bun could be called "ultimate" without a thick spread of icing. We topped the buns with a tangy glaze of cream cheese, confectioners' sugar, and milk. We do not recommend mixing this dough by hand.

dough
4¼ cups (21¼ ounces) all-purpose flour

½ cup (2 ounces) cornstarch

2¼ teaspoons instant or rapid-rise yeast

1½ teaspoons salt

¾ cup (6 ounces) whole milk, room temperature

3 large eggs, room temperature

½ cup (3½ ounces) granulated sugar

12 tablespoons (6 ounces) unsalted butter, softened

filling
1½ cups packed (10½ ounces) light brown sugar

1½ tablespoons ground cinnamon

¼ teaspoon salt

4 tablespoons (2 ounces) unsalted butter, softened

glaze
1½ cups (6 ounces) confectioners' sugar

4 ounces cream cheese, softened

1 tablespoon whole milk

1 teaspoon vanilla extract

continued

1 **For the dough** Whisk flour, cornstarch, yeast, and salt together in bowl of stand mixer. Whisk milk, eggs, and sugar in 4-cup liquid measuring cup until sugar has dissolved.

2 Using dough hook on low speed, slowly add milk mixture to flour mixture and mix until cohesive dough starts to form and no dry flour remains, about 2 minutes, scraping down bowl as needed. Increase speed to medium-low, add butter, 1 tablespoon at a time, and knead until butter is fully incorporated, about 6 minutes. Continue to knead until dough is smooth and elastic and clears sides of bowl, about 3 minutes.

3 Transfer dough to lightly floured counter and knead by hand to form smooth, round ball, about 30 seconds. Place dough seam side down in lightly greased large bowl or container, cover tightly with plastic wrap, and let rise until doubled in size, 2 to 2½ hours.

4 Make foil sling for 13 by 9-inch baking pan by folding 2 long sheets of aluminum foil; first sheet should be 13 inches wide and second sheet should be 9 inches wide. Lay sheets of foil in pan perpendicular to each other, with extra foil hanging over edges of pan. Push foil into corners and up sides of pan, smoothing foil flush to pan, then spray foil with vegetable oil spray.

5 **For the filling** Combine sugar, cinnamon, and salt in bowl. Press down on dough to deflate, then transfer to lightly floured counter. Press and roll dough into 18-inch square. Spread butter over dough, leaving ½-inch border around edges. Sprinkle with sugar mixture, leaving ¾-inch border at top edge, and press lightly to adhere.

6 Roll dough away from you into firm cylinder, keeping roll taut by tucking it under itself as you go. Pinch seam closed, then reshape cylinder as needed to be 18 inches in length with uniform thickness. Using serrated knife, cut cylinder into 8 pieces and arrange cut side down in prepared pan. Cover loosely with greased plastic and let rise until doubled in size, about 1 hour. (Unrisen buns can be refrigerated for at least 16 hours or up to 1 day; let buns sit at room temperature for 1 hour before baking.)

7 Adjust oven rack to middle position and heat oven to 350 degrees. Bake until buns are golden brown and filling is melted, 35 to 40 minutes, rotating dish halfway through baking.

8 **For the glaze** Whisk all ingredients in bowl until smooth. Top buns with ½ cup glaze and let cool in pan for 30 minutes. Using foil overhang, transfer buns to wire rack and top with remaining glaze. Serve warm.

troubleshooting

problem The buns don't bake evenly or they leak.

solution Make sure to roll the dough neatly.

Perhaps the most crucial part of this recipe is the assembly step. Make sure to roll the dough into a fairly neat 18-inch square that will then roll up into a neat cylinder. If the square is misshapen, the cylinder and buns will be misshapen, which means a greater likelihood of uneven cooking or leaking. Also, make sure the cylinder is of even thickness from end to end. If the cylinder tapers, the two buns cut from the ends will be smaller than the rest and will look a bit squat.

problem The glaze soaks into the buns.

solution Glaze the buns in two stages.

Topping the warm buns with some glaze when they come out of the oven allows the sweet cream cheese frosting to seep into and flavor the buns, adding tang. However, if you use all of it at once, the glaze will have mostly disappeared by the time the buns are cool enough to eat. We reserve a portion of the glaze and then retop the buns after they've cooled for the requisite 30 minutes. This ensures gooey buns with a thick layer of glaze.

morning buns

makes 12 buns
rising time 1 to 1½ hours
baking time 45 minutes
total time 3 to 3½ hours
key equipment rolling pin, rimmed baking sheet, 12-cup muffin tin

why this recipe works Unlike cinnamon buns, the filling of which is tucked within an enriched bread dough, morning buns typically start as croissants. A buttery, flaky croissant rolled up with cinnamon sugar? We couldn't think of a reason not to make them—except for the amount of work they required. For an easier path to a sweet breakfast, we thought of the technique used for "blitz," or quick, puff pastry; instead of laminating layers of butter between layers of dough, we cut up the butter, combine it with the flour, and incorporate it with a rolling pin. To adapt this for a flavorful, yeasted, croissant-like pastry, we simply added a packet of yeast, plus a little sugar, to the dough and let the buns rise before baking them. The technique made pastries with many layers, but it also made a mess. To contain the process, we sealed quarter-inch butter slices in a zipper-lock bag with the dry ingredients and then rolled everything right in the bag. Incorporating sour cream into the dough made it more supple and easy to roll, and provided richness without greasiness. A blend of brown and white sugar gave the filling a subtle molasses flavor; orange zest contributed a lovely floral aroma. And we liked the hint of citrus in the filling so much that we exchanged some of the water in the dough with orange juice. If the dough becomes too soft to work with at any point, refrigerate it until it's firm enough to easily handle.

dough

3 cups (15 ounces) all-purpose flour

1 tablespoon granulated sugar

2¼ teaspoons instant or rapid-rise yeast

¾ teaspoon salt

24 tablespoons (12 ounces) unsalted butter, cut into ¼-inch slices and chilled

1 cup (8 ounces) sour cream, chilled

¼ cup (2 ounces) orange juice, chilled

3 tablespoons ice water

1 large egg yolk

filling

½ cup (3½ ounces) granulated sugar

½ cup packed (3½ ounces) light brown sugar

1 tablespoon grated orange zest

2 teaspoons ground cinnamon

1 teaspoon vanilla extract

continued

1 ***For the dough*** Combine flour, sugar, yeast, and salt in 1-gallon zipper-lock bag. Add butter to bag, seal, and shake to coat. Press air out of bag and reseal. Roll over bag several times with rolling pin, shaking bag after each roll, until butter is pressed into large flakes.

2 Transfer mixture to large bowl and stir in sour cream, orange juice, ice water, and egg yolk with wooden spoon until combined. Transfer dough to lightly floured counter and knead by hand to form smooth, round ball, about 30 seconds.

3 Press and roll dough into 20 by 12-inch rectangle, with short side parallel to counter edge. Roll dough away from you into firm cylinder, keeping roll taut by tucking it under itself as you go.

4 With seam side down, flatten cylinder into 12 by 4-inch rectangle. Transfer to parchment paper–lined rimmed baking sheet, cover loosely with greased plastic wrap, and freeze for 15 minutes.

5 ***For the filling*** Line 12-cup muffin tin with paper or foil liners and spray with vegetable oil spray. Combine all ingredients in bowl. Transfer dough to lightly floured counter and roll into 20 by 12-inch rectangle, with long side parallel to counter edge. Sprinkle with sugar mixture, leaving ½-inch border around edges, and press lightly to adhere.

6 Roll dough away from you into firm cylinder, keeping roll taut by tucking it under itself as you go. Pinch seam closed, then reshape cylinder as needed to be 20 inches in length with uniform thickness.

7 Using serrated knife, trim ½ inch dough from each end and discard. Cut cylinder into 12 pieces and place cut side up in muffin cups. Cover loosely with greased plastic and let rise until doubled in size, 1 to 1½ hours. (Unrisen buns can be refrigerated for at least 16 hours or up to 24 hours; let buns sit at room temperature for 1 hour before baking.)

8 Adjust oven rack to middle position and heat oven to 425 degrees. Bake until buns begin to rise, about 5 minutes, then reduce oven temperature to 325 degrees. Continue to bake until buns are deep golden brown, 40 to 50 minutes, rotating muffin tin halfway through baking. Let buns cool in muffin tin for 5 minutes, then transfer to wire rack and discard liners. Serve warm.

troubleshooting

problem The dough lacks distinct layers.

solution Make sure your ingredients are fully chilled.

The key to getting many-leaved buns using this "quick" pastry technique is to roll multiple layers of butter between multiple layers of flour. The butter melts in the oven and creates steam, forcing the layers apart. However, if the dough or the butter is too warm, the butter will simply coat the flour, creating a cohesive dough without the necessary striations. Be sure to fully chill the butter as well as the sour cream and orange juice so that the dough stays cool.

mallorcas

makes 12 buns
rising time 4 to 5 hours
baking time 24 minutes
total time 6 to 7 hours
key equipment stand mixer, 2 rimmed baking sheets, rolling pin, pastry brush

5 cups (25 ounces) all-purpose flour

4 teaspoons instant or rapid-rise yeast

1 teaspoon salt

1 cup (8 ounces) whole milk, room temperature

4 large eggs, room temperature

10 tablespoons (4⅓ ounces) granulated sugar

10 tablespoons (5 ounces) unsalted butter, softened, plus 6 tablespoons (3 ounces) melted

confectioners' sugar

why this recipe works In Puerto Rico, these cloud-like, sweet, nautilus-shaped buns can be found in nearly every bakery. The bun made its way to Puerto Rico from the Spanish Balearic island of Mallorca, thus the name. Eggy mallorca dough is packed with layer upon layer of fat, so the buns are pillowy and delicate, flaky and light. Freshly baked and generously dusted with confectioners' sugar, they make for a heavenly treat alongside coffee. Day-old mallorcas come into their own when split, stuffed with ham and cheese, griddled, and sprinkled once again with confectioners' sugar. To start our development of these feathery buns, we tested both butter and lard. The two fats gave us similar results in terms of texture, so we chose butter because we preferred its flavor. We experimented with various folding techniques to laminate (or create layers of butter within) our dough—the key to achieving a fluffy, feathery texture. We adopted a stream-lined two-step process: First, we stretched the mass of dough thin, brushed it with melted butter, and rolled it like a jelly roll to form layers. Then, after cutting the roll and shaping individual ropes, we brushed the dough with more butter before coiling each rope into a spiral-shaped roll. These two simple brushing and shaping steps created the glorious layers we were after. We do not recommend mixing this dough by hand. If the dough becomes too soft to work with at any point, refrigerate it until it's firm enough to easily handle.

continued

mallorcas, continued

1 Whisk flour, yeast, and salt together in bowl of stand mixer. Whisk milk, eggs, and granulated sugar in 4-cup liquid measuring cup until sugar has dissolved. Using dough hook on low speed, slowly add milk mixture to flour mixture and mix until cohesive dough starts to form and no dry flour remains, about 2 minutes, scraping down bowl as needed.

2 Increase speed to medium-low and knead until dough begins to pull away from sides of bowl but sticks to bottom, about 5 minutes. With mixer running, add softened butter, 1 tablespoon at a time, and knead until butter is fully incorporated, about 5 minutes. Continue to knead until dough is smooth and elastic and clears sides of bowl but sticks to bottom, about 3 minutes.

3 Transfer dough to lightly floured counter and knead by hand to form smooth, round ball, about 30 seconds. Place dough seam side down in lightly greased large bowl or container, cover tightly with plastic wrap, and let rise until doubled in size, 2 to 2½ hours.

4 Line 2 rimmed baking sheets with parchment paper. Press down on dough to deflate. Transfer dough to lightly floured counter, divide in half, and cover loosely with greased plastic. Press and roll 1 piece of dough (keep remaining piece covered) into 18 by 12-inch rectangle, with long side parallel to counter edge.

5 Brush 2 tablespoons melted butter over dough, leaving 1-inch border at top edge. Roll dough away from you into firm cylinder, keeping roll taut by tucking it under itself as you go. Pinch seam closed, then reshape cylinder as needed to be 18 inches in length with uniform thickness. Cover loosely with greased plastic. Repeat with remaining piece of dough and 2 tablespoons melted butter.

6 Using serrated knife, cut each cylinder into 6 pieces and cover loosely with greased plastic. Working with 1 piece of dough at a time (keep remaining pieces covered), stretch and roll into 10-inch rope. Lightly brush rope with melted butter, coil into spiral, and tuck tail end underneath.

7 Arrange rolls on prepared sheets, spaced about 2 inches apart. Using finger, gently poke indentation into center of each spiral. Cover loosely with greased plastic and let rise until nearly doubled in size and dough springs back minimally when poked gently with your knuckle, 2 to 2½ hours.

8 Adjust oven rack to middle position and heat oven to 350 degrees. Bake 1 sheet at a time until rolls are light golden brown, 12 to 15 minutes, rotating sheet halfway through baking. Transfer rolls to wire rack and let cool for 15 minutes. Dust with confectioners' sugar and serve warm.

troubleshooting

problem The buns unravel.

solution Make an indentation in the center of each spiral.

When you're shaping these buns, it's important to finish by poking in the center tail of the spiral before proofing. If the spiral is not reinforced at this point, the center can pop out when this feathery, layered dough expands, creating misshapen mallorcas. This can happen during proofing, as the shaped buns rise, or during baking, when the buns experience oven spring and expand one last time.

st. lucia buns

makes 16 buns
rising time 2 to 3 hours
baking time 15 minutes
total time 3½ to 4½ hours, plus 1 hour cooling time
key equipment 2 rimmed baking sheets, rolling pin, pastry brush

why this recipe works *Lussebullar,* also known as St. Lucia buns, are a staple of St. Lucia Day, which ushers in the holiday season in Sweden. While this Swedish delicacy typically gets its rich yellow color from saffron, a spice revered in times past by royalty, many modern commercial bakeries now rely on artificial food dye. We wanted to re-create the classic saffron-flavored dough, with no funny ingredients. We found through testing that we needed just a small amount of saffron—¼ teaspoon—to give these sweet treats balanced flavor, but this left the color a little lacking. We knew we didn't want to tint our buns with food coloring, so we turned to another yellow spice, turmeric, whose flavor went undetected. Steeping the saffron, along with the turmeric, in boiling water for 15 minutes helped release the full potential of its water-soluble flavor compounds. One-third cup each of sugar and currants (the customary mix-in) gave these buns just enough sweetness. While the dough can be shaped into a variety of traditional forms, we stuck with the most popular "S," or "cat's tail," shape. Brushing the buns with egg wash and giving each an optional sprinkling of pearled sugar created a glossy and festive finish. For an accurate measurement of boiling water, bring a full kettle of water to a boil and then measure out the desired amount. If the dough becomes too soft to work with at any point, refrigerate it until it's firm enough to easily handle.

¼ cup (2 ounces) boiling water

¼ teaspoon saffron threads, crumbled

⅛ teaspoon ground turmeric

3½ cups (17½ ounces) all-purpose flour

2 teaspoons instant or rapid-rise yeast

1 teaspoon salt

¾ cup (6 ounces) whole milk, room temperature

6 tablespoons (3 ounces) unsalted butter, melted

⅓ cup (2⅓ ounces) granulated sugar

1 large egg, room temperature

⅓ cup currants

1 large egg, lightly beaten with 1 tablespoon water and pinch salt

¼ cup pearled sugar (optional)

continued

1 Combine boiling water, saffron, and turmeric in small bowl and let steep for 15 minutes.

2 Whisk flour, yeast, and salt together in bowl of stand mixer. Whisk milk, melted butter, granulated sugar, egg, and saffron mixture in 4-cup liquid measuring cup until sugar has dissolved. Using dough hook on low speed, slowly add milk mixture to flour mixture and mix until cohesive dough starts to form and no dry flour remains, about 2 minutes, scraping down bowl as needed.

3 Increase speed to medium-low and knead until dough is smooth and elastic and clears sides of bowl but sticks to bottom, about 8 minutes. Reduce speed to low, slowly add currants, and mix until incorporated, about 2 minutes.

4 Transfer dough to lightly floured counter and knead by hand to form smooth, round ball, about 30 seconds. Place dough seam side down in lightly greased large bowl or container, cover tightly with plastic wrap, and let rise until increased in size by about half, 1½ to 2 hours.

5 Line 2 rimmed baking sheets with parchment paper. Press down on dough to deflate, then transfer to clean counter. Press and roll dough into 16 by 6-inch rectangle, with long side parallel to counter edge. Using pizza cutter or chef's knife, cut rectangle vertically into 16 (6 by 1-inch) strips and cover loosely with greased plastic.

6 Working with 1 dough strip at a time (keep remaining pieces covered), stretch and roll into 16-inch rope. (If dough resists stretching, let it relax for 5 to 10 minutes before trying to stretch it again.)

7 Coil ends of rope in opposite directions to form tight S shape. Arrange buns on prepared sheets, spaced about 2½ inches apart. Cover loosely with greased plastic and let rise until puffy, 30 minutes to 1 hour.

8 Adjust oven racks to upper-middle and lower-middle positions and heat oven to 350 degrees. Gently brush buns with egg mixture and sprinkle with pearled sugar, if using. Bake until golden brown, 15 to 20 minutes, switching and rotating sheets halfway through baking. Transfer rolls to wire rack and let cool completely, about 1 hour, before serving.

troubleshooting

problem The buns taste flat.

solution Steep the saffron for a full 15 minutes.

This recipe calls for just a modest amount of pricey saffron threads: ¼ teaspoon. When saffron is steeped in hot water, the water takes on a deep yellow hue very quickly. But to fully coax out the saffron flavor don't rush this step. You need to steep the saffron, with the turmeric, for the full 15 minutes called for in the recipe. This will bring out a round saffron flavor in the buns that is just right.

kolaches

makes 16 kolaches
rising time 3 to 4 hours
baking time 25 minutes
total time 4½ to 5½ hours, plus 20 minutes cooling time
key equipment stand mixer, 2 rimmed baking sheets, pastry brush

why this recipe works Brought to Texas by Czech immigrants, these palm-size sweet (and sometimes savory) pastries are a sibling to the Danish and are heaped with either a cheese or a fruit filling. The amount of pride Texans from all over the state have for these treats rivals that of New Yorkers for their bagels, and multiple towns claim the title "kolache capital" and hold kolache festivals. The dough for these much-beloved buns is enriched with eggs and butter (or sometimes shortening), very much like a brioche dough. We cobbled together a working recipe after tasting and trying multiple regional versions, but the base was a little tough and dry, so we upped the fat—by a lot. In addition to the egg, we added two egg yolks. And we nearly doubled the flavorful butter. The fat tenderized the dough and added moisture and richness. Many recipes call for mixing the dough gently, theoretically to keep the buns tender, but we found that lengthy kneading yielded a more supple dough that held air well, giving our kolaches a lighter crumb. For a cheese filling, we found a combination of tangy cream cheese and milkier, slightly salty ricotta was a perfect base, while a little sugar and lemon zest balanced the flavor; 1 tablespoon of flour bound this mix nicely. The finishing touch to these sweet treats is a simple streusel topping that we made by quickly rubbing together flour, sugar, and butter with our fingers. A greased and floured measuring cup makes even indentations for the filling in the formed pastries.

dough
3½ cups (17½ ounces) all-purpose flour

2¼ teaspoons instant or rapid-rise yeast

1½ teaspoons salt

1 cup (8 ounces) whole milk, room temperature

10 tablespoons unsalted butter, melted

⅓ cup (2⅓ ounces) sugar

1 large egg plus 2 large yolks, room temperature

filling
6 ounces cream cheese, softened

3 tablespoons sugar

1 tablespoon all-purpose flour

½ teaspoon grated lemon zest

6 ounces (¾ cup) whole-milk or part-skim ricotta cheese

streusel
2 tablespoons plus 2 teaspoons all-purpose flour

2 tablespoons plus 2 teaspoons sugar

1 tablespoon unsalted butter, cut into 8 pieces and chilled

1 large egg, lightly beaten with 1 tablespoon water and pinch salt

continued

1 **For the dough** Whisk flour, yeast, and salt together in bowl of stand mixer. Whisk milk, melted butter, sugar, and egg and yolks in 4-cup liquid measuring cup until sugar has dissolved. Using dough hook on low speed, slowly add milk mixture to flour mixture and mix until cohesive dough starts to form and no dry flour remains, about 2 minutes, scraping down bowl as needed. Increase speed to medium-low and knead until dough is smooth and elastic and clears sides of bowl but sticks to bottom, about 10 minutes.

2 Transfer dough to lightly floured counter and knead by hand to form smooth, round ball, about 30 seconds. Place dough seam side down in lightly greased large bowl or container, cover tightly with plastic wrap, and let rise until increased in size by about half, 1½ to 2 hours. (Unrisen dough can be refrigerated for at least 8 hours or up to 16 hours; let sit at room temperature for 1 hour before shaping.)

3 **For the filling** Using clean, dry mixer bowl and paddle, mix cream cheese, sugar, flour, and lemon zest on low speed until smooth, about 1 minute. Add ricotta and mix until just combined, about 30 seconds. Transfer mixture to bowl, cover, and refrigerate until ready to use.

4 **For the streusel** Combine flour, sugar, and butter in bowl and rub between your fingers until mixture resembles wet sand. Cover and refrigerate until ready to use.

5 Line 2 rimmed baking sheets with parchment paper. Press down on dough to deflate. Transfer dough to clean counter and stretch into even 16-inch log. Cut log into 16 equal pieces (about 2¼ ounces each) and cover loosely with greased plastic. Working with 1 piece of dough at a time (keep remaining pieces covered), form into rough ball by stretching dough around your thumbs and pinching edges together so that top is smooth. Place ball seam side down on clean counter and, using your cupped hand, drag in small circles until dough feels taut and round.

6 Arrange dough balls seam side down on prepared sheets, spaced about 1½ inches apart. Cover loosely with greased plastic and let rise until increased in size by about half, 1½ to 2 hours.

7 Adjust oven racks to upper-middle and lower-middle positions and heat oven to 350 degrees. Grease and flour bottom of round ⅓-cup dry measuring cup (or 2¼-inch-diameter drinking glass). Press cup firmly into center of each dough round until cup touches sheet to make indentation for filling. (Reflour cup as needed to prevent sticking.)

8 Divide filling evenly among kolaches (about 1½ tablespoons each) and smooth with back of spoon. Gently brush edges with egg mixture and sprinkle with streusel. (Do not sprinkle streusel over filling.) Bake until golden brown, about 25 minutes, switching and rotating sheets halfway through baking. Transfer kolaches to wire rack and let cool for 20 minutes. Serve warm.

variation **fruit-filled kolaches**
Omit cream cheese filling. Combine 10 ounces frozen pineapple, blueberries, or cherries; 5 tablespoons sugar; and 4 teaspoons cornstarch in bowl. Microwave, covered, until bubbling and thickened, about 6 minutes, stirring once halfway through microwaving. Mash with potato masher. Let cool completely and fill kolaches as directed in step 8.

oatmeal raisin bread

makes 1 loaf
rising time 2 to 3 hours
baking time 45 minutes
total time 4 to 5 hours, plus 3 hours cooling time
key equipment small saucepan, 8½ by 4½-inch loaf pan, rimmed baking sheet, water-filled spray bottle, instant-read thermometer

why this recipe works This bread, flavored with oatmeal, sweet raisins, and just a touch of brown sugar, is like a bowl of oatmeal in bread form. It's great toasted up for breakfast or perfect with coffee for an afternoon snack. Mixing the oatmeal into the dough toward the end of kneading proved the perfect way to incorporate it without creating big clumps of oats. The loaf tasted good, but we thought it needed even more oat flavor, so we tried incorporating oat flour into the dough in addition to the meal. This didn't cut it; the loaf tasted no more oaty, and the crumb became dry and crumbly. We found instead that replacing ½ cup of the bread flour with whole-wheat flour complemented the earthy flavor of the oats and ensured that the crumb stayed light and moist. And to give the loaf a hint of what's within, we misted it with water and then rolled it in oats before transferring it to the pan. Misting the oat-rolled loaf in water once again before baking contributed to an appealingly crunchy, golden brown top. Do not substitute quick or instant oats in this recipe. The test kitchen's preferred loaf pan measures 8½ by 4½ inches; if you use a 9 by 5-inch loaf pan, increase the shaped rising time by 20 to 30 minutes and start checking for doneness 10 minutes earlier than advised in the recipe.

1¼ cups (3¾ ounces) old-fashioned rolled oats

¾ cup (6 ounces) water, room temperature

2 cups (11 ounces) bread flour

½ cup (2¾ ounces) whole-wheat flour

2 teaspoons instant or rapid-rise yeast

1½ teaspoons salt

1 cup (8 ounces) whole milk, room temperature

3 tablespoons unsalted butter, melted

2 tablespoons packed brown sugar

½ cup raisins

continued

1 Bring ¾ cup oats and water to simmer in small saucepan over medium heat and cook, stirring occasionally, until oats are softened and water is completely absorbed, about 2 minutes; set aside to cool.

2 Whisk bread flour, whole-wheat flour, yeast, and salt together in bowl of stand mixer. Whisk milk, melted butter, and sugar in 4-cup liquid measuring cup until sugar has dissolved. Using dough hook on low speed, slowly add milk mixture to flour mixture and mix until cohesive dough starts to form and no dry flour remains, about 2 minutes, scraping down bowl as needed.

3 Increase speed to medium-low and knead until dough is smooth and elastic and clears sides of bowl, about 6 minutes. Reduce speed to low, slowly add raisins, then slowly add oatmeal, 2 tablespoons at a time, and mix until mostly incorporated, about 3 minutes.

4 Transfer dough to lightly floured counter. Using your lightly floured hands, knead dough until oatmeal and raisins are evenly distributed and dough forms smooth, round ball, about 30 seconds. Place dough seam side down in lightly greased large bowl or container, cover tightly with plastic wrap, and let rise until doubled in size, 1½ to 2 hours.

5 Grease 8½ by 4½-inch loaf pan. Spread remaining ½ cup oats on rimmed baking sheet. Press down on dough to deflate. Turn dough out onto lightly floured counter (side of dough that was against bowl should now be facing up). Press and stretch dough into 8 by 6-inch rectangle, with long side parallel to counter edge.

6 Roll dough away from you into firm cylinder, keeping roll taut by tucking it under itself as you go. Pinch seam closed. Mist loaf with water on all sides and roll in oats, pressing gently to adhere. Place loaf seam side down in prepared pan, pressing dough gently into corners.

7 Cover loosely with greased plastic and let rise until loaf reaches 1 inch above lip of pan and dough springs back minimally when poked gently with your knuckle, 30 minutes to 1 hour.

8 Adjust oven rack to lower-middle position and heat oven to 350 degrees. Mist loaf with water and bake until golden brown and loaf registers 205 to 210 degrees, 45 to 50 minutes, rotating pan halfway through baking. Let loaf cool in pan for 15 minutes. Remove loaf from pan and let cool completely on wire rack, about 3 hours, before serving.

troubleshooting

problem The loaf is stodgy.

solution Use the right oats.

Do not substitute instant or quick oats for the required old-fashioned oats in this recipe. Instant oats make gluey, gummy oatmeal, and quick oats make pasty, flavorless oatmeal, so it's not surprising that bread made with them would turn out gummy or flavorless, respectively. Old-fashioned oats give the crumb a hearty, flavorful crumb that's not too dense.

problem The oat coating falls off.

solution Mist the loaf with water.

This recipe calls for misting the loaf with water before baking, but you also need to mist the dough before rolling it in the oats. Even though dough has some tack to it, the oats would pop off an otherwise dry loaf during proofing or baking. And don't mist just the top of the loaf; you'll get an uneven coating. Make sure to mist the loaf on all sides.

challah

makes 1 loaf
rising time 2½ to 3½ hours
baking time 20 minutes
total time 3¾ to 4¾ hours, plus 3 hours cooling time
key equipment 2 rimmed baking sheets, pastry brush, instant-read thermometer

why this recipe works Beautifully braided, rich, and lightly sweet, freshly baked challah is delicious on its own or smeared with softened butter. After a few days, it's great dunked in custard and made into French toast for a decadent breakfast. The best challah is rich with eggs, and it has a dark, shiny crust and a firm but light and tender texture. For our recipe, we tried using bread flour, but it made no significant improvement to loaves we made with the typical all-purpose, so we stuck with that. We tested many different egg combinations (challah is known as egg bread, after all); for a tender texture and a rich but not overwhelmingly eggy flavor, we found two whole eggs and an additional yolk to be optimal. We kept with tradition and made the bread dairy-free, using water and oil to hydrate and enrich the crumb instead of the milk and butter found in less authentic versions. (Happily, we found that the challah made with water had a lighter and more appealing texture.) Just ¼ cup of sugar sweetened the loaf and also contributed to its browned exterior. The recommended shape for challah in most recipes is a simple three-rope braid. Shaped this way, however, our eggy dough rose out instead of up. Some recipes call for braiding six strands for a higher loaf, but this can get complicated—unless you have skills in origami. Our solution was to make two three-strand braids, one large and one small, and place the smaller braid on top of the larger one. We brushed the loaf with an egg-water mixture before putting it in the oven to produce an evenly brown, shiny crust—the finishing touch to our handsome challah.

3¼ cups (16¼ ounces) all-purpose flour

2¼ teaspoons instant or rapid-rise yeast

1¼ teaspoons salt

½ cup (4 ounces) water, room temperature

¼ cup (1¾ ounces) vegetable oil

2 large eggs plus 1 large yolk, room temperature

¼ cup (1¾ ounces) sugar

1 large egg, lightly beaten with 1 tablespoon water and pinch salt

1 teaspoon poppy or sesame seeds (optional)

continued

challah, continued

1 Whisk flour, yeast, and salt together in bowl of stand mixer. Whisk water, oil, eggs and yolk, and sugar in 4-cup liquid measuring cup until sugar has dissolved.

2 Using dough hook on low speed, slowly add water mixture to flour mixture and mix until cohesive dough starts to form and no dry flour remains, about 2 minutes, scraping down bowl as needed. Increase speed to medium-low and knead until dough is smooth and elastic and begins to pull away from sides of bowl but sticks to bottom, about 10 minutes.

3 Transfer dough to lightly floured counter and knead by hand to form smooth, round ball, about 30 seconds. Place dough seam side down in lightly greased large bowl or container, cover tightly with plastic wrap, and let rise until increased in size by about half, 1½ to 2 hours.

4 Stack 2 rimmed baking sheets, line with aluminum foil, and spray with vegetable oil spray. Transfer dough to clean counter and divide into 2 pieces, one twice as large as the other (small piece will weigh about 9 ounces, larger piece about 18 ounces). Divide each piece into thirds and cover loosely with greased plastic.

5 Working with 1 piece of dough at a time (keep remaining pieces covered), stretch and roll into 16-inch rope (3 ropes will be much thicker).

6 Arrange 3 thicker ropes side by side, perpendicular to counter edge, and pinch far ends together. Braid ropes into 10-inch loaf and pinch remaining ends together. Repeat braiding remaining ropes into second 10-inch loaf.

7 Transfer larger loaf to prepared sheet, brush top with egg mixture, and place smaller loaf on top. Tuck ends underneath. Cover loosely with greased plastic and let rise until loaf increases in size by about half and dough springs back minimally when poked gently with your knuckle, 1 to 1½ hours.

8 Adjust oven rack to middle position and heat oven to 375 degrees. Brush loaf with remaining egg mixture and sprinkle with poppy seeds, if using. Bake until deep golden brown and loaf registers 190 to 195 degrees, 20 to 25 minutes, rotating sheet halfway through baking. Transfer loaf to wire rack and let cool completely, about 3 hours, before serving.

troubleshooting

problem The loaf's braids come undone.

solution Tuck the ends of the loaf under.

After shaping the loaf of challah, don't forget to tuck the ends under. If you fail to do so, the ends will open up as the loaf expands during proofing and baking, and the braid will begin to unravel. If the braids do come undone as the loaf proofs, pinch the ends back together and tuck them under before baking.

problem The loaf browns too quickly.

solution Tent the loaf with foil.

This loaf's exterior may turn deep golden brown before the interior cooks through. If the loaf seems to be browning too quickly, simply tent it with aluminum foil to shield the crust while the interior finishes baking.

the sweeter side   249

cinnamon swirl bread

makes 2 loaves
resting time 30 minutes
rising time 2¾ to 3¾ hours
baking time 40 minutes
total time 5¾ to 6¾ hours, plus 3 hours cooling time
key equipment stand mixer, rolling pin, water-filled spray bottle, two 8½ by 4½-inch loaf pans, pastry brush, instant-read thermometer

why this recipe works Cinnamon swirl bread always sounds appealing, but this American classic frequently disappoints. Loaves are usually on opposite ends of the cinnamon spectrum: Either they're flavorless, featuring a bare sprinkling of precious filling, or, just as bad, they're overly sweet and ruined by gobs of oozing filling. The bread itself is often an afterthought of pedestrian white bread, or else it's a cakey, dense affair. To make bread worthy of its swirl, we wanted a moderately rich dough, with a lot of structure to encourage a tall loaf and an airy crumb. To achieve these somewhat contradictory goals, we first kneaded our dough until it had fully developed gluten before slowly mixing in softened butter; that way the fat didn't compromise the structure. For a loftier rise, we added a series of folds into our recipe, which incorporated more air. Our balanced filling combined cinnamon, confectioners' sugar, and vanilla. The confectioners' sugar thickened up the filling, as did the starches in a hefty amount of cinnamon. To ensure that the filling stayed put and could be tasted with every bite, we traded the swirl shape for an elegant Russian braid. The test kitchen's preferred loaf pan measures 8½ by 4½ inches; if you use 9 by 5-inch loaf pans, increase the shaped rising time by 20 to 30 minutes and start checking for doneness 10 minutes earlier than advised in the recipe. We do not recommend mixing this dough by hand. If the dough becomes too soft to work with at any point, refrigerate it until it's firm enough to easily handle.

dough

8 tablespoons (4 ounces) unsalted butter, cut into 32 pieces

3¾ cups (20⅔ ounces) bread flour

¾ cup (2¼ ounces) nonfat dry milk powder

1 tablespoon instant or rapid-rise yeast

1½ cups (12 ounces) water, room temperature

⅓ cup (2⅓ ounces) granulated sugar

1 large egg, room temperature

1½ teaspoons salt

1½ cups (7½ ounces) golden raisins

filling

1 cup (4 ounces) confectioners' sugar

3 tablespoons ground cinnamon

1 teaspoon vanilla extract

½ teaspoon salt

1 large egg, lightly beaten with 1 tablespoon water and pinch salt

continued

1 For the dough Toss butter with 1 tablespoon flour in bowl and set aside to soften. Whisk remaining flour, milk powder, and yeast together in bowl of stand mixer. Whisk water, sugar, and egg in 4-cup liquid measuring cup until sugar has dissolved. Using dough hook on low speed, slowly add water mixture to flour mixture and mix until cohesive dough starts to form and no dry flour remains, about 2 minutes, scraping down bowl as needed. Cover bowl tightly with plastic wrap and let dough rest for 20 minutes.

2 Add salt to dough and knead on medium-low speed until dough is smooth and elastic and clears sides of bowl, about 8 minutes. With mixer running, add butter, a few pieces at a time, and knead until butter is fully incorporated, about 4 minutes. Continue to knead until dough is smooth and elastic and clears sides of bowl, 3 to 5 minutes. Reduce speed to low, slowly add raisins, and mix until incorporated, about 1 minute.

3 Transfer dough to lightly greased large bowl or container. Using greased bowl scraper (or your fingertips), fold dough over itself by gently lifting and folding edge of dough toward middle. Turn bowl 45 degrees and fold dough again; repeat turning bowl and folding dough 6 more times (total of 8 folds). Cover tightly with plastic and let dough rise for 45 minutes. Repeat folding, then cover bowl tightly with plastic and let dough rise until nearly doubled in size, 30 minutes to 1 hour.

4 Press down on dough to deflate. Transfer dough to lightly floured counter, divide in half, and cover loosely with greased plastic. Working with 1 piece of dough at a time (keep remaining piece covered), press and roll into 11 by 6-inch rectangle, with short side parallel to counter edge. Stretch and fold dough lengthwise into thirds to form 11 by 3-inch rectangle. Roll dough away from you into firm ball, keeping roll taut by tucking it under itself as you go. Cover balls loosely with greased plastic.

5 For the filling Whisk all together in bowl until well combined. Coat 1 dough ball lightly with flour and place on lightly floured counter. With seam side down, flatten ball with rolling pin into 18 by 7-inch rectangle, with short side parallel to counter edge. Mist surface of dough with water. Sprinkle half of sugar mixture over dough, leaving ¼-inch border on sides and ¾-inch border on top and bottom, and press lightly to adhere. Mist filling with water until entire surface is speckled.

6 Roll dough away from you into firm cylinder, keeping roll taut by tucking it under itself as you go. Pinch seam and ends closed. Dust cylinder lightly on all sides with flour, cover loosely with greased plastic, and let rest for 10 minutes. Repeat with remaining dough ball and filling.

7 Grease two 8½ by 4½-inch loaf pans. Using bench scraper, cut 1 cylinder in half lengthwise. Turn halves cut side up and gently stretch into 14-inch lengths. Arrange strips side by side, perpendicular to counter edge, and pinch far ends together. Take left strip of dough and lay over right strip of dough. Repeat, keeping cut sides up, until pieces of dough are tightly twisted. Pinch remaining ends together. Transfer loaf cut sides up to prepared pan. Press dough gently into corners of pan and push any exposed raisins into seams of braid. Repeat with second loaf. Cover loosely with greased plastic and let rise until loaves reach 1 inch above lip of pans and dough springs back minimally when poked gently with your knuckle, 1½ to 2 hours.

8 Adjust oven rack to middle position and heat oven to 350 degrees. Gently brush loaves with egg mixture and bake until crust is well browned, about 25 minutes, rotating pans halfway through baking. Reduce oven temperature to 325 degrees, tent loaves with aluminum foil, and continue to bake until loaves register 200 to 205 degrees, 15 to 25 minutes. Let loaves cool in pans for 5 minutes. Remove loaves from pans and let cool completely on wire rack, about 3 hours, before serving.

chocolate babka

makes 1 loaf
rising time 3 to 4 hours
resting time 1 hour
baking time 40 minutes
total time 5 to 6 hours, plus 3 hours cooling time
key equipment stand mixer, 8½ by 4½-inch loaf pan, rolling pin, pastry brush, instant-read thermometer

why this recipe works If you don't live within driving distance of New York City, it's hard to get your hands on really great babka. For that reason, we decided to devise a foolproof recipe to use in our own Boston kitchens. While cinnamon filling is also a common choice for babka, we wanted to make a decadent chocolate babka, with a deep, dark filling. By definition, babka is a rich, tender dough, akin to brioche. But go too far in that direction and the dough will collapse under the weight of the filling, leaving large holes in the bread. To add richness yet preserve the loaf's structural integrity, we cut back on the butter found in most traditional recipes and substituted two egg yolks for one whole egg. Chilling the dough after rising ensured that it was firm and pliable enough to fill and twist into its signature shape. For the filling, we used a combination of bittersweet chocolate and cocoa powder, which provided the full, rounded chocolate flavor and appealingly fudgy texture we were looking for. To make sure that the filling stayed put and didn't sink to the bottom of the loaf, we also mixed in confectioners' sugar and an egg white, which helped stiffen it up. The test kitchen's preferred loaf pan measures 8½ by 4½ inches; if you use a 9 by 5-inch loaf pan, increase the shaped rising time by 20 to 30 minutes and start checking for doneness 10 minutes earlier than advised in the recipe. We do not recommend mixing this dough by hand. If the dough becomes too soft to work with at any point, refrigerate it until it's firm enough to easily handle.

dough

2 cups (10 ounces) all-purpose flour

1½ teaspoons instant or rapid-rise yeast

½ teaspoon salt

½ cup (4 ounces) whole milk, room temperature

¼ cup (1¾ ounces) granulated sugar

2 large egg yolks, room temperature

1 teaspoon vanilla extract

8 tablespoons (4 ounces) unsalted butter, softened

filling

2 ounces bittersweet chocolate, chopped

4 tablespoons (2 ounces) unsalted butter

3 tablespoons unsweetened cocoa powder

¼ cup (1 ounce) confectioners' sugar

1 large egg white

1 large egg, lightly beaten with 1 tablespoon water and pinch salt

continued

chocolate babka, continued

1 **For the dough** Whisk flour, yeast, and salt together in bowl of stand mixer. Whisk milk, sugar, egg yolks, and vanilla in 4-cup liquid measuring cup until sugar has dissolved. Using dough hook on low speed, slowly add milk mixture to flour mixture and mix until cohesive dough starts to form and no dry flour remains, about 2 minutes, scraping down bowl as needed.

2 Increase speed to medium-low, add butter, 1 tablespoon at a time, and knead until butter is fully incorporated, about 4 minutes. Continue to knead until dough is smooth and elastic and clears sides of bowl, 10 to 12 minutes.

3 Transfer dough to lightly floured counter and knead by hand to form smooth, round ball, about 30 seconds. Place dough seam side down in lightly greased large bowl or container, cover tightly with plastic wrap, and let rise until increased in size by about half, 1½ to 2 hours. Place in refrigerator until dough is firm, at least 1 hour or up to 24 hours. (If dough is chilled longer than 1 hour, let rest at room temperature for 15 minutes before rolling out in step 5.)

4 **For the filling** Microwave chocolate, butter, and cocoa together in medium bowl at 50 percent power, stirring occasionally, until melted, about 30 seconds. Stir in sugar until combined and let cool completely. Whisk in egg white until fully combined and mixture turns glossy. Measure out and reserve 1 tablespoon filling.

5 Grease 8½ by 4½-inch loaf pan. Press down on dough to deflate, then transfer to lightly floured counter. Press and roll dough into 18 by 14-inch rectangle, with long side parallel to counter edge. Spread remaining filling over dough, leaving ½-inch border around edges.

6 Roll dough away from you into firm cylinder, keeping roll taut by tucking it under itself as you go. Pinch seam closed, then reshape cylinder as needed to be 18 inches in length with uniform thickness. Position cylinder seam side up and spread reserved filling over top. Fold cylinder on top of itself and pinch ends to seal.

7 Gently twist double cylinder twice to form double figure eight. Place loaf seam side down in prepared pan, pressing dough gently into corners. Cover loosely with greased plastic and let rise until loaf is level with lip of pan, 1½ to 2 hours.

8 Adjust oven rack to lower-middle position and heat oven to 350 degrees. Gently brush loaf with egg mixture and bake until deep golden brown and loaf registers 190 to 195 degrees, 40 to 45 minutes, rotating pan halfway through baking. Let loaf cool in pan for 15 minutes. Remove loaf from pan and let cool completely on wire rack, about 3 hours, before serving.

troubleshooting

problem The dough doesn't engage the dough hook in a large mixer.

solution Scrape down the mixer bowl.

Our babka recipe yields a smaller amount of dough than you'll find in many of the other breads in this book—which leaves all the more room for generous ribbons of rich chocolate. Because the yield of dough is modest, bakers with larger stand mixers (our favorite stand mixer is outfitted with a 7-quart bowl) may notice that the dough doesn't always engage with the dough hook. Without proper kneading, the loaf will lack structure. To ensure that the dough is actively kneaded in a large stand mixer, be sure to scrape the bowl down often so that the dough doesn't just stick to the bottom of the bowl for the entire mixing time.

portuguese sweet bread

makes 1 loaf
rising time 4½ to 5½ hours
baking time 30 minutes
total time 6 to 7 hours, plus 3 hours cooling time
key equipment stand mixer, 9-inch round cake pan, pastry brush, instant-read thermometer

4 cups (20 ounces) all-purpose flour

2¼ teaspoons instant or rapid-rise yeast

1 teaspoon salt

¾ cup (6 ounces) water, room temperature

3 large eggs plus 1 large yolk, room temperature

½ cup (3½ ounces) plus 1 tablespoon sugar

½ teaspoon vanilla extract

4 tablespoons (2 ounces) unsalted butter, softened

1 large egg, lightly beaten with 1 tablespoon water and pinch salt

why this recipe works Portuguese sweet bread is a mildly sweet enriched bread with a moderately compact yet delicate crumb and a thin, tender, mahogany-colored crust. It is eggy, yeasty, and buttery like brioche but less rich, and is delicious on its own, dunked into coffee, slathered with jam, or made into French toast. The bread is well known throughout coastal New England and Hawaii, where it is made in bakeries founded by Portuguese immigrant families. While it is baked for holidays (hard-cooked eggs are baked inside for Easter), it is also a daily bread. Portuguese sweet bread comes in many shapes. We liked a large round baked in a cake pan best; it was simple to shape and easy to cut into slices or wedges, and its mushroom top was beautiful to behold. We tested egg amounts and found that three whole eggs plus one yolk gave us a tender, moist crumb; fewer gave us an unappealingly dense texture, and more gave us too much egg flavor. We added just the right amount of sugar to make our bread pleasingly sweet but mild enough to enjoy regularly. A moderate amount of butter (rather than lard) gave us the slight richness we were after, and a touch of vanilla extract added subtle warm tones. In our testing, we had noticed that our loaf was tearing on the sides. This bread experiences a lot of oven spring (the rapid rising of bread after it's placed in a hot oven), so we let the loaf proof 1¾ inches above the lip of the pan to ensure that its oven rise wouldn't be so dramatic. Slashing the loaf around its circumference was another way to eliminate tears by helping the loaf expand before its crust set. We do not recommend mixing this dough by hand.

continued

1 Whisk flour, yeast, and salt together in bowl of stand mixer. Whisk water, eggs and yolk, sugar, and vanilla in 4-cup liquid measuring cup until sugar has dissolved. Using dough hook on low speed, slowly add water mixture to flour mixture and mix until cohesive dough starts to form and no dry flour remains, about 2 minutes, scraping down bowl as needed.

2 Increase speed to medium-low and knead until dough begins to pull away from sides of bowl but sticks to bottom, about 5 minutes. With mixer running, add butter, 1 tablespoon at a time, and knead until butter is fully incorporated, about 2 minutes. Continue to knead until dough is elastic and slightly sticky, about 3 minutes.

3 Transfer dough to lightly floured counter and knead by hand to form smooth, round ball, about 30 seconds. Place dough seam side down in lightly greased large bowl or container, cover tightly with plastic wrap, and let rise until doubled in size, 2 to 2½ hours.

4 Generously grease 9-inch round cake pan. Press down on dough to deflate. Turn dough out onto clean counter (side of dough that was against bowl should now be facing up) and press into 10-inch round. Working around circumference of dough, fold edges toward center until ball forms.

5 Flip dough ball seam side down and, using your cupped hands, drag in small circles on counter until dough feels taut and round and all seams are secured on underside of loaf. Place loaf seam side down in prepared pan. Cover loosely with greased plastic and let rise until loaf reaches 1¾ inches above lip of pan and dough springs back minimally when poked gently with your knuckle, 2½ to 3 hours.

6 Adjust oven rack to lower-middle position and heat oven to 350 degrees. Using sharp paring knife or single-edge razor blade, make one ¼-inch-deep slash with swift, fluid motion around circumference of loaf, level with lip of pan. Lightly brush loaf with egg mixture and bake until deep golden brown and loaf registers 190 to 195 degrees, 30 to 35 minutes, rotating pan halfway through baking. Let loaf cool in pan for 15 minutes. Remove loaf from pan and let cool completely on wire rack, about 3 hours, before serving.

troubleshooting

problem The loaf tears or is misshapen.

solution Let the dough rise to 1¾ inches above the lip of the pan and slash it.

It may seem finicky to have to check that a dough reaches such a specific height; however, it is crucial for this muffin-topped loaf. If you underproof the loaf (that is, if you let it rise to a lower point), it will tear. If you overproof the loaf (that is, if you let it rise to a higher point), the top will lack symmetry and may collapse. To proof the loaf to the perfect point, we recommend using two rulers: Place one on the lip of the pan to measure vertical rise, and place another one horizontally across the top of the dough to ensure that the very center of the dough is 1¾ inches above the lip of the pan. We also slash the loaf around its circumference, level to the lip of the pan, which allows the top to expand uniformly. By slashing around the side, rather than across the top, we preserve the loaf's beautiful, glazed dome.

kugelhopf

makes 1 loaf
rising time 4 to 5 hours
baking time 25 minutes
total time 9¼ to 10¼ hours
key equipment stand mixer, 12-cup nonstick Bundt pan, instant-read thermometer

why this recipe works *Kugelhopf* is a festive, crown-shaped yeasted bread traditionally baked in a heavy earthenware mold. One legend suggests it originated in the Alsatian village of Ribeauvillé, when the Three Kings presented it to a local baker named Kügel, who had hosted them. Other histories point to origins in Vienna, where bakers may have made the bread in the shape of a sultan's turban to celebrate the defeat of the Turks by Hapsburg forces in 1683. For our version, we set out to make a kirsch-scented, raisin- and dried cherry–studded, almond-crusted Kugelhopf typical of Alsace. Classic Alsatian recipes we tested yielded dense, somewhat dry breads that we needed to dunk in coffee or wine to fully enjoy. Several modern versions we tasted were sweeter, airier, moister, and even doughnut-like. Our goal was to develop a Kugelhopf recipe that would please traditional and modern palates alike—not too sweet, yeasty and a tad boozy, light but not fluffy, chewy yet soft, rich but not heavy. Many traditional recipes call for a sponge—a mixture of yeast, flour, and liquid that ferments seprarately and is added to the dough—for flavor, but we found that allowing our dough to ferment slowly (up to 2½ hours) during the initial rise, and folding the dough upon itself twice during that time to redistribute and stimulate the yeast, gave our bread plenty of heady flavor. Adding just the right amount of cherry brandy augmented this complexity. We tested our way through hydration levels and amounts of sugar, butter, and eggs until we landed on the perfect formula to yield a delicate yet satisfying texture and a moderate level of richness. We developed this recipe using our favorite 12-cup Bundt pan, however, we also like using a tradi-tional 10-cup Kugelhopf pan. If using a Kugelhopf pan, the dough will rise ½ inch above the lip of the pan in step 7. We do not recommend mixing this dough by hand.

⅔ cup dried cherries, chopped coarse

⅓ cup golden raisins

¼ cup (2 ounces) kirsch or other cherry-flavored brandy

3½ cups (17½ ounces) all-purpose flour

4 teaspoons instant or rapid-rise yeast

1 teaspoon salt

⅔ cup (5⅓ ounces) whole milk, room temperature

3 large eggs, room temperature

6 tablespoons (2⅔ ounces) granulated sugar

8 tablespoons (4 ounces) butter, softened

¼ cup sliced almonds

confectioners' sugar

continued

kugelhopf, continued

1 Microwave cherries, raisins, and kirsch in covered bowl until steaming, about 1 minute. Let sit until cherries and raisins have softened, about 15 minutes. Drain fruit and reserve kirsch.

2 Whisk flour, yeast, and salt together in bowl of stand mixture. Whisk milk, eggs, granulated sugar, and reserved kirsch in 4-cup liquid measuring cup until sugar has dissolved. Using dough hook on low speed, slowly add milk mixture to flour mixture and mix until cohesive dough starts to form and no dry flour remains, about 2 minutes, scraping down bowl as needed.

3 Increase speed to medium-low and knead until dough begins to pull away from sides of bowl but sticks to bottom, about 5 minutes. With mixer running, add butter, 1 tablespoon at a time, and knead until butter is fully incorporated, about 4 minutes. Continue to knead until dough is elastic and slightly sticky, about 3 minutes. Reduce speed to low, add fruit mixture, and mix until incorporated, about 1 minute. Transfer dough to lightly greased large bowl or container, cover tightly with plastic wrap, and let rise for 30 minutes.

4 Using greased bowl scraper (or your fingertips), fold dough over itself by gently lifting and folding edge of dough toward middle. Turn bowl 90 degrees and fold dough again; repeat turning bowl and folding dough 2 more times (total of 4 folds). Cover tightly with plastic and let rise for 30 minutes. Fold dough again, then cover bowl tightly with plastic and let dough rise until nearly doubled in size, 1 to 1½ hours.

5 Grease 12-cup nonstick Bundt pan and sprinkle bottom with almonds. Press down on dough to deflate, then transfer to lightly floured counter. Using your lightly floured hands, press dough into 8-inch round.

6 Using your fingertips, press through and stretch center of dough to create 2-inch hole.

7 Place dough in prepared pan and gently press into even thickness. Cover loosely with greased plastic and let rise until loaf is level with lip of pan, 2 to 2½ hours.

8 Adjust oven rack to lower-middle position and heat oven to 350 degrees. Bake until golden brown and loaf registers 190 to 195 degrees, 25 to 30 minutes, rotating pan halfway through baking. Let loaf cool in pan for 10 minutes, then invert loaf onto wire rack and let cool completely, about 3 hours. Dust with confectioners' sugar and serve.

troubleshooting

problem The dough looks greasy.

solution Use perfectly room-temperature butter.

We tested adding melted butter and room-temperature butter to our Kugelhopf dough, and the bread made with room-temperature butter had a lighter, stretchier, chewier texture. Room-temperature butter has just the right consistency. If the butter is too soft, it will not incorporate well and will make the dough look greasy and separated. Too-cold butter will get thrown around the mixer bowl and will never distribute evenly through the dough. When we call for room-temperature butter, we're looking for the butter to be between 65 and 67 degrees. Room-temperature butter should easily bend without breaking and give slightly when pressed. Let refrigerated butter sit on the counter for about 30 minutes to achieve the perfect texture.

panettone

makes 2 loaves
resting time 1½ hours
rising time 20 to 21 hours
baking time 1 hour
total time 24 to 25 hours, plus 3 hours cooling time
key equipment stand mixer, two 6 by 4-inch paper panettone molds, rimmed baking sheet, instant-read thermometer

1¼ cups (6¼ ounces) golden raisins

1½ tablespoons grated orange zest plus ¼ cup (2 ounces) juice

5 cups (27½ ounces) bread flour

2 tablespoons instant or rapid-rise yeast

1½ teaspoons salt

2 cups (16 ounces) whole milk, room temperature

4 large eggs plus 3 large yolks, room temperature

⅔ cup (4⅔ ounces) sugar

2 teaspoons vanilla extract

1 teaspoon almond extract

8 tablespoons (4 ounces) unsalted butter, softened

1¼ cups (6 ounces) finely chopped candied orange peel

why this recipe works Originating in Milan, panettone, a tall, luxurious, candied- and dried fruit–filled sweet bread made during the Christmas season, was at one time a specialty of just northern Italy. Now panettone can be found in American supermarkets. Because it's easy to come by, few attempt to make this gift bread at home. And existing recipes often turn out like dense fruitcake instead of the tall, light, and fluffy yet indulgently rich loaves that were once the bread of emperors and popes. We wanted to develop a recipe that was worthy of its regal history yet simple enough to make at home. Panettone is so prized because of its decadent ingredients; we packed the dough with butter, eggs, and extra yolks for richness and a golden color. But all of that fat made the bread dense and crumbly. To remedy this, we used high-protein bread flour and kneaded the dough for a full 8 minutes before incorporating softened butter, a little at a time, so the dough had a strong gluten structure to support all that fat. We stuck with traditional flavorings of golden raisins, candied orange peel, orange zest, and vanilla and almond extract to finish. We gave the rising dough a series of folds and let it ferment overnight in the refrigerator; our panettone relied on elongated fermentation and proofing times to maximize the gas development from the yeast in the dough that gives such a rich bread a remarkably light, fluffy texture and slightly tangy flavor. Because this bread is often given as a gift, our recipe makes two loaves in decorative baking paper. You can find paper panettone molds online or at kitchen supply stores. We do not recommend mixing this dough by hand. Be sure to reduce the oven temperature immediately after putting the loaves in the oven.

continued

1 Microwave raisins and orange juice in covered bowl until steaming, about 1 minute. Let sit until raisins have softened, about 15 minutes. Drain raisins and reserve orange juice.

2 Whisk flour, yeast, and salt together in bowl of stand mixer. Whisk milk, eggs and yolks, sugar, vanilla, almond extract, and reserved orange juice in 4-cup liquid measuring cup until sugar has dissolved. Using dough hook on low speed, slowly add milk mixture to flour mixture and mix until cohesive dough starts to form and no dry flour remains, about 5 minutes, scraping down bowl as needed.

3 Increase speed to medium-low and knead until dough is elastic but still sticks to sides of bowl, about 8 minutes. With mixer running, add butter, 1 tablespoon at a time, and knead until butter is fully incorporated, about 4 minutes. Continue to knead until dough is satiny and elastic and very sticky, about 3 minutes. Reduce speed to low, slowly add candied orange peel, raisins, and orange zest and mix until incorporated, about 3 minutes. Transfer dough to lightly greased large bowl or container, cover tightly with plastic wrap, and let rise for 30 minutes.

4 Using greased bowl scraper (or your fingertips), fold dough over itself by gently lifting and folding edge of dough toward middle. Turn bowl 90 degrees and fold dough again; repeat turning bowl and folding dough 2 more times (total of 4 folds). Cover tightly with plastic and let dough rise for 30 minutes. Fold dough again, then cover bowl tightly with plastic and refrigerate for at least 16 hours or up to 48 hours.

5 Let dough sit at room temperature for 1½ hours. Press down on dough to deflate. Transfer dough to well-floured counter, divide in half, and cover loosely with greased plastic. Press 1 piece of dough (keep remaining piece covered) into 6-inch round. Working around circumference of dough, fold edges toward center until ball forms. Flip ball seam side down and, using your cupped hands, drag in small circles on counter until dough feels taut and round and all seams are secured on underside. Repeat with remaining piece of dough.

6 Place dough rounds into two 6 by 4-inch paper panettone molds, pressing dough gently into corners. Transfer to wire rack set in rimmed baking sheet, cover loosely with greased plastic, and let rise until loaves reach 2 inches above lip of molds and dough springs back minimally when poked gently with your knuckle, 3 to 4 hours.

7 Adjust oven rack to middle position and heat oven to 400 degrees. Using sharp paring knife or single-edge razor blade, make two 5-inch-long, ¼-inch-deep slashes with swift, fluid motion along top of each loaf to form cross.

8 Place baking sheet in oven and reduce oven temperature to 350 degrees. Bake until loaves are deep golden brown, about 40 minutes, rotating sheet halfway through baking. Tent loaves with aluminum foil and continue to bake until loaves register 190 to 195 degrees, 20 to 30 minutes. Let loaves cool completely on wire rack, about 3 hours, before serving.

troubleshooting

problem There are lumps in the dough.

solution Add the liquid slowly.

This dough is highly enriched—that's what makes it so luxurious. The liquid ingredient mixture includes a hefty amount of milk, eggs, and sugar. Be sure to stream this mixture into the dry ingredients slowly when mixing the dough. Work too quickly and the loose, batter-like dough will form lumps. If, however, your dough does develop lumps, it is possible to eradicate them: Turn off the mixer and, using a rubber spatula, press the lumps against the side of the mixer bowl to break them up.

stollen

makes 2 loaves
resting time 30 minutes
rising time 12 hours
baking time 40 minutes
total time 17¼ hours
key equipment stand mixer, 2 rimmed baking sheets, instant-read thermometer, pastry brush

why this recipe works Originating in Dresden in the Middle Ages, stollen is a sweet yeasted bread served at Christmas throughout Germany and Austria. Its characteristic folded shape symbolizes the baby Jesus wrapped in swaddling clothes, and its candied fruit and nuts represent the gifts of the Magi. We sought a buttery, sweet stollen featuring a balanced mix of dried and candied fruits and a perfume of spirits and almonds. To achieve the dense texture and rich flavor we were looking for, we got the best results from a dough enriched with milk, brandy, egg, and a generous amount of butter. We found that melted butter produced the short crumb we wanted. This dough, however, was too wet and sticky to work with. Letting the dough rest overnight in the refrigerator helped firm it up considerably. In addition, the refrigerator rest allowed the dough to ferment slowly so that the baked bread had a wonderful yeasty flavor. After testing a variety of fruits, we chose a combination of brandy-soaked raisins and candied lemon and orange peel for their colorful jewel tones and bright flavor. Many recipes feature a core of marzipan running through the loaf, and we followed suit; we softened our almond filling with butter and water and scented it with a pinch of nutmeg. Infused with liquor, bathed in butter, and liberally coated with confectioners' sugar, stollen keeps well—a perfect treat to share with guests over coffee throughout the holiday season. This recipe makes two loaves, ideal for giving one away as a gift. We do not recommend mixing this dough by hand. If the dough becomes too soft to work with at any point, refrigerate it until it's firm enough to easily handle. The texture and flavor of the stollen improves over time and is best eaten 2 weeks after baking; in plastic wrap, it can be stored at room temperature for up to 1 month.

filling
1 tube (7 ounces) almond paste, cut into 4 pieces
1 tablespoon unsalted butter, softened
1 tablespoon water
pinch nutmeg

dough
1 cup raisins
½ cup (4 ounces) brandy
½ cup chopped candied lemon peel
½ cup chopped candied orange peel
½ cup slivered almonds, toasted
3½ cups (17½ ounces) all-purpose flour
4 teaspoons instant or rapid-rise yeast
1¼ teaspoons salt
1 cup (8 ounces) whole milk, room temperature
10 tablespoons (5 ounces) unsalted butter, melted
½ cup (3½ ounces) granulated sugar
1 large egg, room temperature
1 teaspoon vanilla extract
confectioners' sugar

continued

stollen, continued

1 **For the filling** Using stand mixer fitted with paddle, beat almond paste, butter, water, and nutmeg on medium speed until smooth, about 1 minute. Transfer to bowl, cover, and refrigerate until ready to use.

2 **For the dough** Microwave raisins and brandy in covered bowl until steaming, about 1 minute. Let sit until raisins have softened, about 15 minutes. Drain raisins and reserve brandy. Combine raisins, candied lemon peel, candied orange peel, and almonds in bowl.

3 Whisk flour, yeast, and salt together in clean, dry mixer bowl. Whisk milk, 8 tablespoons melted butter, granulated sugar, egg, vanilla, and reserved brandy in 4-cup liquid measuring cup until sugar has dissolved. Using paddle on low speed, slowly add milk mixture to flour mixture and mix until cohesive dough starts to form and no dry flour remains, about 2 minutes, scraping down bowl as needed. Slowly add fruit mixture and mix until incorporated, about 30 seconds. Transfer dough to lightly greased large bowl or container, cover tightly with plastic wrap, and refrigerate for at least 12 hours or up to 24 hours.

4 Stack 2 rimmed baking sheets, line with aluminum foil, and spray with vegetable oil spray. Transfer filling to well-floured counter, divide in half, and press each half into 7 by 2-inch rectangle; set aside.

5 Transfer dough to well-floured counter, divide in half, and cover loosely with greased plastic. Using your well-floured hands, press 1 piece of dough into 10 by 8-inch rectangle (keep remaining piece covered), with short side parallel to counter edge.

6 Place 1 piece of filling across top edge of dough, leaving 2-inch border at top. Fold dough away from you over filling until folded edge is snug against filling and dough extends 2 inches beyond top edge.

7 Fold top 2 inches of dough back toward center of loaf. Pinch side seams together to seal. Repeat with remaining dough and filling. Transfer loaves to prepared sheet, spaced about 4 inches apart. Cover loosely with greased plastic and let rest for 30 minutes.

8 Adjust oven rack to middle position and heat oven to 350 degrees. Bake until golden brown and loaves register 190 to 195 degrees, 40 to 45 minutes, rotating sheet halfway through baking. Brush loaves with remaining melted butter and dust liberally with confectioners' sugar. Transfer to wire rack and let cool completely, about 3 hours. Dust with additional confectioners' sugar before serving.

troubleshooting

problem The dough doesn't come together.

solution Use the paddle attachment.

Most of our bread recipes call for using the stand mixer dough hook attachment for kneading. However, in order to quickly incorporate all of the fruit and nuts into it (so we don't develop too much gluten and compromise its short, cake-like crumb), you'll want to use the paddle attachment here. The paddle attachment works its way through the whole mass of dough at once, distributing the ingredients evenly as it goes.

almond ring coffee cake

makes 2 cakes
rising time 2½ to 3½ hours
baking time 25 minutes
total time 5 to 6 hours
key equipment stand mixer, 2 rimmed baking sheets, rolling pin, pastry brush

why this recipe works Why buy inferior boxed versions when you can make a better coffee cake ring at home—one with buttery layers of dough, a sweet almond filling, and a smooth glaze? Most yeasted coffee cakes rely on an enriched dough made with milk, butter, and eggs. Because we were filling this cake with a sweet, rich almond filling, we wanted to encase it in something a bit lighter. To that end, we cut the butter used in most recipes in half. We figured we'd sweeten our dough with granulated sugar or brown sugar, as most recipes we researched do. But once we tested other options, we found that honey gave the cake a slight caramel flavor and also added welcome moisture to the dough. For the filling, most recipes bolster cream cheese with ground almonds and sugar, but this made a soft mixture that leaked out of the dough. Worse, the almond flavor was barely perceptible. We had better luck with almond paste. When we mixed the almond paste with a little cream cheese, it formed a luxurious filling that was thick enough to stay put in the dough. Perhaps even more important, it had a rich, nutty flavor that wasn't obscured by the dough. If the dough becomes too soft to work with at any point, refrigerate it until it's firm enough to easily handle.

filling

1 tube (7 ounces) almond paste, cut into 4 pieces

4 ounces cream cheese, softened

½ cup (2 ounces) confectioners' sugar

dough

4¾ cups (23¾ ounces) all-purpose flour

2¼ teaspoons instant or rapid-rise yeast

2 teaspoons salt

1⅓ cups (10⅔ ounces) whole milk, room temperature

8 tablespoons (4 ounces) unsalted butter, melted

⅓ cup (4 ounces) honey

3 large egg yolks

2 teaspoons vanilla extract

topping

2 large eggs, lightly beaten with 2 tablespoons water and pinch salt

½ cup sliced almonds

1½ cups (6 ounces) confectioners' sugar

2 ounces cream cheese, softened

2 tablespoons whole milk

½ teaspoon vanilla extract

continued

1 **For the filling** Using stand mixer fitted with paddle, beat almond paste, cream cheese, and sugar on medium speed until smooth, about 1 minute. Transfer to bowl, cover, and refrigerate until ready to use.

2 **For the dough** Whisk flour, yeast, and salt together in clean, dry mixer bowl. Whisk milk, melted butter, honey, egg yolks, and vanilla in 4-cup liquid measuring cup until honey has dissolved. Using dough hook on low speed, slowly add milk mixture to flour mixture and mix until cohesive dough starts to form and no dry flour remains, about 2 minutes, scraping down bowl as needed. Increase speed to medium-low and knead until dough is smooth and elastic and clears sides of bowl but sticks to bottom, about 8 minutes.

3 Transfer dough to lightly floured counter and knead by hand to form smooth, round ball, about 30 seconds. Place dough seam side down in lightly greased large bowl or container, cover tightly with plastic wrap, and let rise until doubled in size, 1½ to 2 hours.

4 Line 2 rimmed baking sheets with parchment paper. Transfer dough to lightly floured counter, divide in half, and cover loosely with greased plastic. Press and roll 1 piece of dough into 18 by 9-inch rectangle (keep remaining piece covered), with long side parallel to counter edge.

5 Spread half of filling into 1-inch-wide strip above bottom edge of dough, leaving 1-inch border at bottom. Roll dough away from you into firm cylinder, keeping roll taut by tucking it under itself as you go. Pinch seam closed.

6 Transfer cylinder seam side down to prepared sheet. Bring ends snug together to form ring and pinch seam closed. Repeat with remaining dough and filling.

7 Using kitchen shears or sharp knife, make 10 cuts around outside of dough, nearly but not all the way through loaf, spaced 1½ inches apart. Twist each section cut side up. Cover loosely with greased plastic and let rise until rings are nearly doubled in size and dough springs back minimally when poked gently with your knuckle, 1 to 1½ hours. (Unrisen dough rings can be refrigerated for at least 8 hours or up to 12 hours; let sit at room temperature for 1 hour before baking. Alternatively, fully risen rings can be wrapped tightly with greased plastic, followed by aluminum foil, and frozen for up to 1 month; let frozen rings thaw in refrigerator for 12 hours, then let sit at room temperature for 1 hour before baking.)

8 **For the topping** Adjust oven racks to upper-middle and lower-middle positions and heat oven to 375 degrees. Gently brush dough rings with egg mixture and sprinkle with almonds. Bake until cakes are deep golden brown, about 25 minutes, switching and rotating sheets halfway through baking. Let cakes cool on sheet for 1 hour. Meanwhile, whisk sugar, cream cheese, milk, and vanilla together in bowl until smooth. Drizzle glaze over cakes and serve warm or at room temperature.

variation **apricot-orange ring coffee cake**
Omit almond filling. Bring 2 cups dried apricots, 1 cup water, and 3 tablespoons sugar to simmer in medium saucepan over medium heat and cook, stirring occasionally, until apricots are soft and water has nearly evaporated, 16 to 18 minutes. Process apricots, 3 tablespoons grated orange zest, 3 tablespoons orange juice, and 2 tablespoons rum (optional) in food processor until smooth, about 1 minute, scraping down bowl as needed. Transfer mixture to bowl and let cool to room temperature. Cover with plastic wrap and refrigerate until ready to use.

yeasted doughnuts

makes 16 doughnuts and doughnut holes
rising time 2½ to 3 hours
cooking time 6 minutes
total time 3¾ to 4¼ hours
key equipment stand mixer, 2 rimmed baking sheets, rolling pin, doughnut cutter, Dutch oven, instant-read thermometer

3 cups (15 ounces) all-purpose flour

2¼ teaspoons instant or rapid-rise yeast

½ teaspoon salt

⅔ cup (5⅓ ounces) whole milk, room temperature

2 large eggs, room temperature

6 tablespoons (2⅔ ounces) sugar, plus 1 cup for rolling

6 tablespoons (3 ounces) unsalted butter, softened

2 quarts vegetable oil

why this recipe works The yeasted doughnuts found in chain shops look more impressive than they taste; once you get past the sugary coating, the flavor of the crumb is flat and stale. We set out to develop the ultimate yeasted doughnut that we could enjoy fresh from the fryer at home. What we wanted was a lightly sweetened doughnut that was tender on the inside and lightly crisp on the outside. Yeasted doughnuts are simply enriched bread dough that's rolled and cut into circles and fried. When we compared versions made using bread flour and all-purpose, we found that bread flour made the doughnut too dense and chewy, almost like a deep-fried bagel. All-purpose flour yielded a doughnut with a lighter interior. Because we wanted the doughnut's flavor to complement coatings and glazes, we didn't make the dough too sweet. But there was another reason for our light hand with the sugar: burning. Too much sugar could cause the doughnuts to brown too quickly in the hot oil. Likewise, too much butter would result in an overly rich, greasy doughnut, so we kept the butter amount to under a stick. If you don't have a doughnut cutter, you cutter (about 2½ inches) for the doughnuts, and a smaller one (about 1¼ inches) for the holes. We do not recommend mixing this dough by hand. Use a Dutch oven that holds 6 quarts or more for this recipe. The doughnuts are best eaten the day they are made.

continued

1 Whisk flour, yeast, and salt together in bowl of stand mixer. Whisk milk, eggs, and 6 tablespoons sugar in 4-cup liquid measuring cup until sugar has dissolved. Using dough hook on low speed, slowly add milk mixture to flour mixture and mix until cohesive dough starts to form and no dry flour remains, about 2 minutes, scraping down bowl as needed.

2 Increase speed to medium-low, add butter, 1 tablespoon at a time, and knead until butter is fully incorporated, about 3 minutes. Continue to knead until dough is smooth and elastic and clears sides of bowl but sticks to bottom, about 8 minutes.

3 Transfer dough to lightly floured counter and knead by hand to form smooth, round ball, about 30 seconds. Place dough seam side down in lightly greased large bowl or container, cover tightly with plastic wrap, and let rise until nearly doubled in size, 2 to 2½ hours. (Unrisen dough can be refrigerated for at least 8 hours or up to 16 hours; let sit at room temperature for 1 hour before rolling in step 4.)

4 Set wire rack in rimmed baking sheet. Line second sheet with parchment paper and dust lightly with flour. Press down on dough to deflate, then transfer to lightly floured counter. Press and roll dough into 12-inch round, about ½ inch thick.

5 Cut dough using 2½- or 3-inch doughnut cutter, gathering scraps and rerolling them as needed. Place doughnut rings and holes on floured sheet, cover loosely with greased plastic, and let rise until puffy, 30 to 45 minutes.

6 Add oil to large Dutch oven until it measures about 1½ inches deep and heat over medium-high heat to 375 degrees. Working in batches of 4 dough holes and 4 dough rings at a time, fry until golden brown, about 30 seconds per side for holes and 45 to 60 seconds per side for doughnuts.

7 Using wire skimmer or slotted spoon, transfer doughnuts and doughnut holes to prepared wire rack.

8 Spread remaining sugar in shallow dish. Let doughnuts and doughnut holes cool for 10 minutes, then roll in sugar to coat. Serve warm or at room temperature.

variations

yeasted cinnamon-sugar doughnuts
Combine 1 cup sugar with 1 tablespoon ground cinnamon before rolling doughnuts and doughnut holes in step 8.

yeasted vanilla-glazed doughnuts
Omit 1 cup sugar for rolling. While doughnuts are cooling, whisk ½ cup half-and-half, 3 cups confectioners' sugar, sifted, and 1 teaspoon vanilla extract in medium bowl until combined. When doughnuts have cooled, dip 1 side of each doughnut into glaze, let excess drip off, and transfer to wire rack. Let glaze set, about 15 minutes, before serving.

yeasted chocolate-glazed doughnuts
Omit 1 cup sugar for rolling. While doughnuts are cooling, place 4 ounces finely chopped semisweet or bittersweet chocolate in small bowl. Add ½ cup hot half-and-half and whisk together to melt chocolate. Add 2 cups confectioners' sugar, sifted, and whisk until no lumps remain. When doughnuts have cooled, dip 1 side of each doughnut into glaze, let excess drip off, and transfer to wire rack. Let glaze set, about 15 minutes, before serving.

upping your game with sponges
bakery-style artisan loaves

pane francese

makes 2 loaves
resting time 6 hours 20 minutes
rising time 2½ to 3½ hours
baking time 20 minutes
total time 11 to 12 hours, plus 3 hours cooling time
key equipment couche, water-filled spray bottle, rimmed baking sheet, baking stone, 2 (9-inch) disposable aluminum pie plates, 2 quarts lava rocks, pizza peel, flipping board, lame, instant-read thermometer

why this recipe works The Italian cousin to the baguette, *pane francese* (which means "French bread") is a long loaf with a moist and open crumb. Pane francese has a crisp yet forgiving exterior, and it's slightly flatter in shape than a baguette. It's nice for sandwiches or for dipping into olive oil. We started this bread with a sponge, which developed structure, depth of flavor, and a hint of tang in the loaf. After preparing this mixture (made with water, yeast, and 20 percent of the bread's total weight of flour), we let it sit on the counter for 6 to 24 hours before mixing it into the dough. During this period the yeast consumed sugars in the flour. This fermentation process, visible by the rise and collapse of the mixture, created acid as a byproduct, which helps develop the strong gluten network that suppors the loaf's open crumb. Also, extending the overall fermentation time for the dough is what provides great flavor. (For more information on sponges, see page 35.) A repeated series of gentle folds helped develop the gluten structure even further while also incorporating air for an open interior crumb. We proofed the loaf on a *couche*—a heavy linen cloth—to help the wet dough keep its shape. (For more information on couches, see page 5.) We slash the top of rustic loaves like pane francese with a *lame*, a curved-blade tool that gives our scores a dramatic raised edge that bakes up crisp. (For more information on lames, see page 5.) The last step? We preheated pans filled with lava rocks and added water to them to create a steamy oven, which encouraged a crisp crust. (For more information on lava rocks, see page 5.)

sponge
⅔ cup (3⅔ ounces) bread flour
½ cup (4 ounces) water, room temperature
⅛ teaspoon instant or rapid-rise yeast

dough
2⅔ cups (14⅔ ounces) bread flour
1½ teaspoons instant or rapid-rise yeast
1¼ cups (10 ounces) water, room temperature
1 tablespoon extra-virgin olive oil
2¼ teaspoons salt

continued

1 ***For the sponge*** Stir all ingredients in 4-cup liquid measuring cup with wooden spoon until well combined. Cover tightly with plastic wrap and let sit at room temperature until sponge has risen and begins to collapse, about 6 hours (sponge can sit at room temperature for up to 24 hours).

2 ***For the dough*** Whisk flour and yeast together in bowl of stand mixer. Stir water into sponge with wooden spoon until well combined. Using dough hook on low speed, slowly add sponge mixture to flour mixture and mix until cohesive dough starts to form and no dry flour remains, about 2 minutes, scraping down bowl as needed. Cover bowl tightly with plastic and let dough rest for 20 minutes.

3 Add oil and salt to dough and knead on medium-low speed until dough is smooth and elastic and clears sides of bowl, about 5 minutes. Transfer dough to lightly greased large bowl or container, cover tightly with plastic, and let rise for 30 minutes.

4 Using greased bowl scraper (or your fingertips), fold dough over itself by gently lifting and folding edge of dough toward middle. Turn bowl 45 degrees and fold dough again; repeat turning bowl and folding dough 6 more times (total of 8 folds). Cover tightly with plastic and let rise for 30 minutes. Repeat folding, then cover bowl tightly with plastic and let dough rise until nearly doubled in size, 1 to 1½ hours.

5 Mist underside of couche with water, drape over inverted rimmed baking sheet, and dust evenly with flour. Transfer dough to lightly floured counter. Press and stretch dough into 12 by 6-inch rectangle, deflating any gas pockets larger than 1 inch, and divide in half crosswise. Cover loosely with greased plastic.

6 Gently press and stretch 1 piece of dough (keep remaining piece covered) into 7-inch square. Fold top corners of dough diagonally into center of square and press gently to seal. Stretch and fold upper third of dough toward center and press seam gently to seal.

continued

troubleshooting

problem The loaf is bland.

solution Let the sponge sit for at least 6 hours.

Made with just flour, water, yeast, and salt (and a little olive oil), our pane francese gets most of its flavor from a prefermented sponge. Don't undercut the 6- to 24-hour fermentation time; it is essential for developing the slight tang we expect from this loaf. The sponge is ready for use when it rises and then begins to collapse.

problem You don't have a flipping board.

solution Make one from cardboard.

You don't want to deflate the delicate proofed loaf, so you can't pick it up with your hands. A flipping board has a thin edge that you can wedge under the loaf to roll it onto the pizza peel without collapsing the air bubbles. But if you don't have a flipping board, you can fashion one from cardboard: Simply tape two 16 by 4-inch pieces of heavy cardboard together with packaging tape.

problem The loaf sticks to the couche.

solution Mist and flour the couche well.

Although a linen couche is better than a cotton towel for releasing loaves, it can still stick to very wet doughs. Mist the couche with water and dust it well with flour—2 tablespoons does the trick.

7 Stretch and fold dough in half toward you to form rough loaf with tapered ends and pinch seam closed. Roll loaf seam side down. Starting at center of dough and working toward ends, gently and evenly roll and stretch dough until it measures 15 inches long by 2½ inches wide. Moving your hands in opposite directions, use back and forth motion to roll ends of loaf under your palms to form sharp points.

8 Gently slide your hands underneath each end of loaf and transfer seam side up to prepared couche. On either side of loaf, pinch couche into pleat, then cover loosely with large plastic garbage bag. Repeat steps 6 through 7 with remaining piece of dough and place on opposite side of 1 pleat. Fold edges of couche over loaves to cover completely, then carefully place sheet inside garbage bag. Tie, or fold under, open end of bag to fully enclose. Let rise until loaves increase in size by about half and dough springs back minimally when poked gently with your knuckle, 30 minutes to 1 hour (remove loaf from bag to test).

9 One hour before baking, adjust oven racks to lower-middle and lowest positions. Place baking stone on upper rack, place 2 disposable aluminum pie plates filled with 1 quart lava rocks each on lower rack, and heat oven to 450 degrees. Line pizza peel with 16 by 12-inch piece of parchment paper, with long edge perpendicular to handle. Bring 1 cup water to boil.

10 Remove sheet with loaves from bag. Unfold couche, pulling from ends to remove pleats. Dust top of loaves with flour. (If any seams have reopened, pinch closed before dusting with flour.) Gently pushing with side of flipping board, roll 1 loaf over, away from other loaf, so it is seam side down. Using your hand, hold long edge of flipping board between loaf and couche at 45-degree angle, then lift couche with your other hand and flip loaf seam side up onto board. Invert loaf seam side down onto prepared pizza peel, about 2 inches from long edge of parchment, then use flipping board to straighten loaf and reshape as needed. Repeat with second loaf, leaving at least 3 inches between loaves.

11 Carefully pour ½ cup boiling water into 1 disposable pie plate of preheated rocks and close oven door for 1 minute to create steam. Meanwhile, holding lame concave side up at 30-degree angle to loaf, make one ½-inch-deep slash with swift, fluid motion lengthwise along top of loaf, starting and stopping about ½ inch from ends. Repeat with second loaf.

12 Working quickly, slide parchment with loaves onto baking stone and pour remaining ½ cup boiling water into second disposable pie plate of preheated rocks. Bake until crust is golden brown and loaves register 205 to 210 degrees, 20 to 25 minutes, rotating loaves halfway through baking. Transfer loaves to wire rack, discard parchment, and let cool completely, about 3 hours, before serving.

whole-wheat sandwich bread

makes 2 loaves
resting time 8 hours
rising time 2¼ to 3¼ hours
baking time 40 minutes
total time 18 to 19 hours, plus 3 hours cooling time
key equipment two 8½ by 4½-inch loaf pans, water-filled spray bottle, instant-read thermometer

why this recipe works Most recipes for whole-wheat sandwich bread either pay lip service to being "whole wheat," containing so little of the whole-grain stuff that they resemble squishy supermarket loaves, or they call for so much that the bread bakes up coarse and dense. We wanted a sandwich bread with a full-blown nutty (but not bitter) taste and a hearty yet soft crumb. For starters, we knew we wanted to use a sponge for this bread to give it a jump start in flavor development. We preferred bread that contained 60 percent whole-wheat flour (and 40 percent white flour)—more whole-wheat flour than in most recipes. But packing that much whole wheat into our loaf compromised its texture, so we had to take a few structure-building measures. First, we used bread flour for our white flour because of its high protein content. Next, we presoaked the whole-wheat flour before making the dough. Soaking softened the grain's bran, thereby dulling its sharp edges and preventing them from puncturing and deflating the dough. As a bonus, soaking also converted some starches in the grain into sugars, reducing bitterness. (For more information on soakers, see page 34.) To amp up the wheatiness even more, we added toasted wheat germ to our dough. Honey gave our bread an earthy sweetness, and adding both butter and oil softened the loaf's texture. The test kitchen's preferred loaf pan measures 8½ by 4½ inches; if you use a 9 by 5-inch loaf pan, increase the shaped rising time by 20 to 30 minutes and start checking for doneness 10 minutes earlier than advised in the recipe.

soaker
3 cups (16½ ounces) whole-wheat flour
2 cups (16 ounces) whole milk
½ cup (1½ ounces) toasted wheat germ

sponge
2 cups (11 ounces) bread flour
1 cup (8 ounces) water, room temperature
½ teaspoon instant or rapid-rise yeast

dough
6 tablespoons (3 ounces) unsalted butter, softened
¼ cup (3 ounces) honey
2 tablespoons instant or rapid-rise yeast
2 tablespoons vegetable oil
4 teaspoons salt

continued

1 **For the soaker** Stir all ingredients in large bowl with wooden spoon until shaggy mass forms. Transfer dough to lightly floured counter and knead by hand until smooth, about 3 minutes. Return soaker to bowl, cover tightly with plastic wrap, and refrigerate for at least 8 hours or up to 24 hours.

2 **For the sponge** Stir all ingredients in 8-cup liquid measuring cup with wooden spoon until well combined. Cover tightly with plastic wrap and let sit at room temperature until sponge has risen and begins to collapse, about 6 hours (sponge can sit at room temperature for up to 24 hours).

3 **For the dough** Tear soaker into 1-inch pieces and place in bowl of stand mixer fitted with dough hook. Add sponge, butter, honey, yeast, oil, and salt and mix on low speed until cohesive dough starts to form, about 2 minutes, scraping down bowl as needed. Increase speed to medium-low and knead until dough is smooth and elastic and clears sides of bowl but sticks to bottom, about 8 minutes. Transfer dough to lightly greased large bowl or container, cover tightly with plastic, and let rise for 45 minutes.

4 Using greased bowl scraper (or your fingertips), fold dough over itself by gently lifting and folding edge of dough toward middle. Turn bowl 45 degrees and fold dough again; repeat turning bowl and folding dough 6 more times (total of 8 folds). Cover tightly with plastic and let rise until nearly doubled in size, 30 minutes to 1 hour.

5 Grease two 8½ by 4½-inch loaf pans. Press down on dough to deflate. Transfer dough to lightly floured counter, divide in half, and cover loosely with greased plastic. Press and stretch 1 piece of dough (keep remaining piece covered) into 8 by 6-inch rectangle, with long side parallel to counter edge.

6 Roll dough away from you into firm cylinder, keeping roll taut by tucking it under itself as you go. Pinch seam closed and place loaf seam side down in prepared pan, pressing dough gently into corners. Repeat with second piece of dough. Cover loosely with greased plastic and let rise until loaves reach 1 inch above lip of pans and dough springs back minimally when poked gently with your knuckle, 1 to 1½ hours.

7 Adjust oven rack to lower-middle position and heat oven to 350 degrees. Using sharp paring knife or single-edge razor blade, make one ¼-inch-deep slash with swift, fluid motion lengthwise along top of loaf, starting and stopping about ½ inch from ends. Repeat with second loaf.

8 Mist loaves with water and bake until deep golden brown and loaves register 205 to 210 degrees, 40 to 45 minutes, rotating pans halfway through baking. Let loaves cool in pans for 15 minutes. Remove loaves from pans and let cool completely on wire rack, about 3 hours, before serving.

troubleshooting

problem The loaf is dense.

solution Soak the whole-wheat flour for at least 8 hours.

During the 8-hour soaking time, the bran softens so its sharp edges don't cut through strands of gluten. If you don't give the soaker enough time, the bran can compromise the gluten structure, yielding a dense loaf of bread.

problem The soaker doesn't incorporate.

solution Tear the soaker into 1-inch pieces.

The soaker is fairly stiff once it's time to add the sponge and other dough ingredients. If you try to knead a mass of soaker into the sponge, it will never incorporate properly. Breaking the soaker into pieces makes mixing easy.

scali bread

makes 1 loaf
resting time 6 hours
rising time 2½ to 3½ hours
baking time 35 minutes
total time 10 to 11 hours, plus 3 hours cooling time
key equipment 2 rimmed baking sheets, pastry brush, instant-read thermometer

why this recipe works Boasting a soft crust and a relatively fluffy crumb, scali is the bread you want to have next to your big bowl of spaghetti and meatballs. A signature of Boston's Italian American community, scali is sold in most local grocery stores and cafés and is almost always braided and coated with a generous amount of sesame seeds. We thought it was time to introduce this lovely loaf to the rest of the country. Unlike with most loaves in this chapter, in which we want a sturdy, open crumb, we quickly passed over bread flour in favor of all-purpose flour here; the lower-protein flour gave our bread its trademark soft, pillowy texture. Looking to further encourage a soft interior, we also avoided adding multiple folds to this recipe, and we simply kneaded the sponge with the remaining dough ingredients in the mixer until smooth and elastic before letting the dough rise undisturbed. Incorporating 1 tablespoon of olive oil into the dough also helped create a soft crumb, and it provided a pleasing touch of richness to the bread. The addition of a sponge set the flavorful scali apart from other fluffy Italian breads. After dividing the dough into thirds and braiding the pieces into a loaf, we brushed the top with beaten egg and sprinkled on the traditional (but optional) dose of sesame seeds.

sponge
⅔ cup (3⅓ ounces) all-purpose flour
½ cup (4 ounces) water, room temperature
⅛ teaspoon instant or rapid-rise yeast

dough
2⅔ cups (13⅓ ounces) all-purpose flour
2 teaspoons salt
1¼ teaspoons instant or rapid-rise yeast
¾ cup plus 2 tablespoons (7 ounces) water, room temperature
3 tablespoons sugar
1 tablespoon extra-virgin olive oil
1 tablespoon sesame seeds (optional)

1 large egg, lightly beaten with 1 tablespoon water and pinch salt

continued

scali bread, continued

1 **For the sponge** Stir all ingredients in 4-cup liquid measuring cup with wooden spoon until well combined. Cover tightly with plastic wrap and let sit at room temperature until sponge has risen and begins to collapse, about 6 hours (sponge can sit at room temperature for up to 24 hours).

2 **For the dough** Whisk flour, salt, and yeast together in bowl of stand mixer. Stir water, sugar, and oil into sponge with wooden spoon until well combined. Using dough hook on low speed, slowly add sponge mixture to flour mixture and mix until cohesive dough starts to form and no dry flour remains, about 2 minutes, scraping down bowl as needed.

3 Increase speed to medium-low and knead until dough is smooth and elastic and clears sides of bowl, about 8 minutes.

4 Transfer dough to lightly floured counter and knead by hand to form smooth, round ball, about 30 seconds. Place dough seam side down in lightly greased large bowl or container, cover tightly with plastic, and let rise until doubled in size, 1½ to 2 hours.

5 Stack 2 rimmed baking sheets, line with aluminum foil, and spray with vegetable oil spray. Press down on dough to deflate. Transfer dough to lightly floured counter, divide into thirds (about 9½ ounces each), and cover loosely with greased plastic. Working with 1 piece of dough at a time (keep remaining pieces covered), stretch and roll into 10-inch rope.

6 Arrange ropes side by side, perpendicular to counter edge, and pinch far ends together. Braid ropes into 10-inch loaf and pinch remaining ends together.

7 Transfer loaf to prepared sheet and reshape as needed, tucking edges under to form taut 10-inch loaf. Cover loosely with greased plastic and let rise until loaf increases in size by about half and dough springs back minimally when poked gently with your knuckle, 1 to 1½ hours.

8 Adjust oven rack to middle position and heat oven to 350 degrees. Gently brush loaf with egg mixture and sprinkle with sesame seeds, if using. Bake until golden brown and loaf registers 205 to 210 degrees, 35 to 40 minutes, rotating sheet halfway through baking. Transfer loaf to wire rack and let cool completely, about 3 hours, before serving.

troubleshooting

problem The braid comes undone.

solution Be sure to secure the edges.

The attractive big braid on our scali expands during proofing and in the oven, and it can come apart if it's not well secured. Be sure to pinch the ends together after braiding the loaf, and tuck the edges of the loaf under after transferring the loaf to the baking sheet.

pumpernickel

makes 1 loaf
resting time 6 hours
rising time 2½ to 3½ hours
baking time 3 hours
total time 13 to 14 hours, plus 4 hours cooling time
key equipment 13 by 4-inch Pullman loaf pan, pastry brush, instant-read thermometer

why this recipe works Pumpernickel bread is a slightly sweet, dense, dark-colored German bread often used as the base for canapés of smoked salmon and crème fraîche. It is made using pumpernickel flour, which is coarsely ground from the whole rye berry and includes the seed coating, bran, and germ. Traditional German pumpernickels use a sourdough starter to provide tang. We simplified this process by making a basic sponge with some of the pumpernickel flour. This produced an aromatic and flavorful base for our dough without the planning and time commitment a starter requires. We found that a dough made with 25 percent bread flour and 75 percent pumpernickel flour had the richest flavor and the ideal chew; any more bread flour diluted the sweet—even chocolaty—notes of the pumpernickel flour, and any less compromised our loaf's structure. Our flavor additions—instant espresso powder, cocoa powder, molasses, and caraway seeds—enhanced the sweet and bitter notes of the loaf, as well as deepened its color. Unlike with most breads, we didn't want this loaf to achieve a lot of spring in the oven—we desired the tight, dense crumb that's traditional. Baking the bread low (at 250 degrees) and slow (for 3 hours) in a Pullman loaf pan both inhibited it from springing dramatically when it entered the oven and dried out the bread. You can find pumpernickel flour online or in specialty baking stores. Dark rye flour can be substituted for pumpernickel flour; however, do not use pumpernickel meal, which is a more coarsely ground version of the flour. The more neutral pH of Dutch-processed cocoa powder is important for proper gluten development in this dough; do not substitute natural unsweetened cocoa. The texture of this loaf improves over time, and it is best eaten three days after baking.

sponge
1⅓ cups (7⅓ ounces) pumpernickel flour

1 cup (8 ounces) water, room temperature

⅛ teaspoon instant or rapid-rise yeast

dough
3½ cups (19¼ ounces) pumpernickel flour

1½ cups (8¼ ounces) bread flour

¼ cup (¾ ounce) Dutch-processed cocoa powder

1 tablespoon caraway seeds

1 tablespoon salt

1 teaspoon instant or rapid-rise yeast

1 tablespoon instant espresso powder

2 cups (16 ounces) water, room temperature

¼ cup (3 ounces) molasses

2 tablespoons vegetable oil

1 large egg, lightly beaten with 1 tablespoon water and pinch salt

continued

1 **For the sponge** Stir all ingredients in 8-cup liquid measuring cup with wooden spoon until well combined. Cover tightly with plastic wrap and let sit at room temperature until sponge has risen and begins to collapse, about 6 hours (sponge can sit at room temperature for up to 24 hours).

2 **For the dough** Whisk pumpernickel flour, bread flour, cocoa, caraway seeds, salt, and yeast together in bowl of stand mixer. Dissolve espresso powder in water, then whisk molasses, oil, and espresso powder mixture into sponge until well combined (mixture may look curdled). Using dough hook on low speed, slowly add sponge mixture to flour mixture and mix until cohesive dough starts to form and no dry flour remains, about 2 minutes, scraping down bowl as needed.

3 Increase speed to medium-low and knead until dough is smooth, about 8 minutes. (Dough will resemble cookie dough.)

4 Dust counter with pumpernickel flour. Transfer dough to counter and knead by hand to form smooth, round ball, about 30 seconds. Place dough seam side down in lightly greased large bowl or container, cover tightly with plastic, and let rise until increased in size by about half, 1 to 1½ hours.

5 Grease 13 by 4-inch Pullman loaf pan. Press down on dough to deflate. Lightly dust counter with pumpernickel flour. Turn out dough onto counter (side of dough that was against bowl should now be facing up). Press dough into 12 by 10-inch rectangle, with long side parallel to counter edge.

6 Roll dough away from you into firm cylinder, keeping roll taut by tucking it under itself as you go. Pinch seam closed and place loaf seam side down in prepared pan, pressing dough gently into corners.

7 Cover loosely with greased plastic and let rise until loaf reaches ½ inch below lip of pan and dough springs back minimally when poked gently with your knuckle, 1½ to 2 hours.

8 Adjust oven rack to lower-middle position and heat oven to 250 degrees. Using sharp paring knife or single-edge razor blade, make one ½-inch-deep slash with swift, fluid motion lengthwise along top of loaf, starting and stopping about ½ inch from ends. Gently brush loaf with egg mixture and bake, uncovered, until crust is very dark brown and dry and loaf registers 205 to 210 degrees, about 3 hours, rotating pan halfway through baking. Let loaf cool in pan for 15 minutes. Remove loaf from pan and let cool completely on wire rack, about 4 hours, before serving.

troubleshooting

problem The loaf is underbaked.

solution Bake for the full 3 hours.

It can be difficult to judge the doneness of dark pumpernickel bread, and you should not use temperature as your main guide. You want this heavy dough to dry out fully in the oven, so the 3-hour baking time is critical. Because the loaf is baked for so long and at such a low temperature, it will reach the proper temperature range long before it is fully baked—about an hour or so into the baking time. If you pull the loaf at this time, it will have a soft, brownie-like texture. Make sure the crust is very dark brown and looks dry before you take it out of the oven. And let the loaf cool for the full 4 hours—longer than for other breads—to allow it to continue to dry out and set up.

pain de campagne

makes 1 loaf
resting time 6 hours 20 minutes
rising time 3 to 4 hours
baking time 45 minutes
total time 11 to 12 hours, plus 3 hours cooling time
key equipment water-filled spray bottle, large linen
towel, 5-quart colander, baking stone, 2 (9-inch) disposable
aluminum pie plates, 2 quarts lava rocks, pizza peel, lame,
instant-read thermometer

why this recipe works *Pain de campagne* is a round country bread that's a mealtime staple in French homes, and it can be found in nearly every boulangerie. We wanted to develop a recipe for a rustic boule as good as any on a French table—one with a hearty crust, an irregular crumb, a wholesome chew, and a deep, slightly tangy flavor. Traditionally, this country bread is made with part whole-wheat flour and part bread flour; using just a small amount of whole-wheat flour (20 percent of the total weight of flour) gave us decent wheaty flavor and didn't make the loaf overly dense. Still, we were hoping for a loaf with a deeper taste. We make most of the sponges in this book with 20 percent of the weight of flour, but we wondered if adding more sponge could boost flavor. Indeed, mixing 50 percent of the dough's total flour into the sponge gave us sweet notes and a bit more tang. But we found that we couldn't surpass 50 percent; when we used more sponge to start our bread, the loaf lacked structure. (The acid that is created in a fermented sponge is beneficial for developing a strong gluten network only up to a point. In the presence of too much acid, the gluten structure breaks down.) You can substitute a round *banneton*, or proofing basket, for the towel-lined colander. (For more information on bannetons, see page 37.) For a more decorative crust, you can slash this loaf in step 11 using either of the techniques shown on page 36.

sponge

1⅔ cups (9⅛ ounces) bread flour

1 cup (8 ounces) water, room temperature

⅛ teaspoon instant or rapid-rise yeast

dough

1 cup (5½ ounces) bread flour

⅔ cup (3⅔ ounces) whole-wheat flour

1½ teaspoons instant or rapid-rise yeast

¾ cup (6 ounces) water, room temperature

2½ teaspoons salt

continued

1 **For the sponge** Stir all ingredients in 8-cup liquid measuring cup with wooden spoon until well combined. Cover tightly with plastic wrap and let sit at room temperature until sponge has risen and begins to collapse, about 6 hours (sponge can sit at room temperature for up to 24 hours).

2 **For the dough** Whisk bread flour, whole-wheat flour, and yeast together in bowl of stand mixer. Stir water into sponge with wooden spoon until well combined.

3 Using dough hook on low speed, slowly add sponge mixture to flour mixture and mix until cohesive dough starts to form and no dry flour remains, about 2 minutes, scraping down bowl as needed. Cover bowl tightly with plastic and let dough rest for 20 minutes.

4 Add salt to dough and knead on medium-low speed until dough is smooth and elastic and clears sides of bowl but sticks to bottom, about 5 minutes. Transfer dough to lightly greased large bowl or container, cover tightly with plastic, and let rise for 30 minutes.

5 Using greased bowl scraper (or your fingertips), fold dough over itself by gently lifting and folding edge of dough toward middle. Turn bowl 45 degrees and fold dough again; repeat turning bowl and folding dough 6 more times (total of 8 folds). Cover tightly with plastic and let rise for 30 minutes. Repeat folding and rising. Fold dough again, then cover bowl tightly with plastic and let dough rise until nearly doubled in size, 1 to 1½ hours.

6 Mist underside of large linen or cotton tea towel with water. Line 5-quart colander with towel and dust evenly with flour. Transfer dough to lightly floured counter (side of dough that was against bowl should now be against counter). Press and stretch dough into 10-inch round, deflating any gas pockets larger than 1 inch.

continued

troubleshooting

problem The loaf is misshapen.

solution Use the right size colander.

Colanders come in different variations. To mimic a round proofing banneton (for more information on bannetons, see page 37), you'll want to make sure your colander is 5 quarts and roughly 11 inches in diameter and 4 inches deep (this is fairly standard). Since the wet dough relies on the colander for shape during proofing, wider colanders will yield short, squat loaves.

problem The dough sticks to the colander.

solution Line the colander with a towel.

Wet dough will stick to a colander (and become pocked with tiny holes) if it sits directly on the metal surface. Lining the colander with a floured towel makes the loaf easy to release. Make sure to use a linen towel or cotton tea towel; the dough can stick to terry cloth. Also, don't substitute a glass bowl for the colander. The bowl will trap moisture and cause the loaf to stick to the towel.

7 Working around circumference of dough, fold edges toward center until ball forms. Flip dough ball seam side down and, using your cupped hands, drag in small circles on counter until dough feels taut and round and all seams are secured on underside of loaf.

8 Place loaf seam side up in prepared colander and pinch any remaining seams closed. Loosely fold edges of towel over loaf to enclose, then place colander in large plastic garbage bag. Tie, or fold under, open end of bag to fully enclose. Let rise until loaf increases in size by about half and dough springs back minimally when poked gently with your knuckle, 30 minutes to 1 hour (remove loaf from bag to test).

9 One hour before baking, adjust oven racks to lower-middle and lowest positions. Place baking stone on upper rack, place 2 disposable aluminum pie plates filled with 1 quart lava rocks each on lower rack, and heat oven to 450 degrees. Bring 1 cup water to boil.

10 Remove colander from garbage bag, unfold edges of towel, and dust top of loaf with flour. (If any seams have reopened, pinch closed before dusting with flour.) Lay 16 by 12-inch sheet of parchment paper on top of loaf. Using 1 hand to support parchment and loaf, invert loaf onto parchment and place on counter. Gently remove colander and towel. Transfer parchment with loaf to pizza peel.

11 Carefully pour ½ cup boiling water into 1 disposable pie plate of preheated rocks and close oven door for 1 minute to create steam. Meanwhile, holding lame concave side up at 30-degree angle to loaf, make two 7-inch-long, ½-inch-deep slashes with swift, fluid motion along top of loaf to form cross.

12 Working quickly, slide parchment with loaf onto baking stone and pour remaining ½ cup boiling water into second disposable pie plate of preheated rocks. Bake until crust is dark brown and loaf registers 205 to 210 degrees, 45 to 50 minutes, rotating loaf halfway through baking. Transfer loaf to wire rack, discard parchment, and let cool completely, about 3 hours, before serving.

troubleshooting

problem The loaf doesn't rise to the proper height.

solution Place the colander and loaf in a large plastic garbage bag.

The holes in the colander provide just enough air circulation around the loaf to dry the outside of the dough, which contributes to a superb crust once the loaf is baked. But you still need to protect the dough from the surrounding environment to prevent it from forming a tough skin. A skin on loaves hinders rise, so the bread does not gain enough height and the interior crumb can be compressed. To protect the loaf in the colander as it proofs, don't simply cover it with plastic wrap; fit the colander inside a large plastic garbage bag and tie or fold the bag closed.

rustic wheat berry bread

makes 1 loaf
resting time 12 hours 20 minutes
rising time 3 to 4 hours
baking time 35 minutes
total time 17 to 18 hours, plus 3 hours cooling time
key equipment food processor, water-filled spray bottle, large linen towel, 5-quart colander, baking stone, 2 (9-inch) disposable aluminum pie plates, 2 quarts lava rocks, pizza peel, lame, instant-read thermometer

why this recipe works We love the flavor and texture that whole-wheat flour gives bread. Some artisan bakers take this concept further, making breads with flour that they grind from whole wheat berries. You might think a bread made with homemade flour sounds a bit unnecessary, and we sure did—until we tried it. While whole-wheat flour has a tinge of bitterness, freshly ground wheat berries give bread a robust flavor with superlatively toasty, sweet notes. To start our own recipe for a rustic loaf made from wheat berries, we needed to figure out the best way to pulverize them. We thought the blender would work, but we had to grind the berries in batches to achieve an even texture. We were also concerned that the generous amount of homemade whole-wheat flour in our recipe (45 percent of the total flour weight) might compromise the structure. So we decided on a two-part solution: First, we soaked our wheat berries in water (for 12 to 24 hours) to soften the bran; the mixture then transformed quickly into a paste in the food processor. Second, we combined our mash with bread flour and a sponge, both of which contributed to a strong gluten network. You can find whole wheat berries in the natural- or bulk-foods section of the grocery store. You can substitute a round *banneton*, or proofing basket, for the towel-lined colander. (For more information on bannetons, see page 37.) For a more decorative crust, you can slash this loaf in step 11 using either of the techniques shown on page 36.

soaker

1¼ cups (8 ounces) wheat berries

1 cup (8 ounces) water, room temperature

sponge

¾ cup (4⅛ ounces) bread flour

½ cup (4 ounces) water, room temperature

¼ teaspoon instant or rapid-rise yeast

dough

¼ cup (2 ounces) water, room temperature

1 cup (5½ ounces) bread flour

2½ teaspoons instant or rapid-rise yeast

1 tablespoon honey

1 tablespoon extra-virgin olive oil

1¼ teaspoons salt

continued

rustic wheat berry bread, continued

1 **For the soaker** Combine wheat berries and water in bowl, cover tightly with plastic wrap, and let sit at room temperature until grains are fully hydrated and softened, at least 12 hours or up to 24 hours.

2 **For the sponge** Stir all ingredients in 4-cup liquid measuring cup with wooden spoon until well combined. Cover tightly with plastic wrap and let sit at room temperature until sponge has risen and begins to collapse, about 6 hours (sponge can sit at room temperature for up to 24 hours).

3 **For the dough** Process soaked wheat berries, remaining soaking liquid, and water in food processor until grains are finely ground, about 4 minutes, scraping down sides of bowl as needed.

4 Whisk flour and yeast together in bowl of stand mixer. Stir wheat berry mixture and honey into sponge with wooden spoon until well combined. Using dough hook on low speed, slowly add sponge mixture to flour mixture and mix until cohesive dough starts to form and no dry flour remains, about 2 minutes, scraping down bowl as needed. Cover bowl tightly with plastic and let dough rest for 20 minutes.

5 Add oil and salt to dough and knead on medium-low speed until dough is smooth and elastic and clears sides of bowl but sticks to bottom, about 5 minutes. Transfer dough to lightly greased large bowl or container, cover tightly with plastic, and let rise for 30 minutes.

6 Using greased bowl scraper (or your fingertips), fold dough over itself by gently lifting and folding edge of dough toward middle. Turn bowl 45 degrees and fold dough again; repeat turning bowl and folding dough 6 more times (total of 8 folds). Cover tightly with plastic and let rise for 30 minutes. Repeat folding and rising. Fold dough again, then cover bowl tightly with plastic and let dough rise until nearly doubled in size, 1 to 1½ hours.

continued

troubleshooting

problem The wheat berries don't completely break down.

solution Soak the berries for at least 12 hours.

Hard wheat berries need to be fully hydrated before you can grind them to a mash in the food processor. To ensure fine results, don't undercut the 12-hour soaking period. This wait also has other bonuses. Soaking the whole grain softens its bran, giving your bread good structure for a nice texture. It also unlocks flavorful sugars in the grain.

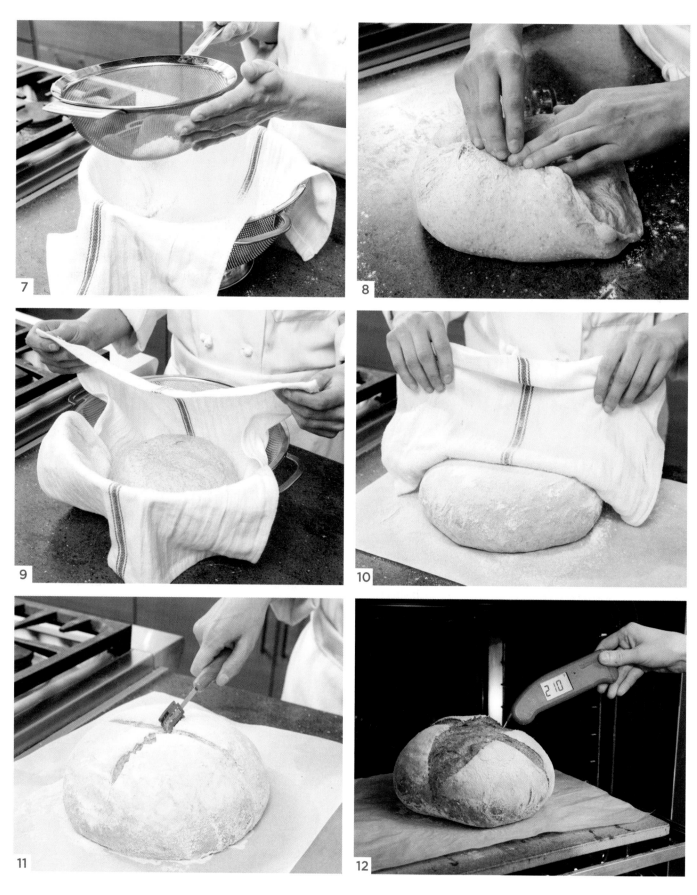

rustic wheat berry bread, continued

7 Mist underside of large linen or cotton tea towel with water. Line 5-quart colander with towel and dust evenly with flour. Transfer dough to lightly floured counter (side of dough that was against bowl should now be against counter). Press and stretch dough into 10-inch round, deflating any gas pockets larger than 1 inch.

8 Working around circumference of dough, fold edges toward center until ball forms. Flip dough ball seam side down and, using your cupped hands, drag in small circles on counter until dough feels taut and round and all seams are secured on underside of loaf.

9 Place loaf seam side up in prepared colander and pinch any remaining seams closed. Loosely fold edges of towel over loaf to enclose, then place colander in large plastic garbage bag. Tie, or fold under, open end of bag to fully enclose. Let rise until loaf increases in size by about half and dough springs back minimally when poked gently with your knuckle, 30 minutes to 1 hour (remove loaf from bag to test).

10 One hour before baking, adjust oven racks to lower-middle and lowest positions. Place baking stone on upper rack, place 2 disposable aluminum pie plates filled with 1 quart lava rocks each on lower rack, and heat oven to 450 degrees. Bring 1 cup water to boil. Remove colander from plastic bag, unfold edges of towel, and dust top of loaf with flour. (If any seams have reopened, pinch closed before dusting with flour.) Lay 16 by 12-inch sheet of parchment paper on top of loaf. Using 1 hand to support parchment and loaf, invert loaf onto parchment and place on counter. Gently remove colander and towel. Transfer parchment with loaf to pizza peel.

11 Carefully pour ½ cup boiling water into 1 disposable pie plate of preheated rocks and close oven door for 1 minute to create steam. Meanwhile, holding lame concave side up at 30-degree angle to loaf, make two 7-inch-long, ½-inch-deep slashes with swift, fluid motion along top of loaf to form cross.

12 Working quickly, slide parchment with loaf onto baking stone and pour remaining ½ cup boiling water into second disposable pie plate of preheated rocks. Bake until crust is dark brown and loaf registers 205 to 210 degrees, 35 to 40 minutes, rotating loaf halfway through baking. Transfer loaf to wire rack, discard parchment, and let cool completely, about 3 hours, before serving.

troubleshooting

problem Whole wheat berries are unavailable.

solution Substitute whole-wheat flour.

Grinding your own wheat berries for this bread will give the loaf superlative flavor. But to make this rustic whole-wheat bread without the berries, simply substitute an equal weight amount of store-bought whole-wheat flour for the wheat berries. Soak the flour in the water for the 12 hours specified for the wheat berries, skip processing, and stir the mixture into the sponge as directed in step 4. The soaker will be slightly thicker than if it had been made with wheat berries, but it will still incorporate easily into the sponge.

cheddar and black pepper bread

makes 1 loaf
resting time 6 hours 20 minutes
rising time 3½ to 4½ hours
baking time 35 minutes
total time 11½ to 12½ hours, plus 3 hours cooling time
key equipment water-filled spray bottle, large linen towel, 5-quart colander, baking stone, 2 (9-inch) disposable aluminum pie plates, 2 quarts lava rocks, pizza peel, lame, instant-read thermometer

why this recipe works We loved the idea of a yeasted cheese bread. We imagined something decadent, featuring bold cheddar flavor and a lingering finish of complementary black pepper. We wanted a rustic loaf that we could cut into generous chunks to dunk into a bowl of homey tomato soup. Big cheese flavor was a must, but to load our loaf with the most cheese, we had to hurdle a few obstacles. We started by kneading a generous amount of shredded cheddar into the dough, but this produced a crumb that was very delicate. That's because the fatty cheese coated the gluten strands, preventing them from linking up. Next, we tried spiraling the shredded cheese into the dough by rolling the dough into a square, sprinkling it with shredded cheese, forming the dough into a jelly roll, and then coiling the roll. This created pockets of melted cheese throughout, which we loved, but the crumb itself no longer had flavor. More problematic, excess melting cheese busted out of the loaf and oozed grease from the bread, smoking up the oven. To get the best of both worlds—a flavorful crumb and pockets of melted cheese—we kneaded just half of the cheese into the bread and then spiraled in the remaining cheese for gooey goodness that didn't escape. Look for a cheddar aged for about one year. (Avoid cheddar aged for longer; it won't melt well.) Use the large holes of a box grater to shred the cheddar. You can substitute a round *banneton*, or proofing basket, for the towel-lined colander. (For more information on bannetons, see page 37.)

sponge
⅔ cup (3⅔ ounces) bread flour
½ cup (4 ounces) water, room temperature
⅛ teaspoon instant or rapid-rise yeast

dough
2⅓ cups (12¾ ounces) bread flour
1¼ teaspoons instant or rapid-rise yeast
1¼ teaspoons coarsely ground pepper
1 cup (8 ounces) water, room temperature
2 teaspoons salt
8 ounces cheddar cheese, shredded, room temperature (2 cups)

continued

cheddar and black pepper bread, continued

1 **For the sponge** Stir all ingredients in 4-cup liquid measuring cup with wooden spoon until well combined. Cover tightly with plastic wrap and let sit at room temperature until sponge has risen and begins to collapse, about 6 hours (sponge can sit at room temperature for up to 24 hours).

2 **For the dough** Whisk flour, yeast, and ¾ teaspoon pepper together in bowl of stand mixer. Stir water into sponge with wooden spoon until well combined. Using dough hook on low speed, slowly add sponge mixture to flour mixture and mix until cohesive dough starts to form and no dry flour remains, about 2 minutes, scraping down bowl as needed. Cover bowl tightly with plastic and let dough rest for 20 minutes.

3 Add salt to dough and knead on medium-low speed until dough is smooth and elastic and clears sides of bowl, about 5 minutes. Reduce speed to low, slowly add 1 cup cheddar, ¼ cup at a time, and mix until just incorporated, about 30 seconds. Transfer dough to lightly greased large bowl or container, cover tightly with plastic, and let rise for 30 minutes.

4 Using greased bowl scraper (or your fingertips), fold dough over itself by gently lifting and folding edge of dough toward middle. Turn bowl 45 degrees and fold dough again; repeat turning bowl and folding dough 6 more times (total of 8 folds). Cover tightly with plastic and let rise for 30 minutes. Repeat folding and rising every 30 minutes, 3 more times. After fourth set of folds, cover bowl tightly with plastic and let dough rise until nearly doubled in size, 1 to 1½ hours.

5 Mist underside of large linen or cotton tea towel with water. Line 5-quart colander with towel and dust evenly with flour. Transfer dough to lightly floured counter (side of dough that was against bowl should now be against counter). Press and stretch dough into 10-inch square, deflating any gas pockets larger than 1 inch.

6 Sprinkle remaining 1 cup cheddar evenly over dough, leaving ½-inch border around edges. Roll dough away from you into snug cylinder. Pinch seam closed.

continued

troubleshooting

problem The bread is greasy or grainy.

solution Use a young cheddar.

Extra-sharp, long-aged cheddars may have great flavor—in fact, we use extra-sharp cheddar in our Quick Cheese Bread (page 41)—but they simply won't work in this yeasted bread. Cut into cubes for our quick bread, the cheese doesn't cause much of a problem. But aged cheddars have a tendency to separate when they melt, marring the loaf with swirls of crumbly, dry cheese and causing grease to spill out. Why? The moisture level of a cheese dictates how well it melts, and this decreases with age. When a young, moist cheese is heated, its casein (the primary protein in cheese) matrix remains intact and holds on to fat. But as a cheese ages and dries out, its casein binds more tightly together, making it more difficult to liquefy. When the clumpy bonded structure finally does break down, it is unable to contain the fat, so it leaks out.

7 Turn cylinder seam side up and roll away from you into snug spiral, ending with tail end on bottom. Pinch side seams together to seal.

8 Using your cupped hands, drag dough in small circles on counter until dough feels taut and round and all seams are secured on underside of loaf. (Some cheese may become exposed.)

9 Place loaf seam side up in prepared colander and pinch any remaining seams closed. Loosely fold edges of towel over loaf to enclose, then place colander in large plastic garbage bag. Tie, or fold under, open end of bag to fully enclose. Let rise until loaf increases in size by about half and dough springs back minimally when poked gently with your knuckle, 30 minutes to 1 hour (remove loaf from bag to test).

10 One hour before baking, adjust oven racks to lower-middle and lowest positions. Place baking stone on upper rack, place 2 disposable aluminum pie plates filled with 1 quart lava rocks each on lower rack, and heat oven to 450 degrees. Bring 1 cup water to boil. Remove colander from garbage bag, unfold edges of towel, and dust top of loaf with flour. (If any seams have reopened, pinch closed before dusting with flour.) Lay 16 by 12-inch sheet of parchment paper on top of loaf. Using 1 hand to support parchment and loaf, invert loaf onto parchment and place on counter. Gently remove colander and towel. Transfer parchment with loaf to pizza peel.

11 Carefully pour ½ cup boiling water into 1 disposable pie plate of preheated rocks and close oven door for 1 minute to create steam. Meanwhile, holding lame concave side up at 30-degree angle to loaf, make two 7-inch-long, ½-inch-deep slashes with swift, fluid motion along top of loaf to form cross. Sprinkle top of loaf with remaining ½ teaspoon pepper.

12 Working quickly, slide parchment with loaf onto baking stone and pour remaining ½ cup boiling water into second disposable pie plate of preheated rocks. Bake until crust is dark brown and loaf registers 205 to 210 degrees, 35 to 40 minutes, rotating loaf halfway through baking. Transfer loaf to wire rack, discard parchment, and let cool completely, about 3 hours, before serving.

troubleshooting

problem The cheese bursts out of the top of the loaf.

solution Slash the loaf with a cross.

For the other breads in this chapter, you can either adorn the top with the simple slashing directions provided (a cross for round loaves, or boules, and three diagonal slashes for long loaves, or bâtards), or you can choose one of the more decorative, advanced designs on page 36. But for our Cheddar and Black Pepper Bread, you'll want to stick to the cross. More intricate designs cause this complexly spiraled loaf to expand irregularly, resulting in cheese oozing out of the bread.

caramelized onion bread

makes 1 loaf
cooking time 17 minutes
resting time 6 hours 20 minutes
rising time 3¼ to 4¼ hours
baking time 45 minutes
total time 11½ to 12½ hours, plus 3 hours cooling time
key equipment 12-inch nonstick skillet, water-filled spray bottle, large linen towel, 5-quart colander, baking stone, 2 (9-inch) disposable aluminum pie plates, 2 quarts lava rocks, pizza peel, lame, instant-read thermometer

why this recipe works Flavor-packed caramelized onions are one of our favorite ingredients. So we dreamed of incorporating them into a crusty, chewy, artisan-style loaf with a sweet-and-savory profile. For concentrated onion flavor, we loaded 3 cups of onions into the recipe; along with brown sugar, thyme, and garlic, they cooked down to a deep golden brown. Finely chopped onions worked best—larger pieces left us with soggy pockets of uncooked dough surrounding the onions after baking. However, we found it difficult to mix such a large volume into the dough at the end of kneading; the slippery onions just slid off of the developed dough. To solve this problem, we mixed half of the onions with the wet ingredients at the beginning of mixing, where they incorporated easily and broke down during kneading to lend more flavor to the crumb. We reserved the remaining half to mix in at the end of kneading, which was just the right amount to incorporate evenly and provide textural contrast. Yellow onions are our favorite variety here; they offer a good balance of flavor and a firm but yielding texture. You can use white or red onions, but they vary in flavor. Vidalia onions have a high water content and make the dough too wet. You can substitute a round *banneton*, or proofing basket, for the towel-lined colander. (For more information on bannetons, see page 37.) For a more decorative crust, you can slash this loaf in step 11 using either of the techniques shown on page 36.

sponge
⅔ cup (3⅔ ounces) bread flour
½ cup (4 ounces) water, room temperature
⅛ teaspoon instant or rapid-rise yeast

dough
2 tablespoons extra-virgin olive oil
3 cups finely chopped onions
2 garlic cloves, minced
2 teaspoons minced fresh thyme or ½ teaspoon dried
2 teaspoons packed brown sugar
Salt and pepper
2⅓ cups (12¾ ounces) bread flour
1¼ teaspoons instant or rapid-rise yeast
¾ cup plus 2 tablespoons (7 ounces) water, room temperature

continued

caramelized onion bread, continued

1 For the sponge Stir all ingredients in 4-cup liquid measuring cup with wooden spoon until well combined. Cover tightly with plastic wrap and let sit at room temperature until sponge has risen and begins to collapse, about 6 hours (sponge can sit at room temperature for up to 24 hours).

2 For the dough Heat oil in 12-inch nonstick skillet over medium heat until shimmering. Stir in onions, garlic, thyme, sugar, ½ teaspoon salt, and ¼ teaspoon pepper. Cover and cook, stirring occasionally, until onions are softened and have released their juice, 3 to 5 minutes. Remove lid and continue to cook, stirring often, until juice evaporates and onions are deep golden brown, 10 to 15 minutes. Transfer onion mixture to bowl and let cool completely before using.

3 Whisk flour and yeast together in bowl of stand mixer. Stir water and half of onion mixture into sponge with wooden spoon until well combined. Using dough hook on low speed, slowly add sponge mixture to flour mixture and mix until cohesive dough starts to form and no dry flour remains, about 2 minutes, scraping down bowl as needed. Cover bowl tightly with plastic and let dough rest for 20 minutes.

4 Add 1½ teaspoons salt to dough and knead on medium-low speed until dough is smooth and elastic and clears sides of bowl, about 5 minutes. Reduce speed to low, slowly add remaining onion mixture, 1 tablespoon at a time, and mix until mostly incorporated, about 1 minute. Transfer dough to lightly greased large bowl or container, cover tightly with plastic, and let rise for 30 minutes.

5 Using greased bowl scraper (or your fingertips), fold dough over itself by gently lifting and folding edge of dough toward middle. Turn bowl 45 degrees and fold dough again; repeat turning bowl and folding dough 6 more times (total of 8 folds). Cover tightly with plastic and let rise for 30 minutes. Repeat folding and rising. Fold dough again, then cover bowl tightly with plastic and let dough rise until nearly doubled in size, 45 minutes to 1¼ hours.

6 Mist underside of large linen or cotton tea towel with water. Line 5-quart colander with towel and dust evenly with flour. Transfer dough to lightly floured counter (side of dough that was against bowl should now be against counter). Press and stretch dough into 10-inch round, deflating any gas pockets larger than 1 inch.

continued

troubleshooting

problem The bread is gummy.

solution Use the right onion variety.

Onions vary in flavor, yes, but also in moisture content. We had success using yellow, white, and red onions in this bread (though tasters preferred the flavor of yellow onions), but our bread spread and had a gummy crumb when we tried using supersweet Vidalia onions. Vidalia onions have a high moisture content and therefore increased the hydration level of our dough.

7 Working around circumference of dough, fold edges toward center until ball forms. Flip dough ball seam side down and, using your cupped hands, drag in small circles on counter until dough feels taut and round and all seams are secured on underside of loaf.

8 Place loaf seam side up in prepared colander and pinch any remaining seams closed. Loosely fold edges of towel over loaf to enclose, then place colander in large plastic garbage bag. Tie, or fold under, open end of bag to fully enclose. Let rise until loaf increases in size by about half and dough springs back minimally when poked gently with your knuckle, 1 to 1½ hours (remove loaf from bag to test).

9 One hour before baking, adjust oven racks to lower-middle and lowest positions. Place baking stone on upper rack, place 2 disposable aluminum pie plates filled with 1 quart lava rocks each on lower rack, and heat oven to 425 degrees. Bring 1 cup water to boil.

10 Remove colander from bag, unfold edges of towel, and dust top of loaf with flour. (If any seams have reopened, pinch closed before dusting with flour.) Lay 16 by 12-inch sheet of parchment paper on top of loaf. Using 1 hand to support parchment and loaf, invert loaf onto parchment and place on counter. Gently remove colander and towel. Transfer parchment with loaf to pizza peel.

11 Carefully pour ½ cup boiling water into 1 disposable pie plate of preheated rocks and close oven door for 1 minute to create steam. Meanwhile, holding lame concave side up at 30-degree angle to loaf, make two 7-inch-long, ½-inch-deep slashes with swift, fluid motion along top of loaf to form cross.

12 Working quickly, slide parchment with loaf onto baking stone and pour remaining ½ cup boiling water into second disposable pie plate of preheated rocks. Bake until crust is dark brown and loaf registers 205 to 210 degrees, 45 to 50 minutes, rotating loaf halfway through baking. Transfer loaf to wire rack, discard parchment, and let cool completely, about 3 hours, before serving.

troubleshooting

problem The onions don't incorporate.

solution Add the onions in two batches.

If you add all of the caramelized onions at the end of mixing, like we often do for other bread mix-ins like olives or dried fruit, the mass of slippery pieces will fail to get incorporated and will just fall off of the dough. Instead, add half to the dough at the beginning with the wet ingredients to flavor the crumb, and the remaining half at the end to add texture.

upping your game with sponges

fig and fennel bread

makes 1 loaf
resting time 6 hours 20 minutes
rising time 3½ to 4½ hours
baking time 40 minutes
total time 12 to 13 hours, plus 3 hours cooling time
key equipment couche, water-filled spray bottle, rimmed baking sheet, baking stone, 2 (9-inch) disposable aluminum pie plates, 2 quarts lava rocks, pizza peel, flipping board, lame, instant-read thermometer

why this recipe works Having mastered many of the techniques for creating the ideal structure, chew, and flavor in our breads, we put our heads together to come up with a novel artisan-style bread to wow company. We wanted a grown-up loaf to accompany cheese and charcuterie plates, and we agreed that the sophisticated combination of sweet, earthy figs and complementary fennel was a distinguished flavor profile. Simply folding chopped dried figs and fennel seeds into a white loaf worked, but the bread was timid, so we swapped out some of the bread flour for rye flour, which added interest. As we learned when developing our recipe for Pain de Campagne (page 303), mixing more of the dough's total flour weight into the sponge gave us even more depth of flavor and structure, which was beneficial to our rye-enhanced loaf. Using precisely 32 percent of the flour in this sponge gave the bread the best chew; any less and the bread was too delicate. Happy with the texture and refined flavors of our bread, we turned our attention to the crust. To develop a more rustic appearance and a unique crunch, we rolled the loaf in cornmeal before its final proof. While any variety of dried figs will work, we especially liked the flavor of Calimyrna figs in this bread. Use light or medium rye flour; dark rye flour is overpowering. Toast the fennel seeds in a dry skillet over medium heat until fragrant (about 1 minute), and then remove the pan from the heat so the fennel seeds don't scorch. For a more decorative crust, you can slash this loaf in step 11 using either of the techniques shown on page 36.

sponge

1 cup (5½ ounces) bread flour

¾ cup (6 ounces) water, room temperature

⅛ teaspoon instant or rapid-rise yeast

dough

1 cup plus 2 tablespoons (6¼ ounces) bread flour

1 cup (5½ ounces) light or medium rye flour

1½ teaspoons instant or rapid-rise yeast

1 cup (8 ounces) water, room temperature

1 tablespoon fennel seeds, toasted

2 teaspoons salt

1 cup dried figs, stemmed and chopped coarse

cornmeal

continued

fig and fennel bread, continued

1 **For the sponge** Stir all ingredients in 4-cup liquid measuring cup with wooden spoon until well combined. Cover tightly with plastic wrap and let sit at room temperature until sponge has risen and begins to collapse, about 6 hours (sponge can sit at room temperature for up to 24 hours).

2 **For the dough** Whisk bread flour, rye flour, and yeast together in bowl of stand mixer. Stir water into sponge with wooden spoon until well combined. Using dough hook on low speed, slowly add sponge mixture to flour mixture and mix until cohesive dough starts to form and no dry flour remains, about 2 minutes, scraping down bowl as needed. Cover bowl tightly with plastic and let dough rest for 20 minutes.

3 Add fennel seeds and salt to dough and knead on medium-low speed until dough is smooth, elastic, and slightly sticky, about 5 minutes. Reduce speed to low, slowly add figs, ¼ cup at a time, and mix until mostly incorporated, about 1 minute. Transfer dough to lightly greased large bowl or container, cover tightly with plastic, and let rise for 30 minutes.

4 Using greased bowl scraper (or your fingertips), fold dough over itself by gently lifting and folding edge of dough toward middle. Turn bowl 45 degrees and fold dough again; repeat turning bowl and folding dough 6 more times (total of 8 folds). Cover tightly with plastic and let rise for 30 minutes. Repeat folding and rising every 30 minutes, 3 more times. After fourth set of folds, cover bowl tightly with plastic and let dough rise until nearly doubled in size, 1 to 1½ hours.

5 Mist underside of couche with water, drape over inverted rimmed baking sheet, and dust liberally and evenly with cornmeal. Transfer dough to lightly floured counter (side of dough that was against bowl should now be against counter). Press and stretch dough into 10-inch square, deflating any gas pockets larger than 1 inch.

6 Fold top and bottom corners of dough diagonally into center of square and press gently to seal. Stretch and fold upper and bottom thirds of dough toward center and press gently to seal.

continued

troubleshooting

problem The flavor of the loaf is overpowering.

solution **Use the right rye flour.**

Don't use just any rye flour you see for this recipe. Rye flour comes in several varieties. We use light or medium rye flour in this recipe. Dark or pumpernickel varieties overwhelm the flavors of the fig and fennel and make the crumb taste too intense. (For more information on rye flour, see page 6).

problem The figs don't incorporate.

solution **Add the figs slowly.**

Even once chopped, the figs will bounce around the mixer bowl and fail to make their way into the dough if you don't add them slowly. With the mixer on low speed, add the figs to the kneaded dough just ¼ cup at a time.

problem The loaf is amorphous.

solution **Reshape the loaf after transferring it to the peel.**

This big loaf gets its sophisticated bâtard shape from being formed into a long diamond. Inevitably, the taut shape will become slightly undone when the loaf is flipped from the couche onto the pizza peel. Be sure to reshape the loaf on the peel so it has a taut shape and can rise evenly in the oven.

7 Stretch and fold dough in half toward you to form rough 12 by 5-inch diamond-shaped loaf, and pinch seam.

8 Gently slide your hands underneath each end of loaf and transfer seam side up to prepared couche. On either side of loaf, pinch couche into pleat, then fold remaining edges of couche over loaf to cover completely. Carefully place sheet inside large plastic garbage bag. Tie, or fold under, open end of bag to fully enclose. Let rise until loaf increases in size by about half and dough springs back minimally when poked gently with your knuckle, 30 minutes to 1 hour (remove loaf from bag to test).

9 One hour before baking, adjust oven racks to lower-middle and lowest positions. Place baking stone on upper rack, place 2 disposable aluminum pie plates filled with 1 quart lava rocks each on lower rack, and heat oven to 450 degrees. Line pizza peel with 16 by 12-inch piece of parchment paper, with long edge perpendicular to handle. Bring 1 cup water to boil.

10 Remove sheet with loaf from bag. Unfold couche, pulling from ends to remove pleats. Dust top of loaf with cornmeal. (If any seams have reopened, pinch closed before dusting with cornmeal.) Gently pushing with side of flipping board, roll loaf over so it is seam side down. Using your hand, hold long edge of flipping board between loaf and couche at 45-degree angle, then lift couche with your other hand and flip loaf seam side up onto board. Invert loaf seam side down onto prepared pizza peel. Reshape loaf as needed, tucking edges under to form taut diamond shape.

11 Carefully pour ½ cup boiling water into 1 disposable pie plate of preheated rocks and close oven door for 1 minute to create steam. Meanwhile, holding lame concave side up at 30-degree angle to loaf, make three 6-inch-long, ½-inch-deep diagonal slashes with swift, fluid motion across top of loaf, starting and stopping about ½ inch from edges and spacing slashes about 2 inches apart.

12 Working quickly, slide parchment with loaf onto baking stone and pour remaining ½ cup boiling water into second pie plate of preheated rocks. Bake until crust is dark brown and loaf registers 205 to 210 degrees, 40 to 45 minutes, rotating loaf halfway through baking. Transfer loaf to wire rack, discard parchment, and let cool completely, about 3 hours, before serving.

sage-polenta bread

makes 1 loaf
cooking time 7 minutes
resting time 6 hours 20 minutes
rising time 2 to 2½ hours
baking time 45 minutes
total time 10¼ to 10¾ hours, plus 3 hours cooling time
key equipment small saucepan, couche, water-filled spray bottle, rimmed baking sheet, baking stone, 2 (9-inch) disposable aluminum pie plates, 2 quarts lava rocks, pizza peel, flipping board, lame, instant-read thermometer

why this recipe works We thought the savory corn flavor and toothsome texture of polenta would be an interesting addition to an Italian loaf for the dinner table. To start our development, we had to determine what type of polenta to use and how best to add it to the dough. We tested both raw instant polenta (which is ground finely and preprocessed for quicker cooking) and traditional coarse-ground polenta, which we added raw as well as cooked into porridge. Instant polenta yielded a disastrous loaf, as the finely ground grains sucked up the available water in the dough, leaving the loaf chalky and dry. Coarse-ground polenta was much more successful; incorporated dry, however, it remained gritty in the loaf. Polenta cooked for just a few minutes on the stovetop offered a soft, pillowy texture with just the right amount of chew. Since polenta increases dramatically in volume once it's cooked, we found we could not stir all of it into the dough after kneading. Instead, we added it in two stages, incorporating half with the wet ingredients at the beginning of mixing, and the remaining half at the end. This method resulted in pleasant pockets of cooked polenta swirled throughout a hearty loaf. In keeping with the Italian flavors, we added fresh sage to the dough, which brought out the polenta's savory notes. Finally, we coated the loaf with dry polenta, which gave the bread a crunchy, golden exterior. Do not substitute instant polenta or prepared polenta (sold in a tube) here. For a more decorative crust, you can slash this loaf in step 11 using either of the techniques shown on page 36.

sponge
⅔ cup (3⅔ ounces) bread flour
½ cup (4 ounces) water, room temperature
¼ teaspoon instant or rapid-rise yeast

dough
1¼ cups plus 2 tablespoons (11 ounces) water, room temperature
¼ cup (1¼ ounces) plus 1 tablespoon coarse-ground polenta
2⅓ cups (12¾ ounces) bread flour
2¼ teaspoons instant or rapid-rise yeast
2 tablespoons extra-virgin olive oil
4 teaspoons minced fresh sage
1½ teaspoons salt

continued

1 **For the sponge** Stir all ingredients in 4-cup liquid measuring cup with wooden spoon until well combined. Cover tightly with plastic wrap and let sit at room temperature until sponge has risen and begins to collapse, about 6 hours (sponge can sit at room temperature for up to 24 hours).

2 **For the dough** Bring ¾ cup water and ¼ cup polenta to simmer in small saucepan over medium heat and cook, stirring frequently, until polenta is softened and water is completely absorbed, about 3 minutes; let cool completely before using.

3 Whisk flour and yeast together in bowl of stand mixer. Break cooked polenta into small pieces with wooden spoon. Stir half of polenta and remaining water into sponge until well combined. Using dough hook on low speed, slowly add sponge mixture to flour mixture and mix until cohesive dough starts to form and no dry flour remains, about 2 minutes, scraping down bowl as needed. Cover bowl tightly with plastic and let dough rest for 20 minutes.

4 Add oil, sage, and salt to dough and knead on medium-low speed until dough is smooth and elastic and clears sides of bowl, about 5 minutes. Reduce speed to low, slowly add remaining cooked polenta, 1 tablespoon at a time, and mix until mostly incorporated, about 1 minute. Transfer dough to lightly greased large bowl or container, cover tightly with plastic, and let rise for 30 minutes.

5 Using greased bowl scraper (or your fingertips), fold dough over itself by gently lifting and folding edge of dough toward middle. Turn bowl 45 degrees and fold dough again; repeat turning bowl and folding dough 6 more times (total of 8 folds). Cover tightly with plastic and let rise for 30 minutes. Repeat folding, then cover bowl tightly with plastic and let dough rise until nearly doubled in size, 30 minutes to 1 hour.

6 Mist underside of couche with water and drape over inverted rimmed baking sheet. Dust couche evenly with flour, then sprinkle with remaining polenta. Transfer dough to lightly floured counter (side of dough that was against bowl should now be against counter). Press and stretch dough into 10-inch square, deflating any gas pockets larger than 1 inch. Fold top and bottom corners of dough diagonally into center of square and press gently to seal.

continued

troubleshooting

problem The loaf is dry and coarse.

solution Don't use instant polenta.

We tested various polenta varieties for our recipe and found that you can't just use what you have on hand. Instant polenta yielded a very dry, chalky loaf of bread. Why? The grains for instant polenta are ground so fine that they suck up all of the available water in the dough. That water not only moistens the loaf, it helps bolster the gluten structure so the polenta-packed loaf has chew. In addition to using coarse-ground polenta, we found that it's best to cook the polenta before adding it to the dough for bread with just the right chewy-soft texture.

7 Stretch and fold upper and bottom thirds of dough toward center and press gently to seal. Stretch and fold dough in half toward you to form rough 12 by 4½-inch diamond-shaped loaf, and pinch seam closed.

8 Gently slide your hands underneath each end of loaf and transfer seam side up to prepared couche. On either side of loaf, pinch couche into pleat, then fold remaining edges of couche over loaf to cover completely. Carefully place sheet inside large plastic garbage bag. Tie, or fold under, open end of bag to fully enclose. Let rise until loaf increases in size by about half and dough springs back minimally when poked gently with your knuckle, about 30 minutes (remove loaf from bag to test).

9 One hour before baking, adjust oven racks to lower-middle and lowest positions. Place baking stone on upper rack, place 2 disposable aluminum pie plates filled with 1 quart lava rocks each on lower rack, and heat oven to 425 degrees. Line pizza peel with 16 by 12-inch piece of parchment paper, with long edge perpendicular to handle. Bring 1 cup water to boil.

10 Remove sheet with loaf from bag. Unfold couche, pulling from ends to remove pleats. Dust top of loaf with flour. (If any seams have reopened, pinch closed before dusting with flour.) Gently pushing with side of flipping board, roll loaf over so it is seam side down. Using your hand, hold long edge of flipping board between loaf and couche at 45-degree angle, then lift couche with your other hand and flip loaf seam side up onto board. Invert loaf seam side down onto prepared pizza peel. Reshape loaf as needed, tucking edges under to form taut diamond shape.

11 Carefully pour ½ cup boiling water into 1 disposable pie plate of preheated rocks and close oven door for 1 minute to create steam. Meanwhile, holding lame concave side up at 30-degree angle to loaf, make three 6-inch-long, ½-inch-deep diagonal slashes with swift, fluid motion across top of loaf, starting and stopping about ½ inch from edges and spacing slashes about 2 inches apart.

12 Working quickly, slide parchment with loaf onto baking stone and pour remaining ½ cup boiling water into second disposable pie plate of preheated rocks. Bake until crust is deep golden brown and loaf registers 205 to 210 degrees, 45 to 50 minutes, rotating loaf halfway through baking. Transfer loaf to wire rack, discard parchment, and let cool completely, about 3 hours, before serving.

honey-spelt bread

makes 1 loaf
resting time 12 hours 20 minutes
rising time 2½ to 3 hours
baking time 30 minutes
total time 16½ to 17 hours, plus 3 hours cooling time
key equipment food processor, couche, water-filled spray bottle, rimmed baking sheet, baking stone, 2 (9-inch) disposable aluminum pie plates, 2 quarts lava rocks, pizza peel, flipping board, lame, instant-read thermometer

why this recipe works Spelt is an ancient grain—it's a cousin of modern wheat but has been cultivated for more than 8,000 years. In ancient Greek mythology, the goddess Demeter gifted spelt to the Greeks, who then taught other civilizations how to grow it and cook with it. Spelt's popularity spread throughout Central Europe during the Bronze and Iron Ages, and remains popular there today. Cultivation of spelt was eventually largely replaced by modern wheat, but the grain has recently experienced a resurgence in popularity. Hardier and nuttier than common wheat, spelt lends a rich, sweet flavor to baked goods. Because of its high water solubility, its nutrients are also more quickly absorbed by the body, making it a healthful grain full of fiber, protein, and vitamins. We wanted to make a delicious rustic bread that would take advantage of this unique grain's qualities. For superior flavor, we followed the lead of our Rustic Wheat Berry Bread (page 308) and made our own spelt flour by soaking whole spelt berries overnight to soften their hard outer shells, and then pureeing them into a mash. Combining the spelt with some bread flour gave us a sturdy loaf with wheaty flavor and a pleasant chew. This loaf tasted great, but we thought that the addition of honey could complement the earthy grain. A full quarter cup enhanced the spelt's natural sweetness and gave the loaf a deep brown color, bringing this ancient grain into the modern age. You can find whole spelt berries in the natural- or bulk-foods section of the grocery store. For a more decorative crust, you can slash this loaf in step 11 using any of the techniques shown on page 36.

soaker

1¼ cups (8 ounces) spelt berries

1 cup (8 ounces) water, room temperature

sponge

¾ cup (4⅛ ounces) bread flour

½ cup (4 ounces) water, room temperature

¼ teaspoon instant or rapid-rise yeast

dough

1 cup (5½ ounces) bread flour

2½ teaspoons instant or rapid-rise yeast

¼ cup (3 ounces) honey

1 tablespoon extra-virgin olive oil

1½ teaspoons salt

continued

honey-spelt bread, continued

1 For the soaker Combine spelt berries and water in bowl, cover tightly with plastic wrap, and let sit at room temperature until grains are fully hydrated and softened, at least 12 hours or up to 24 hours.

2 For the sponge Stir all ingredients in 4-cup liquid measuring cup with wooden spoon until well combined. Cover tightly with plastic wrap and let sit at room temperature until sponge has risen and begins to collapse, about 6 hours (sponge can sit at room temperature for up to 24 hours).

3 For the dough Whisk flour and yeast together in bowl of stand mixer. Process soaked spelt berries and remaining soaking liquid in food processor until grains are finely ground, about 4 minutes, scraping down sides of bowl as needed. Stir spelt berry mixture and honey into sponge with wooden spoon until well combined. Using dough hook on low speed, slowly add sponge mixture to flour mixture and mix until cohesive dough starts to form and no dry flour remains, about 2 minutes, scraping down bowl as needed. Cover bowl tightly with plastic and let dough rest for 20 minutes.

4 Add oil and salt to dough and knead on medium-low speed until dough is smooth and elastic and clears sides of bowl but sticks to bottom, about 5 minutes. Transfer dough to lightly greased large bowl or container, cover tightly with plastic, and let rise for 30 minutes.

5 Using greased bowl scraper (or your fingertips), fold dough over itself by gently lifting and folding edge of dough toward middle. Turn bowl 45 degrees and fold dough again; repeat turning bowl and folding dough 6 more times (total of 8 folds). Cover tightly with plastic and let rise for 30 minutes. Repeat folding, then cover bowl tightly with plastic and let dough rise until nearly doubled in size, 1 to 1½ hours.

6 Mist underside of couche with water, drape over inverted rimmed baking sheet, and dust evenly with flour. Transfer dough to lightly floured counter (side of dough that was against bowl should now be against counter). Press and stretch dough into 10-inch square, deflating any gas pockets larger than 1 inch. Fold top and bottom corners of dough diagonally into center of square and press gently to seal.

continued

troubleshooting

problem Whole spelt berries are not available.

solution Substitute spelt flour.

Just like in our Rustic Wheat Berry Bread recipe (page 308), if you cannot find whole spelt berries for this recipe, you can substitute an equal weight amount of store-bought spelt flour, though the sweet wheat flavor will be less deep. Soak the flour in the water for the 12 hours specified for the spelt berries, skip processing, and stir the mixture into the sponge as directed in step 3.

7 Stretch and fold upper and bottom thirds of dough toward center and press gently to seal. Stretch and fold dough in half toward you to form rough 12 by 5-inch diamond-shaped loaf, and pinch seam closed.

8 Gently slide your hands underneath each end of loaf and transfer seam side up to prepared couche. On either side of loaf, pinch couche into pleat, then fold remaining edges of couche over loaf to cover completely. Carefully place sheet inside large plastic garbage bag. Tie, or fold under, open end of bag to fully enclose. Let rise until loaf increases in size by about half and dough springs back minimally when poked gently with your knuckle, about 30 minutes (remove loaf from bag to test).

9 One hour before baking, adjust oven racks to lower-middle and lowest positions. Place baking stone on upper rack, place 2 disposable aluminum pie plates filled with 1 quart lava rocks each on lower rack, and heat oven to 450 degrees. Line pizza peel with 16 by 12-inch piece of parchment paper, with long edge perpendicular to handle. Bring 1 cup water to boil.

10 Remove sheet with loaf from bag. Unfold couche, pulling from ends to remove pleats. Dust top of loaf with flour. (If any seams have reopened, pinch closed before dusting with flour.) Gently pushing with side of flipping board, roll loaf over so it is seam side down. Using your hand, hold long edge of flipping board between loaf and couche at 45-degree angle, then lift couche with your other hand and flip loaf seam side up onto board. Invert loaf seam side down onto prepared pizza peel. Reshape loaf as needed, tucking edges under to form taut diamond shape.

11 Carefully pour ½ cup boiling water into 1 disposable pie plate of preheated rocks and close oven door for 1 minute to create steam. Meanwhile, holding lame concave side up at 30-degree angle to loaf, make three 6-inch-long, ½-inch-deep diagonal slashes with swift, fluid motion across top of loaf, starting and stopping about ½ inch from edges and spacing slashes about 2 inches apart.

12 Working quickly, slide parchment with loaf onto baking stone and pour remaining ½ cup boiling water into second disposable pie plate of preheated rocks. Bake until crust is dark brown and loaf registers 205 to 210 degrees, 30 to 35 minutes, rotating loaf halfway through baking. Transfer loaf to wire rack, discard parchment, and let cool completely, about 3 hours, before serving.

ciabatta

makes 2 loaves
resting time 6 hours
rising time 2 to 2½ hours
baking time 25 minutes
total time 9½ to 10 hours, plus 3 hours cooling time
key equipment stand mixer, baking stone, pizza peel, water-filled spray bottle, instant-read thermometer

why this recipe works Unless your source is an artisanal bakery, most loaves of ciabatta just aren't very good. We wanted homemade ciabatta with an airy texture, full flavor, and perfect lift. Ciabatta, like many rustic breads, starts with a sponge. (We settled on 30 percent sponge and 70 percent dough as the ideal proportion for the right tang for this bread.) But beyond the sponge, ciabatta has unique characteristics. First, the dough is extremely wet—even more hydrated than other rustic breads—which gives this loaf its signature holes. Second, ciabatta has a light, springy texture; we achieved this by using all-purpose flour instead of the bread flour we use for most rustic breads. Because this dough is so hydrated, it's necessary to begin kneading with the stand mixer's paddle attachment instead of the dough hook, and to incorporate a series of folds to reinforce the structure and make it easier to work with. While we wanted large holes in our bread, we could end up with a loaf that was more air than bread if they were too large. In researching this problem, we found that some ciabatta recipes included milk. And indeed, ciabatta made with milk boasted unifom medium-size bubbles. Curious about why this addition worked, we learned that milk contains a protein fragment called glutathione, which weakens the gluten strands slightly. A small amount of milk reduced the size of the bubbles just enough. As you make this bread, keep in mind that the dough is wet and very sticky. The key to manipulating it is working quickly and gently; rough handling will result in flat, tough loaves. When possible, use a bowl scraper or a large rubber spatula to move the dough. If you have to use your hands, make sure they are well floured. We do not recommend mixing this dough by hand.

sponge
1 cup (5 ounces) all-purpose flour
½ cup (4 ounces) water, room temperature
⅛ teaspoon instant or rapid-rise yeast

dough
2 cups (10 ounces) all-purpose flour
1½ teaspoons salt
½ teaspoon instant or rapid-rise yeast
¾ cup (6 ounces) water, room temperature
¼ cup (2 ounces) whole milk, room temperature

continued

1 **For the sponge** Stir all ingredients in 4-cup liquid measuring cup with wooden spoon until well combined. Cover tightly with plastic wrap and let sit at room temperature until sponge has risen and begins to collapse, about 6 hours (sponge can sit at room temperature for up to 24 hours).

2 **For the dough** Whisk flour, salt, and yeast together in bowl of stand mixer. Stir water and milk into sponge with wooden spoon until well combined. Using paddle on low speed, slowly add sponge mixture to flour mixture and mix until cohesive dough starts to form and no dry flour remains, about 2 minutes, scraping down bowl as needed. Increase speed to medium-low and continue to mix until dough becomes uniform mass that collects on paddle and pulls away from sides of bowl, 4 to 6 minutes.

3 Remove paddle and fit stand mixer with dough hook. Knead on medium-low speed until dough is smooth and shiny (dough will be very sticky), about 10 minutes. Transfer dough to lightly greased large bowl or container, cover tightly with plastic, and let rise until doubled in size, 30 minutes to 1 hour.

4 Using greased bowl scraper (or rubber spatula), fold dough over itself by gently lifting and folding edge of dough toward middle. Turn bowl 45 degrees and fold dough again; repeat turning bowl and folding dough 6 more times (total of 8 folds). Cover tightly with plastic and let rise for 30 minutes. Repeat folding, then cover bowl tightly with plastic and let dough rise until nearly doubled in size, about 30 minutes.

5 One hour before baking, adjust oven racks to lower-middle and lowest positions. Place baking stone on upper rack and heat oven to 450 degrees. Dust two 12 by 6-inch pieces of parchment paper liberally with flour. Transfer dough to well-floured counter (side of dough that was against bowl should now be against counter). Liberally dust top of dough with flour and divide in half. Turn 1 piece of dough cut side up and dust with flour. Using your well-floured hands, press and stretch dough into 12 by 6-inch rectangle, with short side parallel to counter edge, being careful not to deflate dough completely.

6 Stretch and fold top and bottom thirds of dough over middle like business letter to form rough 7 by 4-inch loaf. Pinch seams closed. Transfer loaf seam side down to 1 sheet of prepared parchment and cover loosely with greased plastic. Repeat with second piece of dough. Let loaves sit until puffy and surface of loaves develops small bubbles, about 30 minutes.

7 Transfer parchment with loaves to pizza peel. Using your floured fingertips, evenly poke entire surface of each loaf to form 10 by 6-inch rectangle. Mist loaves with water.

8 Working quickly, slide each piece of parchment with loaf onto baking stone. Bake, misting loaves with water twice more during first 5 minutes of baking time, until crust is deep golden brown and loaves register 210 to 212 degrees, 25 to 30 minutes, rotating loaves halfway through baking. Transfer loaves to wire rack, discard parchment, and let cool completely, about 2 hours, before serving.

durum bread

makes 1 loaf
resting time 6 hours 20 minutes
rising time 2½ to 3 hours
baking time 30 minutes
total time 10¼ to 10¾ hours, plus 3 hours cooling time
key equipment stand mixer, baking stone, 2 (9-inch) dispos-able aluminum pie plates, 2 quarts lava rocks, pizza peel, lame, instant-read thermometer

why this recipe works Italian loaves made with durum flour boast an open, airy crumb, a warm, golden color, a chewy texture, and a sweet, nutty flavor. Most recipes call for a combination of durum and bread flours. We tested eight different ratios of the two flours (including one loaf made from 100 percent durum flour) and preferred the loaf made with 60 percent durum flour. With too much bread flour, the loaf lacked the unique color and flavor of the durum; with too much durum, the bread lost some of its pasta-like chewiness. We tested different hydration levels, and tasters universally favored the highest hydration we could work with for a chewy, open crumb: 90 percent. Though handling this clingy dough can be challenging, we found that after folding it onto itself several times during the initial proofing period, the gluten strands elongated and the dough became more supple. But the loaf was still difficult to shape. To make the process fuss-free, we trans-ferred our proofed dough directly onto a piece of floured parchment paper. A simple stretching of the dough with well-floured hands, followed by a couple of folds, yielded an elegant slipper-shaped loaf—ready to be split to make panini, sliced into pieces for bruschetta, swabbed through the juicy remnants of a meal, or even dunked into a fruity wine. Be sure to use durum flour, not semolina flour. You can find durum flour online or in specialty baking stores. As you make this bread, keep in mind that the dough is wet and very sticky. The key to manipulating it is working quickly and gently; rough handling will result in flat, tough loaves. When possible, use a bowl scraper or large rubber spatula to move the dough. If you have to use your hands, make sure they are well floured. We do not recommend mixing this dough by hand.

sponge

¾ cup (4⅛ ounces) bread flour

½ cup (4 ounces) water, room temperature

¼ teaspoon instant or rapid-rise yeast

dough

2 cups (9½ ounces) durum flour

½ cup (2¾ ounces) bread flour

2½ teaspoons instant or rapid-rise yeast

1⅓ cups (10⅔ ounces) water, room temperature

1½ teaspoons salt

continued

1 **For the sponge** Stir all ingredients in 4-cup liquid measuring cup with wooden spoon until well combined. Cover tightly with plastic wrap and let sit at room temperature until sponge has risen and begins to collapse, about 6 hours (sponge can sit at room temperature for up to 24 hours).

2 **For the dough** Whisk durum flour, bread flour, and yeast together in bowl of stand mixer. Stir water into sponge with wooden spoon until well combined. Using paddle on low speed, slowly add sponge mixture to flour mixture and mix until cohesive dough starts to form and no dry flour remains, about 2 minutes, scraping down bowl as needed. Remove paddle, cover bowl tightly with plastic, and let dough rest for 20 minutes.

3 Fit stand mixer with dough hook. Add salt to dough and knead on medium-low speed until dough is smooth and elastic and clears sides of bowl but sticks to bottom, about 5 minutes. Transfer dough to lightly greased large bowl or container, cover tightly with plastic, and let rise for 30 minutes.

4 Using greased bowl scraper (or rubber spatula), fold dough over itself by gently lifting and folding edge of toward middle. Turn bowl 45 degrees and fold dough again; repeat turning bowl and folding dough 6 more times (total of 8 folds). Cover tightly with plastic and let rise for 30 minutes. Repeat folding, then cover bowl tightly with plastic and let dough rise until nearly doubled in size, 1 to 1½ hours.

5 One hour before baking, adjust oven racks to lower-middle and lowest positions. Place baking stone on upper rack, place 2 disposable aluminum pie plates filled with 1 quart lava rocks each on lower rack, and heat oven to 450 degrees. Place 16 by 12-inch piece of parchment paper on counter, with long edge of paper parallel to counter edge, and dust liberally with bread flour. Transfer dough to prepared parchment (side of dough that was against bowl should now be against parchment). Using your well-floured hands, press and stretch dough into 14 by 9-inch rectangle, being careful not to deflate it completely.

6 Stretch and fold top and bottom thirds of dough over middle like business letter to form rough 14 by 4-inch loaf. Pinch seams closed, then flip loaf seam side down. Reshape loaf as needed, tucking edges under to form taut torpedo shape with rounded ends. Transfer parchment with loaf to pizza peel. Cover loosely with greased plastic and let rise until loaf increases in size by about half and dough springs back minimally when poked gently with your knuckle, about 30 minutes. Bring 1 cup water to boil.

7 Carefully pour ½ cup boiling water into 1 disposable pie plate of preheated rocks and close oven door for 1 minute to create steam. Meanwhile, holding lame concave side up at 30-degree angle to loaf, make one ½-inch-deep slash with swift, fluid motion lengthwise along top of loaf, starting and stopping about 1½ inches from ends.

8 Working quickly, slide parchment with loaf onto baking stone and pour remaining ½ cup boiling water into second disposable pie plate of preheated rocks. Bake until crust is deep golden brown and loaf registers 210 to 212 degrees, 30 to 35 minutes, rotating loaf halfway through baking. Transfer loaf to wire rack, discard parchment, and let cool completely, about 3 hours, before serving.

troubleshooting

problem The dough sticks.

solution Use flour liberally.

This dough is very wet for a reason—the high hydration level gives the loaf a dramatic chewy, open crumb structure. So to work around this, we don't shape this bread like we do other loaves; instead, using very well-floured hands, we stretch and fold it into shape on a very well-floured piece of parchment paper to avoid contact with the counter. Once shaped and proofed, the loaf can then be slid onto the baking stone with the floured parchment to avoid further handling.

rosemary focaccia

makes two 9-inch round loaves
resting time 7 hours
rising time 1½ to 2 hours
baking time 25 minutes
total time 9¾ to 10¼ hours, plus 30 minutes cooling time
key equipment baking stone, 2 (9-inch) round cake pans, pastry brush

why this recipe works Focaccia can easily disappoint when it turns out heavy, thick, and flavorless. We wanted a light, airy loaf, crisp-crusted and topped with just a smattering of herbs. For a bubbly crumb, we turned to a no-knead method to build our dough. We employed a high proportion of water to flour and a long resting period, which let the natural enzymes in the wheat replicate the effect of kneading. As with our Almost No-Knead Bread (page 52) and our No-Knead Brioche (page 94), we don't knead our focaccia per se. But we do fold it while it rises to prevent squat loaves. Gently turning the dough over itself at regular intervals accomplishes three things: It brings the wheat proteins into closer proximity with one another, keeping the process going at maximum clip; it aerates the dough, replenishing the oxygen that the yeasts consume during fermentation; and it elongates and redistributes the bubbles. After turning our dough three times in the process, we ended up with a well-risen focaccia with a tender, moist crumb. Olive oil is a key ingredient in focaccia, but we found that if we added it straight to the dough, it could turn the bread dense and cake-like. Instead, we baked the bread in round cake pans, where a couple of table-spoons of oil coating the exterior could be contained. Before baking, we poked the dough surface 25 to 30 times to pop large air bubbles and allow any extra gas to escape. Then we sprinkled the dough with a healthy dose of chopped fresh rosemary. Out of the oven, our focaccia boasted a crackly, crisp bottom, a deeply browned top, and an interior that was open and airy. It is important to use fresh, not dried, rosemary. Be sure to reduce the temperature immediately after putting the loaves in the oven.

sponge
½ cup (2½ ounces) all-purpose flour
⅓ cup (2⅔ ounces) water, room temperature
¼ teaspoon instant or rapid-rise yeast

dough
2½ cups (12½ ounces) all-purpose flour
1¼ cups (10 ounces) water, room temperature
1 teaspoon instant or rapid-rise yeast
Kosher salt
¼ cup (1¾ ounces) extra-virgin olive oil
2 tablespoons chopped fresh rosemary

continued

rosemary focaccia, continued

1 **For the sponge** Stir all ingredients in large bowl with wooden spoon until well combined. Cover tightly with plastic wrap and let sit at room temperature until sponge has risen and begins to collapse, about 6 hours (sponge can sit at room temperature for up to 24 hours).

2 **For the dough** Stir flour, water, and yeast into sponge with wooden spoon until well combined. Cover bowl tightly with plastic and let dough rest for 15 minutes.

3 Stir 2 teaspoons salt into dough with wooden spoon until thoroughly incorporated, about 1 minute. Cover bowl tightly with plastic and let dough rest for 30 minutes.

4 Using greased bowl scraper (or rubber spatula), fold dough over itself by gently lifting and folding edge of dough toward middle. Turn bowl 45 degrees and fold dough again; repeat turning bowl and folding dough 6 more times (total of 8 folds). Cover tightly with plastic and let rise for 30 minutes. Repeat folding and rising. Fold dough again, then cover bowl tightly with plastic and let dough rise until nearly doubled in size, 30 minutes to 1 hour.

5 One hour before baking, adjust oven rack to upper-middle position, place baking stone on rack, and heat oven to 500 degrees. Coat two 9-inch round cake pans with 2 tablespoons oil each. Sprinkle each pan with ½ teaspoon salt. Transfer dough to lightly floured counter and dust top with flour. Divide dough in half and cover loosely with greased plastic. Working with 1 piece of dough at a time (keep remaining piece covered), shape into 5-inch round by gently tucking under edges.

6 Place dough rounds seam side up in prepared pans, coat bottoms and sides with oil, then flip rounds over. Cover loosely with greased plastic and let dough rest for 5 minutes.

7 Using your fingertips, gently press each dough round into corners of pan, taking care not to tear dough. (If dough resists stretching, let it relax for 5 to 10 minutes before trying to stretch it again.) Using fork, poke surface of dough 25 to 30 times, popping any large bubbles. Sprinkle 1 tablespoon rosemary evenly over top of each loaf, cover loosely with greased plastic, and let dough rest until slightly bubbly, about 10 minutes.

8 Place pans on baking stone and reduce oven temperature to 450 degrees. Bake until tops are golden brown, 25 to 30 minutes, rotating pans halfway through baking. Let loaves cool in pans for 5 minutes. Remove loaves from pans and transfer to wire rack. Brush tops with any oil remaining in pans and let cool for 30 minutes. Serve warm or at room temperature.

variation **focaccia with caramelized red onion, pancetta, and oregano**
Cook 4 ounces finely chopped pancetta in 12-inch skillet over medium heat, stirring occasionally, until well rendered, about 10 minutes. Using slotted spoon, transfer pancetta to medium bowl. Add 1 chopped red onion and 2 tablespoons water to fat left in skillet and cook over medium heat until onion is softened and lightly browned, about 12 minutes. Transfer onion to bowl with pancetta and stir in 2 teaspoons minced fresh oregano; let mixture cool completely before using. Substitute pancetta mixture for rosemary.

raising the
bar
project
recipes
worth the
time

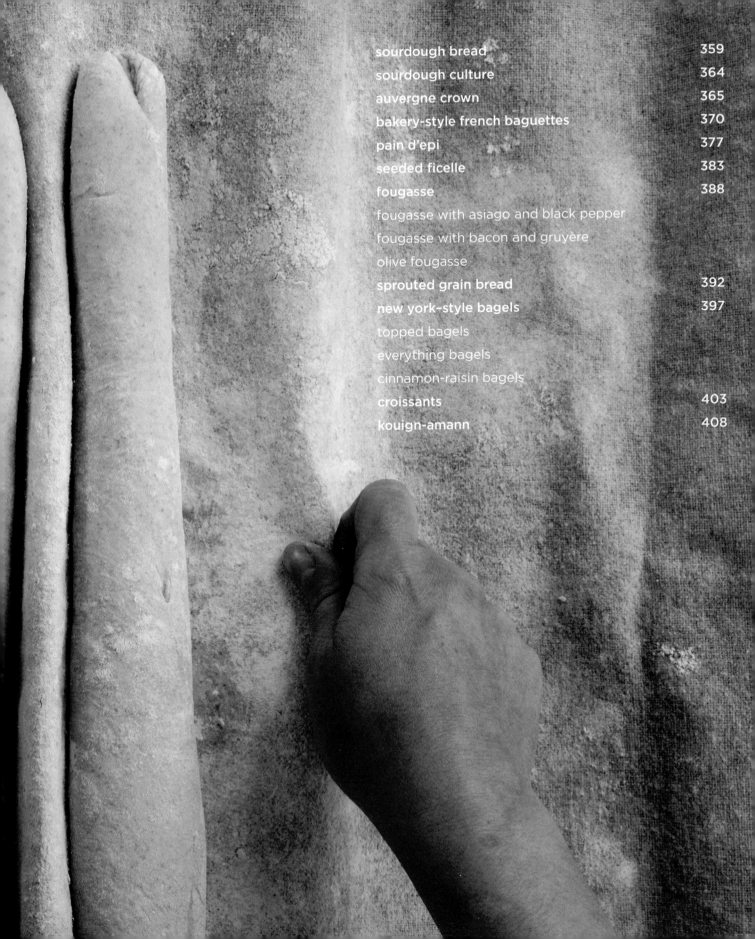

sourdough bread

makes 1 loaf
resting time 21 hours 35 minutes to 22 hours 35 minutes
rising time 17½ to 18½ hours
baking time 1 hour
total time 42 to 43 hours, plus 3 hours cooling time
key equipment large linen towel, 5-quart colander, baking stone, 2 (9-inch) disposable aluminum pie plates, 2 quarts lava rocks, pizza peel, lame, instant-read thermometer

why this recipe works Despite the "sour" in its name, sourdough breads need not be sour in flavor. What "sourdough" means is that the bread is fermented with a naturally occuring mixture of bacteria and yeasts, rather than with commericial yeast. Many think that sourdough is more complicated than other breads, but once you have a healthy sourdough culture to use, it isn't all that different. Though creating a culture from scratch takes a few weeks of patience, it is dead simple to do. And it's well worth the wait: Sourdough breads are among the best the baking world has to offer—crusty without, moist and chewy within, complexly flavored, and superbly long-lasting (the mild acidity that gives sourdough some of its flavor also helps to stave off staling). Once your culture is active, the method for making sourdough is not that different from other loaves we've made using commercial yeast. We used a mixture of higher-protein all-purpose flour and whole-wheat flour for complex flavor. We sift the whole-wheat flour to remove excess bran, ensuring a light and airy loaf. For convenience and the deepest flavor, we shape the loaf and give it an overnight proof in the fridge. For more information on sourdough cultures, see page 35. If you can't find King Arthur all-purpose flour, you can substitute bread flour. Take care when removing the linen towel from the loaf in step 10, as it may stick slightly to the dough. You can substitute a round *banneton* or proofing basket for the towel-lined colander. (For more information on bannetons, see page 37.) For a more decorative crust, you can slash this loaf in step 11 using either of the techniques shown on page 36.

starter
¾ cup (3¾ ounces) King Arthur Unbleached All-Purpose Flour
¼ cup plus 2 tablespoons (3 ounces) water, room temperature
⅓ cup (2⅔ ounces) Sourdough Culture (page 364)

dough
1 cup (5½ ounces) whole-wheat flour
2 cups (10 ounces) all-purpose flour
1¼ cups (10 ounces) water, room temperature
1¾ teaspoons salt

continued

1 *For the starter* Stir all ingredients together in 4-cup liquid measuring cup with wooden spoon until cohesive dough starts to form and no dry flour remains. Cover bowl tightly with plastic wrap, let sit at room temperature for 5 hours, then refrigerate for 16 to 24 hours. (Alternatively, starter can sit at room temperature until doubled in size, 8 to 12 hours, and be used immediately; do not refrigerate.)

2 *For the dough* Sift whole-wheat flour through fine-mesh strainer into bowl of stand mixer; discard bran remaining in strainer. Whisk all-purpose flour into whole-wheat flour. Stir water into starter with wooden spoon until well combined. Using dough hook on low speed, slowly add starter mixture to flour mixture and mix until cohesive dough starts to form and no dry flour remains, about 2 minutes, scraping down bowl as needed. Cover bowl tightly with plastic and let dough rest for 20 minutes.

3 Add salt to dough and mix on low speed until incorporated, about 2 minutes. Transfer dough to lightly greased large bowl or container, cover tightly with plastic, and let rise for 30 minutes.

4 Using greased bowl scraper (or your fingertips), fold dough over itself by gently lifting and folding edge of dough toward middle. Turn bowl 45 degrees and fold dough again; repeat turning bowl and folding dough 6 more times (total of 8 folds). Cover tightly with plastic and let rise for 30 minutes. Repeat folding and rising every 30 minutes, 3 more times.

5 After fourth set of folding and rising, turn out dough onto lightly floured counter (side of dough that was against bowl should now be against counter). Press and stretch dough into 10-inch round, deflating any gas pockets larger than 1 inch. Working around circumference of dough, fold edges toward center until ball forms. Cover loosely with greased plastic and let rest for 15 minutes.

6 Line 5-quart colander with large linen or cotton tea towel and dust liberally with flour. Repeat pressing and folding of dough to re-form ball, then flip dough ball seam side down and, using your cupped hands, drag in small circles on counter until dough feels taut and round and all seams are secured on underside of loaf.

continued

troubleshooting

problem The lame drags.

solution Try greasing the lame.

To get clean-looking cuts, we slash loaves quickly and decisively to prevent the lame from dragging. Properly slashed loaves expand uniformly in the oven. If you have a hard time making slashes without the lame catching, you can try greasing it. Spray the lame (or knife or single-edge razor blade for simple loaves) with vegetable oil spray before slashing.

problem You don't have lava rocks.

solution Fill a pan with boiling water.

We tested multiple ways to create steam in the oven, and nothing turned out crusts as crisp and crackly as our lava rock method. For the best bread, we highly recommend you use them. However, if you don't want to buy lava rocks, you can get satisfactory crust (it will be chewier and less crunchy) by using a water pan. Before baking, place an empty loaf pan or cake pan on the lower rack instead of the pans of lava rocks and bring 1 cup of water to boil. When you slide the loaf onto the baking stone, pour the boiling water into the empty pan and shut the oven door.

sourdough bread, continued

7 Place loaf seam side up in prepared colander and pinch any remaining seams closed. Loosely fold edges of towel over loaf to enclose, then place colander in large plastic garbage bag. Tie, or fold under, open end of bag to fully enclose. Let loaf sit at warm room temperature for 1 hour, then refrigerate for at least 12 hours or up to 16 hours.

8 Remove loaf from refrigerator and let rise (still inside plastic bag) at warm room temperature until nearly doubled in size and dough springs back minimally when poked gently with your knuckle, 2 to 3 hours (remove loaf from bag to test).

9 One hour before baking, adjust oven racks to lower-middle and lowest positions. Place baking stone on upper rack, place 2 disposable aluminum pie plates filled with 1 quart lava rocks each on lower rack, and heat oven to 475 degrees. Bring 1 cup water to boil.

10 Remove colander from garbage bag, unfold edges of towel, and dust top of loaf with flour. (If any seams have reopened, pinch closed before dusting with flour.) Lay 16 by 12-inch sheet of parchment paper on top of loaf. Using 1 hand to support parchment and loaf, invert loaf onto parchment and place on counter. Gently remove colander and towel. Transfer parchment with loaf to pizza peel.

11 Carefully pour ½ cup boiling water into 1 disposable pie plate of preheated rocks and close oven door for 1 minute to create steam. Meanwhile, holding lame concave side up at 30-degree angle to loaf, make two 7-inch-long, ½-inch-deep slashes with swift, fluid motion along top of loaf to form cross.

12 Working quickly, slide parchment with loaf onto baking stone and pour remaining boiling water into second disposable pie plate of preheated rocks. Bake loaf for 15 minutes, then reduce oven temperature to 425 degrees. Rotate loaf and continue to bake until crust is dark brown and loaf registers 210 to 212 degrees, 45 to 50 minutes, rotating loaf halfway through baking. Transfer loaf to wire rack, discard parchment, and let cool completely, about 3 hours, before serving.

troubleshooting

problem The loaf doesn't rise.

solution Let the dough sit at a warm room temperature for the right amount of time.

Sourdoughs can take much longer to rise than doughs leavened with commercial yeast. That's because sourdough bacteria and yeast metabolize starch much more slowly than baker's yeast, and they also prefer slightly higher temperatures for proofing. For the first rise, let the loaf rise at a warm room temperature (about 75 to 78 degrees), such as above your refrigerator or near a radiator. If you do not have a warm spot, you can place the loaf on the middle oven rack and set a pan of hot water beneath it. This creates a warm, steamy environment—a "proofing box"—that encourages the dough to rise and keeps it from drying out. And for the second rise, before baking, this loaf takes longer to proof than most. The dough gets a lot of flavor from proofing overnight in the refrigerator, but it doesn't expand very much during this period. It's only after the yeasts warm up again that they begin to produce enough carbon dioxide to give the loaf good volume. Once the loaf has about doubled in size and the dough springs back minimally when poked gently with your knuckle, it is ready to bake. This should take 2 to 3 hours, again at a warm room temperature. Utilize the oven once again if necessary.

sourdough culture

makes about 6½ ounces sourdough culture
total time 13 to 18 days

why this recipe works This recipe yields enough culture to make our Sourdough Bread (page 359) or Auvergne Crown with enough left to continue maintaining it for future use. Filtered water limits the amount of chlorine in the culture, which can weaken the growth of organisms. Don't let the culture go for more than 48 hours without feeding in step 2. Don't be alarmed if your culture has an unpleasant aroma in step 1; it will decrease in intensity and become more pleasant. For more information on sourdough cultures, see page 35.

4½ cups (24¾ ounces) whole-wheat flour
5 cups (25 ounces) all-purpose flour, plus extra as needed
Filtered water, room temperature

1 **Establish culture** Whisk whole-wheat flour and 4½ cups (22½ ounces) all-purpose flour together in large bowl or container. Stir 1 cup (5 ounces) flour mixture and ⅔ cup (5⅓ ounces) water in medium bowl with wooden spoon until well combined and no dry flour remains. Cover tightly with plastic wrap and let sit at room temperature until culture is established (mixture will be bubbly and have an intense aroma), 48 to 72 hours. Cover and set aside remaining flour mixture for feeding culture.

2 **Feed culture** Stir ¼ cup (2 ounces) culture, ½ cup (2½ ounces) flour mixture, and ¼ cup (2 ounces) water together in clean bowl with wooden spoon until well combined and no dry flour remains; discard remaining culture. Cover tightly with plastic and let sit at room temperature for 24 hours.

3 **Refresh culture** Repeat feeding culture every 24 hours until culture is pleasantly aromatic and rises and falls within an 8- to 12-hour period after being fed, 10 to 14 days. (You may have flour mixture left over.) Sourdough culture is now ready to use (or move to storage).

4 **Store and maintain culture** Stir ¼ cup (2 ounces) culture, ¼ cup (2 ounces) water, and remaining ½ cup (2½ ounces) all-purpose flour together in clean bowl with wooden spoon until well combined and no dry flour remains; discard remaining culture. Let culture sit at room temperature for 5 hours, then transfer to clean container, cover loosely, and refrigerate. Once a week, remove culture from refrigerator and repeat maintenance with ¼ cup (2 ounces) culture, ¼ cup (2 ounces) water, and ½ cup (2½ ounces) all-purpose flour. Let culture sit at room temperature for 5 hours before transferring to clean container and refrigerating.

troubleshooting

problem The culture has gone longer than a week without a maintenance feeding.

solution Refresh the culture.

If you have neglected your culture for longer than a week (or if you otherwise have one you aren't sure about), refresh it by combining ½ cup (2½ ounces) all-purpose flour, ¼ cup (2 ounces) water, and ¼ cup (2 ounces) of culture in a bowl. Cover tightly with plastic wrap and let sit at room temperature. Repeat refreshing twice daily (approximately every 12 hours) until the culture rises and falls within an 8- to 12-hour period after refreshing. (A spoonful of healthy, fully proofed culture should float in water.) The refreshed culture can be used or prepared for maintenance as directed in step 3.

auvergne crown

makes 1 loaf
resting time 21 hours 35 minutes
rising time 17½ hours
baking time 35 minutes
total time 47½ hours, plus 3 hours cooling time
key equipment 2 rimmed baking sheets, couche, 2 (9-inch) disposable aluminum pie plates, 2 quarts lava rocks, baking stone, instant-read thermometer

why this recipe works The Auvergne Crown, or *couronne auvergnate*, is a large, crusty, ring-shaped loaf made with white flour and leavened with a sourdough culture. It can be found in boulangeries throughout France, but it originated in the Auvergne region of central France, an area known as the source of most of the country's grain. Unlike simple white breads, the Auvergne Crown is deeply flavorful, owing to its mildly tangy, aromatic sourdough starter and a long, slow fermentation process. We experimented with several approaches to forming this 100 percent white-flour sourdough bread into its unique crown shape. We started by rolling the dough into a log, or folding it into a baguette shape, before bending it into a ring, but the results were inconsistent: The crust was uneven, the width variable, and the holes in the crumb too irregular. We had the best results when we shaped the dough into a taut boule and stretched a hole through the center before placing the loaf on a liberally floured *couche* to proof. (For more information on couches, see page 5.) Happily, this process was easier, too. An inverted bowl placed under the couche helped maintain the crown shape. Since this is a rustic loaf, we wanted a deep-brown crust, so we let the loaf bake for longer—35 to 40 minutes—and we used the crust's rich, toasty appearance in addition to the interior temperature to guide us when gauging doneness. Take care when removing the couche from the loaf in step 10, as it may stick slightly to the dough. If you can't find King Arthur all-purpose flour, you can substitute bread flour.

starter
1 cup (5 ounces) all-purpose flour
½ cup (4 ounces) water, room temperature
½ cup (4 ounces) Sourdough Culture (page 364)

dough
1¾ cups (14 ounces) water, room temperature
4½ cups (22½ ounces) King Arthur Unbleached All-Purpose Flour
1 tablespoon salt

continued

1 For the starter Stir all ingredients together in 4-cup liquid measuring cup with wooden spoon until cohesive dough starts to form and no dry flour remains. Cover tightly with plastic wrap, let sit at room temperature for 5 hours, then refrigerate for 16 to 24 hours. (Alternatively, starter can sit at room temperature for 8 to 12 hours and be used immediately; do not refrigerate.)

2 For the dough Stir water into starter with wooden spoon until well combined. Place flour in bowl of stand mixer. Using dough hook on low speed, slowly add starter mixture to flour and mix until cohesive dough starts to form and no dry flour remains, about 2 minutes, scraping down bowl as needed. Cover bowl tightly with plastic and let dough rest for 20 minutes. Add salt to dough and mix on low speed until incorporated, about 2 minutes. Transfer dough to lightly greased large bowl or container, cover tightly with plastic, and let rise for 30 minutes.

3 Using greased bowl scraper (or your fingertips), fold dough over itself by gently lifting and folding edge of dough toward middle. Turn bowl 45 degrees and fold dough again; repeat turning bowl and folding dough 6 more times (total of 8 folds). Cover tightly with plastic and let rise for 30 minutes. Repeat folding and rising every 30 minutes, 3 more times.

4 After fourth set of folding and rising, turn out dough onto lightly floured counter (side of dough that was against bowl should now be against counter). Press and stretch dough into 10-inch round, deflating any gas pockets larger than 1 inch.

5 Working around circumference of dough, fold edges toward center until ball forms. Cover loosely with greased plastic and let rest for 15 minutes.

6 Place 4-inch bowl that has been inverted in center of rimmed baking sheet, then drape couche over bowl and dust liberally with flour. Repeat pressing and folding of dough to re-form ball, then flip dough ball seam side down and, using your cupped hands, drag in small circles on counter until dough feels taut and round and all seams are secured on underside of loaf.

7 Using your fingertips, press through and stretch center of dough to create 5-inch hole. Invert dough ring onto prepared couche and pinch any remaining seams closed. Fold edges of couche over loaf to cover completely, then carefully place sheet inside large plastic garbage bag. Tie, or fold under, open end of bag to fully enclose. Let loaf sit at warm room temperature for 1 hour, then refrigerate for at least 12 hours or up to 16 hours.

8 Remove loaf from refrigerator and let rise (still inside plastic bag) at warm room temperature until nearly doubled in size and dough springs back minimally when poked gently with your knuckle, about 4 hours (remove from bag to test with knuckle).

continued

troubleshooting

problem The loaf burns.

solution Reduce the oven temperature partway through baking.

This large loaf bakes longer than many other rustic breads. To achieve good oven spring (the rise that dough experiences when it first hits a hot oven). To ensure a lofty—not squat—crown, we start the loaf at a high temperature—475 degrees. But you can't bake the loaf at this temperature for the entire time it takes to cook through. After 40 minutes of baking at this temperature, the loaf would be charred. We reduce the oven temperature to 425 degrees after the loaf has baked for 15 minutes. If you forget to do so, your loaf will have a bitter crust.

auvergne crown, continued

9 One hour before baking, adjust oven racks to lower-middle and lowest positions. Place baking stone on upper rack, place 2 disposable aluminum pie plates filled with 1 quart lava rocks each on lower rack, and heat oven to 475 degrees. Bring 1 cup water to boil on stovetop.

10 Remove sheet with loaf from garbage bag, unfold edges of couche, and dust top of loaf with flour. Lay 16 by 12-inch sheet of parchment paper on top of loaf. Gently place second rimmed baking sheet on top of parchment and invert loaf onto parchment. Carefully, remove top baking sheet, bowl, and couche. Reshape loaf as needed, tucking edges under to form taut ring shape.

11 Carefully pour ½ cup boiling water into 1 disposable pie plate of preheated rocks and close oven door for 1 minute to create steam. Meanwhile, using sharp paring knife or single-edge razor blade, make one ½-inch-deep slash around outer circumference of loaf, about 1 inch from outer edge. Make second ½-inch-deep slash around inner circumference of loaf, about 1 inch from inner edge.

12 Working quickly, slide parchment with loaf onto baking stone and pour remaining boiling water into second disposable pie plate of preheated rocks. Bake loaf for 15 minutes, then reduce oven temperature to 425 degrees. Rotate loaf and continue to bake until crust is dark brown and loaf registers 210 to 212 degrees, 20 to 25 minutes. Transfer loaf to wire rack, discard parchment, and let cool completely, about 3 hours, before serving.

bakery-style french baguettes

makes 4 loaves
resting time 1 to 1½ hours
rising time 18½ to 19 hours
baking time 17 minutes
total time 21¼ to 22¼ hours, plus 20 minutes cooling time
key equipment rimmed baking sheet, couche, water-filled spray bottle, baking stone, pizza peel, flipping board, lame, 2 (16 by 12-inch) disposable aluminum roasting pans

¼ cup (1⅓ ounces) whole-wheat flour

3 cups (15 ounces) King Arthur Unbleached All-Purpose Flour

1½ teaspoons salt

1 teaspoon instant or rapid-rise yeast

1 teaspoon diastatic malt powder (optional)

1½ cups (12 ounces) water, room temperature

why this recipe works A great baguette is hard to come by outside of France. The ideal: a moist, wheaty interior punctuated with irregular holes, and a deeply browned crust so crisp it shatters into shards. But home cooks rarely attempt to make baguettes since existing recipes provide little instruction and explanation. We wanted to create a detailed, authentic recipe for the home oven. First order of business: the mixing method. We chose a hybrid approach for the ideal structure and open crumb: We mixed the dough in a stand mixer and then folded the dough several times during the first rising period. We got the best flavor when we then gave the folded dough a slow rise—16 to 48 hours—in the fridge. We added a little diastatic malt powder to our dough to boost exterior browning and flavor; during the dough's long refrigerator stay, the yeast consumed nearly all of the available sugars, and the malt powder unlocked more sugar by converting starches in the flour. A little whole-wheat flour provided even more depth. For a shatteringly crisp, flavorful crust, we covered the bread with a disposable roasting pan while it baked so it could cook in its own steam. If you can't find King Arthur all-purpose flour, you can substitute bread flour. This recipe makes enough dough for four loaves, which can be baked anytime during the 16- to 48-hour window after placing the dough in the refrigerator in step 3. The baguettes are best eaten within 4 hours of baking.

continued

1 Sift whole-wheat flour through fine-mesh strainer into bowl of stand mixer; discard bran remaining in strainer.

2 Whisk all-purpose flour, salt, yeast, and malt powder, if using, into mixer bowl. Using dough hook on low speed, slowly add water to flour mixture and mix until cohesive dough starts to form and no dry flour remains, 5 to 7 minutes, scraping down bowl as needed. Transfer dough to lightly greased large bowl or container, cover tightly with plastic wrap, and let rise for 30 minutes.

3 Using greased bowl scraper (or your fingertips), fold dough over itself by gently lifting and folding edge of dough toward middle. Turn bowl 45 degrees and fold dough again; repeat turning bowl and folding dough 6 more times (total of 8 folds). Cover tightly with plastic and let rise for 30 minutes. Repeat folding and rising every 30 minutes, 3 more times. After fourth set of folds, cover bowl tightly with plastic and refrigerate for at least 16 hours or up to 48 hours.

4 Transfer dough to lightly floured counter, press into 8-inch square (do not deflate), and divide in half. Return 1 piece of dough to bowl, cover tightly with plastic, and refrigerate (dough can be shaped and baked anytime within 48-hour window). Divide remaining dough in half crosswise, transfer to lightly floured rimmed baking sheet, and cover loosely with greased plastic. Let rest until no longer cool to touch, 30 minutes to 1 hour.

5 Working with 1 piece of dough at a time (keep remaining piece covered), roll into loose 3- to 4-inch-long cylinder on lightly floured counter. Cover loosely with greased plastic and let rest for 30 minutes.

6 Mist underside of couche with water, drape over second rimmed baking sheet that has been inverted, and dust evenly with flour. Gently press 1 dough cylinder into 6 by 4-inch rectangle on lightly floured counter, with long side parallel to counter edge. Fold upper quarter of dough toward center and press gently to seal. Rotate dough 180 degrees and repeat folding step to form 8 by 2-inch rectangle.

7 Fold dough in half toward you, using thumb of your other hand to create crease along center of dough, sealing with heel of your hand as you work your way along loaf. Without pressing down on loaf, use heel of your hand to reinforce seal (do not seal ends of loaf).

8 Cup your hand over center of dough and roll dough back and forth gently to tighten (it should form dog-bone shape).

continued

troubleshooting

problem The bread is bitter and dense.

solution Sift the whole-wheat flour.

We add ¼ cup of whole-wheat flour to the dough to deepen the flavor. But the sharp-edged bran in the whole-wheat flour can cut through the loaf's gluten structure for a squat loaf, and also impart a bitter flavor. The solution? Simply sift the bran out of the whole-wheat flour, so your bread gets nutty—not bitter—flavor without any textural defects.

9 Starting at center of dough and working toward ends, gently and evenly roll and stretch dough until it measures 15 inches long by 1¼ inches wide. Moving your hands in opposite directions, use back and forth motion to roll ends of loaf under your palms to form sharp points.

10 Transfer loaf seam side up to prepared couche. On either side of loaf, pinch edges of couche into pleat, then cover loosely with large plastic garbage bag.

11 Repeat steps 6 through 10 with remaining piece of dough and place on opposite side of pleat. Fold edges of couche over loaves to cover completely, then carefully place sheet inside garbage bag. Tie, or fold under, open end of bag to fully enclose. Let loaves rise until nearly doubled in size and dough springs back minimally when poked gently with your knuckle, 30 minutes to 1 hour (remove from bag to test with knuckle).

12 One hour before baking, adjust oven rack to lower-middle position, place baking stone on rack, and heat oven to 500 degrees. Line pizza peel with 16 by 12-inch piece of parchment paper, with long edge of paper perpendicular to handle. Unfold couche, pulling from ends to remove pleats. Gently pushing with side of flipping board, roll 1 loaf over, away from other loaf, so it is seam side down.

13 Using your hand, hold long edge of flipping board between loaf and couche at 45-degree angle, then lift couche with your other hand and flip loaf seam side up onto board.

14 Invert loaf seam side down onto prepared pizza peel, about 2 inches from long edge of parchment, then use flipping board to straighten loaf. Repeat with remaining loaf, leaving at least 3 inches between loaves.

15 Holding lame concave side up at 30-degree angle to loaf, make three 4-inch-long, ½-inch-deep slashes with swift, fluid motion along length of loaf. Repeat with second loaf.

16 Slide parchment with loaves onto baking stone. Cover loaves with stacked inverted disposable pans and bake for 5 minutes. Carefully remove pans and continue to bake until loaves are deep golden brown, 12 to 15 minutes, rotating loaves halfway through baking. Transfer loaves to wire rack, discard parchment, and let cool for 20 minutes. Serve warm or at room temperature.

troubleshooting

problem The bread has a uniform crumb.

solution Shape the loaves gently.

One of the hallmarks of a good French baguette is its open, uneven crumb structure. Be sure to use a gentle hand when following the shaping steps; otherwise, you'll press out the air that forms the irregular, open, airy holes in these loaves.

pain d'epi

makes 4 loaves
resting time 1 to 1½ hours
rising time 18½ to 19 hours
baking time 17 minutes
total time 21¼ to 22¼ hours, plus 20 minutes cooling time
key equipment rimmed baking sheet, couche, water-filled spray bottle, baking stone, pizza peel, flipping board, kitchen shears, 2 (16 by 12-inch) disposable aluminum roasting pans

¼ cup (1⅓ ounces) whole-wheat flour

3 cups (15 ounces) King Arthur Unbleached All-Purpose Flour

1½ teaspoons salt

1 teaspoon instant or rapid-rise yeast

1 teaspoon diastatic malt powder (optional)

1½ cups (12 ounces) water, room temperature

why this recipe works Baguettes have an iconic shape, but there are more shapes and sizes of this crusty, open-crumbed loaf to explore, including our Seeded Ficelle (page 383) and this striking wheat stalk–shaped loaf called *pain d'epi*. This loaf boasts not only a gorgeous appearance, but a uniquely impressive crust as well. Why? All of those cuts and angles leave more surface to crisp in the oven. Stateside, these loaves are found only in the highest-quality bread bakeries, so you may never think to attempt replicating these loaves, with their intricate design, at home. But once you've mastered our Bakery-Style French Baguettes (page 370), making pain d'epi doesn't actually take much extra effort, and adapting our baguette shaping technique was simple. We followed our baguette recipe until it was time to score the loaves. Instead of turning to our lame, we broke out our kitchen shears, cutting into the loaves at an angle to create attached lobes that resembled the stalks of wheat. If you can't find King Arthur all-purpose flour, you can substitute bread flour. This recipe makes enough dough for four loaves, which can be baked anytime during the 16- to 48-hour window after placing the dough in the refrigerator in step 2. The pain d'epi are best eaten within 4 hours of baking.

continued

pain d'epi, continued

1 Sift whole-wheat flour through fine-mesh strainer into bowl of stand mixer; discard bran remaining in strainer. Whisk all-purpose flour, salt, yeast, and malt powder, if using, into mixer bowl. Using dough hook on low speed, slowly add water to flour mixture and mix until cohesive dough starts to form and no dry flour remains, 5 to 7 minutes, scraping down bowl as needed. Transfer dough to lightly greased large bowl or container, cover tightly with plastic wrap, and let rise for 30 minutes.

2 Using greased bowl scraper (or your fingertips), fold dough over itself by gently lifting and folding edge of dough toward middle. Turn bowl 45 degrees and fold dough again; repeat turning bowl and folding dough 6 more times (total of 8 folds). Cover tightly with plastic and let rise for 30 minutes. Repeat folding and rising every 30 minutes, 3 more times. After fourth set of folds, cover bowl tightly with plastic and refrigerate for at least 16 hours or up to 48 hours.

3 Transfer dough to lightly floured counter, press into 8-inch square (do not deflate), and divide in half. Return 1 piece of dough to bowl, cover tightly with plastic, and refrigerate (dough can be shaped and baked anytime within 48-hour window). Divide remaining dough in half crosswise, transfer to lightly floured rimmed baking sheet, and cover loosely with greased plastic. Let rest until no longer cool to touch, 30 minutes to 1 hour.

4 Working with 1 piece of dough at a time (keep remaining piece covered), roll into loose 3- to 4-inch-long cylinder on lightly floured counter. Cover loosely with greased plastic and let rest for 30 minutes.

5 Mist underside of couche with water, drape over second rimmed baking sheet that has been inverted, and dust evenly with flour. Gently press 1 dough cylinder into 6 by 4-inch rectangle on lightly floured counter, with long side parallel to counter edge. Fold upper quarter of dough toward center and press gently to seal. Rotate dough 180 degrees and repeat folding step to form 8 by 2-inch rectangle.

6 Fold dough in half toward you, using thumb of your other hand to create crease along center of dough, sealing with heel of your hand as you work your way along loaf. Without pressing down on loaf, use heel of your hand to reinforce seal (do not seal ends of loaf).

7 Cup your hand over center of dough and roll dough back and forth gently to tighten (it should form dog-bone shape).

8 Starting at center of dough and working toward ends, gently and evenly roll and stretch dough until it measures 15 inches long by 1¼ inches wide. Moving your hands in opposite directions, use back and forth motion to roll ends of loaf under your palms to form sharp points.

continued

troubleshooting

problem The crust is pale and dull-tasting.

solution Use diastatic malt powder.

During the long proofing time, nearly all the sugars in this dough are consumed by the yeast. Since sugars are responsible for browning and caramelization, this will leave the crust pale and dull-tasting. Adding diastatic malt powder, derived from a naturally occurring enzyme that converts the starches in flour into sugar, guarantees a supply of sugar at baking time and thus a crust that browns and caramelizes. Purchase diastatic malt powder (available from Amazon for $7.63 for 1 pound), not plain malt powder or malt syrup.

9 Transfer loaf seam side up to prepared couche. On either side of loaf, pinch edges of couche into pleat, then cover loosely with large plastic garbage bag.

10 Repeat steps 5 through 9 with remaining piece of dough and place on opposite side of pleat. Fold edges of couche over loaves to cover completely, then carefully place sheet inside garbage bag. Tie, or fold under, open end of bag to fully enclose. Let loaves rise until nearly doubled in size and dough springs back minimally when poked gently with your knuckle, 30 minutes to 1 hour (remove from bag to test with knuckle).

11 One hour before baking, adjust oven rack to lower-middle position, place baking stone on rack, and heat oven to 500 degrees. Line pizza peel with 16 by 12-inch piece of parchment paper, with long edge of paper perpendicular to handle. Unfold couche, pulling from ends to remove pleats. Gently pushing with side of flipping board, roll 1 loaf over, away from other loaf, so it is seam side down.

12 Using your hand, hold long edge of flipping board between loaf and couche at 45-degree angle, then lift couche with your other hand and flip loaf seam side up onto board.

13 Invert loaf seam side down onto prepared pizza peel, about 2 inches from long edge of parchment, then use flipping board to straighten loaf. Repeat with remaining loaf, leaving at least 3 inches between loaves.

14 Using kitchen shears, cut into loaf at 45-degree angle, about 3 inches from end of loaf, nearly but not all the way through loaf.

15 Arrange cut section at 30-degree angle in either direction. Repeat every 3 inches, pulling sections out toward alternating sides to create wheat stalk shape. Repeat with second loaf.

16 Slide parchment with loaves onto baking stone. Cover loaves with stacked inverted disposable pans and bake for 5 minutes. Carefully remove pans and continue to bake until loaves are deep golden brown, 12 to 15 minutes, rotating loaves halfway through baking. Transfer loaves to wire rack, discard parchment, and let cool for 20 minutes. Serve warm or at room temperature.

troubleshooting

problem The loaves are too chewy or tender.

solution Use the right flour.

All-purpose flour is all-purpose, right? Although we develop our recipes with Gold Medal Unbleached All-Purpose Flour, we specifically call for King Arthur Unbleached All-Purpose Flour in a handful of recipes in this book for the best results. King Arthur all-purpose flour has a higher protein content than does Gold Medal and most other brands of all-purpose flour—yet it is lower in protein than bread flour. Some of our artisan-style breads get folded—for an airier crumb—and given an extended refrigerator rise—for great flavor. Both of these techniques also develop more gluten in doughs. So if you use high-protein bread flour, your loaves may become too chewy, and therefore tough. Conversely, though, using regular all-purpose flour might not be enough to give the bread structure. If you can't find King Arthur Unbleached All-Purpose flour, substitute bread flour.

seeded ficelle

makes 4 loaves
resting time 1 to 1½ hours
rising time 18½ to 19 hours
baking time 13 minutes
total time 21¼ to 22¼ hours, plus 15 minutes cooling time
key equipment 2 rimmed baking sheets, couche, water-filled spray bottle, baking stone, pizza peel, flipping board, lame, 2 (16 by 12-inch) disposable aluminum roasting pans

2 cups (10 ounces) King Arthur Unbleached All-Purpose Flour

1 teaspoon salt

¾ teaspoon instant or rapid-rise yeast

¾ teaspoon diastatic malt powder (optional)

1 cup (8 ounces) water, room temperature

3 tablespoons poppy seeds

3 tablespoons sesame seeds

2 teaspoons fennel seeds

why this recipe works The French word *ficelle* means "string," thus the loaf that takes this name resembles a long, skinny, stick-like baguette made from a "string" of dough. Because it is so thin, a loaf of ficelle maximizes the ratio of crackly crust to tender, chewy interior, making it perfect for slicing for hors d'oeuvres, dipping in oil, or cutting down the middle to make elegant sandwiches. As a starting point, we scaled down our Bakery-Style French Baguette recipe (page 370)—and eliminated the whole-wheat flour—to make four petite sticks. Ficelles are sometimes rolled in seeds before being proofed and baked, and we liked the crunch and flavor that a mixture of poppy, sesame, and fennel seeds provided. Since these small loaves bake through quickly, we once again added a small amount of diastatic malt powder to boost exterior browning during the loaves' short stint in the oven. And although we typically take the temperature of our breads to help assess doneness, we chose to forgo using a thermometer here—these loaves are so thin that it's difficult to insert the probe into them and get an accurate reading. Instead, we relied on a clear visual cue: When the loaves are deep golden brown and the crust is dry and crackly, they're done baking. If you can't find King Arthur all-purpose flour, you can substitute bread flour. This recipe makes enough dough for four loaves, which can be baked anytime during the 16- to 48-hour window after placing the dough in the refrigerator in step 2. The ficelles are best eaten within 4 hours of baking.

continued

1 Whisk flour, salt, yeast, and malt powder, if using, together in bowl of stand mixer. Using dough hook on low speed, slowly add water to flour mixture and mix until cohesive dough starts to form and no dry flour remains, 5 to 7 minutes, scraping down bowl as needed. Transfer dough to lightly greased large bowl or container, cover tightly with plastic wrap, and let rise for 30 minutes.

2 Using greased bowl scraper (or your fingertips), fold dough over itself by gently lifting and folding edge of dough toward middle. Turn bowl 45 degrees and fold dough again; repeat turning bowl and folding dough 6 more times (total of 8 folds). Cover tightly with plastic and let rise for 30 minutes. Repeat folding and rising every 30 minutes, 3 more times. After fourth set of folds, cover bowl tightly with plastic and refrigerate for at least 16 hours or up to 48 hours.

3 Transfer dough to lightly floured counter, press into 8-inch square (do not deflate), and divide in half. Return 1 piece of dough to bowl, cover tightly with plastic, and refrigerate (dough can be shaped and baked anytime within 48-hour window). Divide remaining dough in half crosswise, transfer to lightly floured rimmed baking sheet, and cover loosely with greased plastic. Let rest until no longer cool to touch, 30 minutes to 1 hour.

4 Working with 1 piece of dough at a time (keep remaining piece covered), roll into loose 3- to 4-inch-long cylinder on lightly floured counter. Cover loosely with greased plastic and let rest for 30 minutes.

5 Combine poppy seeds, sesame seeds, and fennel seeds in bowl. Spread half of seed mixture on second rimmed baking sheet; reserve remaining seed mixture for second half of dough. Mist underside of couche with water, drape over rimmed baking sheet that has been inverted, and dust evenly with flour.

6 Gently press 1 dough cylinder into 6 by 4-inch rectangle on lightly floured counter, with long side parallel to counter edge. Fold upper quarter of dough toward center and press gently to seal. Rotate dough 180 degrees and repeat folding step to form 8 by 2-inch rectangle.

7 Fold dough in half toward you, using thumb of your other hand to create crease along center of dough, sealing with heel of your hand as you work your way along loaf. Without pressing down on loaf, use heel of your hand to reinforce seal (do not seal ends of loaf).

8 Cup your hand over center of dough and roll dough back and forth gently to tighten (it should form dog-bone shape). Starting at center of dough and working toward ends, gently and evenly roll and stretch dough until it measures 15 inches long by 1 inch wide. Moving your hands in opposite directions, use back and forth motion to roll ends of loaf under your palms to form sharp points.

continued

troubleshooting

problem The seed coating is uneven.

solution Spray all sides of the loaf with water.

Rolling the ficelle in a mixture of poppy seeds, sesame seeds, and fennel seeds gives these skinny baguettes a distinctive crust. To ensure an even coating of seeds, make sure that you mist all sides of the dough—not just the top—with water so that the seed mixture adheres after you roll the loaves in it.

9 Mist loaf with water on all sides and roll in seed mixture, pressing gently to adhere.

10 Transfer loaf seam side up to prepared couche. On either side of loaf, pinch edges of couche into pleat, then cover loosely with large plastic garbage bag.

11 Redistribute seeds on sheet into even layer. Repeat steps 6 through 10 with remaining piece of dough and place on opposite side of pleat. Fold edges of couche over loaves to cover completely, then carefully place sheet inside plastic bag. Tie, or fold under, open end of bag to fully enclose. Let loaves rise until nearly doubled in size and dough springs back minimally when poked gently with your knuckle, 30 minutes to 1 hour (remove from bag to test with knuckle).

12 One hour before baking, adjust oven rack to lower-middle position, place baking stone on rack, and heat oven to 500 degrees. Line pizza peel with 16 by 12-inch piece of parchment paper, with long edge of paper perpendicular to handle. Unfold couche, pulling from ends to remove pleats. Gently pushing with side of flipping board, roll 1 loaf over, away from other loaf, so it is seam side down.

13 Using your hand, hold long edge of flipping board between loaf and couche at 45-degree angle, then lift couche with your other hand and flip loaf seam side up onto board.

14 Invert loaf seam side down onto prepared pizza peel, about 2 inches from long edge of parchment, then use flipping board to straighten loaf. Repeat with remaining loaf, leaving at least 3 inches between loaves.

15 Holding lame concave side up at 30-degree angle to loaf, make three 4-inch-long, ½-inch-deep slashes with swift, fluid motion along length of loaf. Repeat with second loaf.

16 Slide parchment with loaves onto baking stone. Cover loaves with stacked inverted disposable pans and bake for 5 minutes. Carefully remove pans, rotate loaves, and continue to bake until loaves are deep golden brown, 8 to 10 minutes. Transfer loaves to wire rack, discard parchment, and let cool for 15 minutes. Serve warm or at room temperature.

fougasse

makes 2 loaves
resting time 30 minutes to 1 hour
rising time 18½ minutes to 19 hours
baking time 36 minutes
total time 20¾ to 21¾ hours, plus 20 minutes cooling time
key equipment 2 rimmed baking sheets, rolling pin, pizza cutter, baking stone, pastry brush

¼ cup (1 ⅓ ounces) whole-wheat flour

3 cups (15 ounces) King Arthur Unbleached All-Purpose Flour

1½ teaspoons salt

1 teaspoon instant or rapid-rise yeast

1½ cups (12 ounces) water, room temperature

cornmeal or semolina flour

¼ cup (1¾ ounces) extra-virgin olive oil

1 tablespoon chopped fresh rosemary

2 teaspoons coarse sea salt

why this recipe works If ever there was a bread made for crust lovers, it has to be fougasse. Revered by professional bakers, this loaf is still relatively unknown to everyday cooks, at least outside its home territory of Provence. It is related by name and pedigree to focaccia, which comes from just over the border in Italy. But unlike its Italian cousin, fougasse gets an elegant twist: After being stretched and flattened, the dough is given a series of cuts, usually in fanciful geometric patterns, to create multiple openings in the finished flatbread and give it a leaf shape. As pretty as the sculpted breads are, the openings are not just for aesthetics: They dramatically increase the crust-to-crumb ratio so that nearly every bite includes an equal share of crisp crust and tender, airy interior. The cuts also help the bread bake very quickly. Most bakeries don't make a separate dough for fougasse. Instead, they simply repurpose extra dough from some other product, such as baguettes. We decided to follow suit and started with our Bakery-Style French Baguette recipe (page 370), and then changed up the shaping. To make shaping the fougasse easy, we rolled it out with a rolling pin so that the dough was level, transferred it to parchment, and cut into it with a pizza cutter, which proved the perfect-size implement. The fougasse looked flawless, but the substantial crust was too hard and tough. We tried adding olive oil to the dough, as we'd seen in some recipes, to soften it, but this eliminated any crispness. Brushing the dough with oil before it went into the oven worked much better, producing a delicate, almost fried crunch and even browning that complemented a rosemary and sea salt topping. If you can't find King Arthur all-purpose flour, you can substitute bread flour. The fougasses are best eaten within 4 hours of baking.

continued

1 Sift whole-wheat flour through fine-mesh strainer into bowl of stand mixer; discard bran remaining in strainer. Whisk all-purpose flour, salt, and yeast into mixer bowl. Using dough hook on low speed, slowly add water to flour mixture and mix until cohesive dough starts to form and no dry flour remains, 5 to 7 minutes, scraping down bowl as needed. Transfer dough to lightly greased large bowl or container, cover tightly with plastic wrap, and let rise for 30 minutes.

2 Using greased bowl scraper (or your fingertips), fold dough over itself by gently lifting and folding edge of dough toward middle. Turn bowl 45 degrees and fold dough again; repeat turning bowl and folding dough 6 more times (total of 8 folds). Cover tightly with plastic and let rise for 30 minutes. Repeat folding and rising every 30 minutes, 3 more times. After fourth set of folds, cover bowl tightly with plastic and refrigerate for at least 16 hours or up to 48 hours.

3 Transfer dough to lightly floured counter, press into 8-inch round (do not deflate), and divide in half. Working with 1 piece of dough at a time, gently stretch and fold over 3 sides of dough to create rough triangle with 5-inch sides. Transfer triangles seam side down to lightly floured rimmed baking sheet, cover loosely with greased plastic, and let rest until no longer cool to the touch, 30 minutes to 1 hour.

4 Invert second rimmed baking sheet, line with parchment paper, and dust liberally with cornmeal. Transfer 1 piece of dough to lightly floured counter and gently roll into triangular shape with 8-inch base and 10-inch sides, about ½ inch thick. Transfer dough to prepared sheet, with base facing short side of sheet.

5 Using pizza cutter, make 6-inch-long cut down center of triangle, through dough to sheet, leaving about 1½ inches at either end.

6 Make three 2- to 3-inch diagonal cuts through dough on each side of center cut, leaving 1-inch border on each end of cuts, to create leaf-vein pattern (cuts should not connect to one another or to edges of dough).

7 Gently stretch dough toward sides of sheet to widen cuts and emphasize leaf shape; overall size of loaf should measure about 10 by 12 inches. Cover loosely with greased plastic and let rise until nearly doubled in size, 30 minutes to 1 hour. Twenty minutes after shaping first loaf, repeat steps 4 through 7 with second piece of dough. (Staggering shaping of loaves will allow them to be baked in succession.)

8 One hour before baking, adjust oven rack to lower-middle position, place baking stone on rack, and heat oven to 450 degrees. Brush top and sides of first loaf with 2 tablespoons oil. Sprinkle loaf evenly with 1½ teaspoons rosemary and 1 teaspoon sea salt. Slide parchment with loaf onto baking stone and bake until deep golden brown, 18 to 22 minutes, rotating loaf halfway through baking. Transfer loaf to wire rack, discard parchment, and let cool for 20 minutes. Serve warm or at room temperature. Repeat topping and baking second loaf.

variations **fougasse with asiago and black pepper** Omit rosemary and sea salt. Sprinkle each loaf with 1 teaspoon coarsely ground pepper and ½ cup finely grated Asiago cheese before baking.

fougasse with bacon and gruyère

Cook 4 slices thick-cut bacon, cut into ½-inch pieces, in 10-inch nonstick skillet over medium heat, stirring occasionally, until crispy, 6 to 8 minutes. Using slotted spoon, transfer bacon to paper towel–lined plate. Omit rosemary and sea salt. Add bacon to mixer bowl with flour in step 1. Sprinkle each loaf with ½ cup shredded Gruyère cheese before baking.

olive fougasse

Add 1 cup coarsely chopped pitted kalamata olives to mixer bowl with flour in step 1.

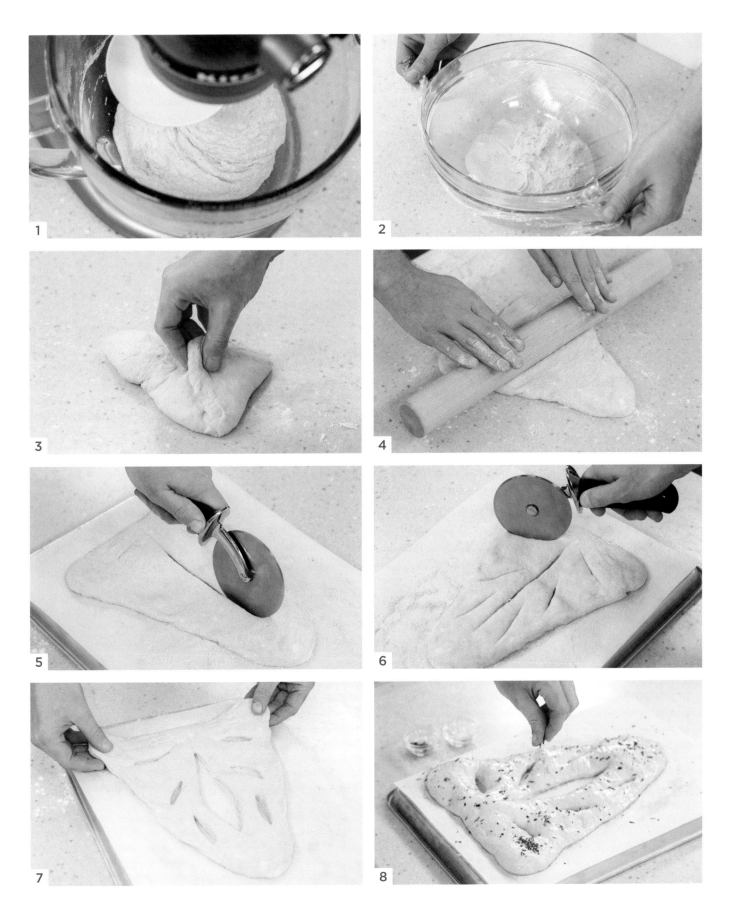

sprouted grain bread

makes 1 loaf
resting time 36 hours 20 minutes to 84 hours 20 minutes
rising time 2 to 2½ hours
baking time 40 minutes
total time 39½ to 88 hours, plus 3 hours cooling time
key equipment food processor, stand mixer, 2 rimmed baking sheets, pastry brush, instant-read thermometer

why this recipe works Sprouted grain bread is a hearty, nutty-tasting, whole-grain-filled loaf you can feel good about eating. When grains begin to sprout, or germinate, their vitamin content increases dramatically, so this bread is packed with nutritious benefits. You can find several expensive brands of sprouted grain breads at the market, but we found them to be dry and bland. To develop our own recipe, we first had to determine which types of grains and legumes work best. Corn and chickpeas tasted sour and were dense, but wheat berries, lentils, and quinoa all made great loaves. We also found that many recipes omit the flour or substitute vital wheat gluten (isolated gluten protein from wheat flour) for flour. Bread made with just sprouted grains turned out leaden; vital wheat gluten built structure but imparted off-flavors. We bolstered our loaf with bread flour for a hearty but not heavy crumb. For the best texture, we pureed most of the sprouted grains and added them to the wet ingredients, holding back just a half cup to mix in whole after kneading. To complement the earthy grains, we also stirred a mix of toasted sunflower, pumpkin, and sesame seeds into the dough, and sprinkled additional seeds and quinoa on top for a loaf that was as delicious as it was healthful. We do not recommend mixing this dough by hand. Toast the sunflower seeds, pepitas, and sesame seeds in a dry skillet over medium heat until fragrant (about 1 minute), and then remove the pan from the heat so the seeds won't scorch. Be sure to reduce the temperature immediately after putting the loaf in the oven.

2½ cups (20 ounces) water, room temperature

¾ cup (4¾ ounces) wheat berries

¼ cup (1¼ ounces) plus 1 teaspoon prewashed white quinoa

¼ cup (1¾ ounces) brown lentils, picked over and rinsed

3 tablespoons plus 1 teaspoon sunflower seeds, toasted

2 tablespoons plus 1 teaspoon pepitas, toasted

1 tablespoon plus 1 teaspoon sesame seeds, toasted

2 cups (11 ounces) bread flour

1 tablespoon instant or rapid-rise yeast

3 tablespoons honey

2 teaspoons salt

1 large egg, lightly beaten with 1 tablespoon water and pinch salt

continued

1 Combine 2 cups water, wheat berries, ¼ cup quinoa, and lentils in large bowl, cover tightly with plastic wrap, and let soak at room temperature until grains and lentils are fully hydrated and softened, at least 12 hours or up to 24 hours. Drain grains through fine-mesh strainer, then return to bowl. Cover and let sit at room temperature, rinsing and draining grains daily, until small sprouts appear on each type of grain, 1 to 3 days. (Do not wait for every individual grain to sprout; you should see just a few examples of each grain.)

2 Transfer ½ cup sprouted grains to medium bowl. Stir in 3 tablespoons sunflower seeds, 2 tablespoons pepitas, and 1 tablespoon sesame seeds; set aside. Process remaining sprouted grains in food processor until finely ground, about 3 minutes, scraping down sides of bowl as needed.

3 Whisk flour and yeast together in bowl of stand mixer. Whisk processed grain mixture, honey, and remaining water together in 4-cup liquid measuring cup. Using dough hook on low speed, slowly add processed grain mixture to flour mixture and mix until cohesive dough starts to form and no dry flour remains, about 2 minutes, scraping down bowl as needed. Cover bowl tightly with plastic wrap and let dough rest for 20 minutes.

4 Add salt to dough and knead on medium-low speed until dough is smooth and elastic and clears sides of bowl, about 5 minutes. Reduce speed to low, slowly add grain-seed mixture, ¼ cup at a time, and mix until mostly incorporated, about 2 minutes. Transfer dough to lightly floured counter. Using your lightly floured hands, knead dough until grains and seeds are evenly distributed and dough forms smooth, round ball, about 30 seconds. Place dough seam side down in lightly greased large bowl or container, cover tightly with plastic wrap, and let rise until doubled in size, 1½ to 2 hours.

5 Stack 2 rimmed baking sheets, line with aluminum foil, and spray with vegetable oil spray. Press down on dough to deflate. Turn dough out onto lightly floured counter (side of dough that was against bowl should now be facing up). Press and stretch dough into 6-inch square. Fold top corners of dough diagonally into center and press gently to seal. Stretch and fold upper third of dough toward center and press seam gently to seal. Stretch and fold dough in half toward you to form rough 8 by 4-inch loaf, and pinch seam closed. Roll loaf seam side down.

6 Gently slide your hands underneath each end of loaf and transfer to prepared sheet. Reshape loaf as needed, tucking edges under to form taut torpedo shape. Cover loosely with greased plastic and let rise until loaf increases in size by about half and dough springs back minimally when poked gently with your knuckle, about 30 minutes.

7 Adjust oven rack to middle position and heat oven to 425 degrees. Combine remaining quinoa, sunflower seeds, pepitas, and sesame seeds in bowl. Using sharp paring knife or single-edge razor blade, make three 4-inch-long, ½-inch-deep diagonal slashes with swift, fluid motion across top of loaf, starting and stopping about 1 inch from edges and spacing slashes about 2 inches apart.

8 Gently brush loaf with egg mixture and sprinkle with seed mixture. Place loaf in oven, reduce oven temperature to 375 degrees, and bake until deep golden brown and loaf registers 205 to 210 degrees, 40 to 45 minutes, rotating sheet halfway through baking. Transfer loaf to wire rack and let cool completely, about 3 hours, before serving.

new york-style bagels

makes 8
rising time 17 hours
resting time 25 minutes
baking time 20 minutes
total time 19½ hours, plus 15 minutes cooling time
key equipment food processor, 2 rimmed baking sheets, rolling pin, baking stone, Dutch oven

why this recipe works Proper New York bagels have a fine, uniform crumb, a substantial chew, a complex sweetness (derived from the addition of malt syrup), and a thin, crackly crust. We wanted to be able to enjoy New York bagels anywhere. To get the right amount of chew, we turned to high-protein bread flour and supplemented it with vital wheat gluten. We also incorporated some gluten-strengthening shaping techniques: We rolled the dough, formed it into a rope, and twisted the rope before shaping it into a ring. Formed bagels are usually refrigerated for about a day to minimize the yeast's gas production and create lots of flavor. It's traditional to then boil them before baking to "wake up" the yeast. This process also hydrates and cooks the starches on the bagel's exterior to create the glossy, crisp crust. We spiked our boiling water with baking soda and sugar, which helped the bagels brown quickly. To build on that crust, we baked the bagels on a wire rack set in a rimmed baking sheet that we then placed on a preheated baking stone. And we poured boiling water into the pan to create steam. This recipe works best with King Arthur bread flour, although other bread flours will work. Vital wheat gluten and malt syrup are available in most supermarkets in the baking and syrup aisles, respectively. If you cannot find malt syrup, substitute 4 teaspoons of molasses. We do not recommend mixing this dough by hand. The bagels are best eaten within a day of baking; fully cooled bagels can be transferred to zipper-lock bags and frozen for up to 1 month.

1 cup plus 2 tablespoons (9 ounces) ice water

2 tablespoons malt syrup

2⅔ cups (14⅔ ounces) King Arthur Unbleached Bread Flour

4 teaspoons vital wheat gluten

2 teaspoons instant or rapid-rise yeast

2 teaspoons salt

¼ cup (1¼ ounces) cornmeal

¼ cup (1¾ ounces) sugar

1 tablespoon baking soda

continued

1 Whisk ice water and malt syrup in 2-cup liquid measuring cup until malt syrup has dissolved. Pulse flour, wheat gluten, and yeast in food processor until combined, about 5 pulses. With processor running, slowly add ice water mixture until dough is just combined and no dry flour remains, about 20 seconds. Let dough rest for 10 minutes.

2 Add salt to dough and process until dough forms shaggy mass that clears sides of bowl (dough may not form 1 single mass), 45 to 90 seconds, stopping processor and redistributing dough as needed.

3 Transfer dough to clean counter and knead by hand to form smooth, round ball, about 30 seconds. Divide dough into quarters, cut each quarter in half (about 3½ ounces each), and cover loosely with greased plastic wrap.

4 Working with 1 piece of dough at a time (keep remaining pieces covered), form into rough ball by stretching dough around your thumbs and pinching edges together so that top is smooth. Place ball seam side down on clean counter and, using your cupped hand, drag in small circles until dough feels taut and round. Let dough balls rest on counter, covered, for 15 minutes.

5 Sprinkle rimmed baking sheet with cornmeal. Coat 1 dough ball with flour and place on lightly floured counter. Press and roll into 5-inch round of even thickness. Roll dough toward you into tight cylinder.

6 Starting at center of cylinder and working toward ends, gently and evenly roll and stretch dough into 8- to 9-inch-long rope. Do not taper ends. Rolling ends of dough under your hands in opposite directions, twist rope to form tight spiral.

continued

troubleshooting

problem The bagels lack chew.

solution Don't skip the vital wheat gluten.

Both New York bagels and pizza get their chew from high-gluten flour. This product, a staple in bread bakeries and available only via mail order, contains a high proportion (14 to 15 percent) of the gluten-forming proteins that make bagels extra-chewy. Fortunately, there is another, more widely available, product you can add to strengthen the dough at home. Vital wheat gluten, a powdered form of wheat gluten, is often used by professional bakers to create a stronger network and thus a chewier product. Without it, your bagels will be just rounds of standard bread.

problem The bagels are pale.

solution Add baking soda and sugar to the boiling water.

While boiling the bagels before baking them wakes up the yeast and helps them achieve good spring in the oven, it also contributes to the bagels' crisp, shiny crust. Browning is influenced by pH—acidic foods don't darken as readily as alkaline ones do—so we add a tablespoon of alkaline baking soda, plus a little sugar, to the boiling water. Don't forget to add these ingredients to the water; they help the bagels bake up with their signature glossy tan and lightly crisp exterior.

7 Without untwisting spiral, wrap rope around your fingers, overlapping ends of dough by about 2 inches under your palm, to create ring shape. Pinch ends of dough gently together.

8 With overlap under your palm, press and roll seam using circular motion on counter to fully seal. Transfer ring to prepared sheet and cover loosely with greased plastic.

9 Repeat steps 5 through 8 with remaining dough balls and transfer to prepared sheet, spaced about 1 inch apart. Cover bagels tightly with greased plastic, let sit at room temperature for 1 hour, then refrigerate for at least 16 or up to 24 hours.

10 One hour before baking, adjust oven rack to upper-middle position, place baking stone on rack, and heat oven to 450 degrees. Bring 4 quarts water, sugar, and baking soda to boil in Dutch oven. Set wire rack in second rimmed baking sheet and spray rack with vegetable oil spray. Transfer 4 bagels to boiling water and cook for 20 seconds.

11 Using wire skimmer or slotted spoon, flip bagels over and cook 20 seconds longer. Transfer bagels to prepared wire rack, with cornmeal side facing down. Repeat with remaining 4 bagels.

12 Place sheet with bagels on preheated baking stone and pour ½ cup boiling water into bottom of sheet. Bake until tops of bagels are beginning to brown, 10 to 12 minutes. Using metal spatula, flip bagels and continue to bake until golden brown, 10 to 12 minutes longer. Remove sheet from oven and let bagels cool on wire rack for at least 15 minutes. Serve warm or at room temperature.

variations **topped bagels**
Place ½ cup poppy seeds, sesame seeds, caraway seeds, dehydrated onion flakes, dehydrated garlic flakes, or coarse sea salt in bowl. Press tops of just-boiled bagels (side without cornmeal) gently into topping and return to wire rack, topping side up.

everything bagels
Combine 2 tablespoons poppy seeds, 2 tablespoons sesame seeds, 1 tablespoon dehydrated onion flakes, 2 teaspoons dehydrated garlic flakes, 2 teaspoons caraway seeds, and ½ teaspoon coarse sea salt in bowl. Press tops of just-boiled bagels (side without cornmeal) gently into topping mixture and return to wire rack, topping side up.

cinnamon-raisin bagels
After transferring dough to counter in step 3, sprinkle ⅔ cup raisins over top and knead by hand until raisins are evenly distributed and dough forms smooth, round ball, about 1 minute. Divide and shape dough into balls as directed. Combine 1 teaspoon sugar and 1 teaspoon ground cinnamon in bowl. Before rolling dough rounds into cylinders in step 5, sprinkle ¼ teaspoon sugar-cinnamon mixture over each round, leaving ½-inch border around edges.

croissants

makes 22
resting time 6 hours
rising time 2½ to 3 hours
baking time 20 minutes
total time 11 to 11½ hours, plus 15 minutes cooling time
key equipment rolling pin, 3 rimmed baking sheets, pastry brush

4¼ cups (21¼ ounces) King Arthur Unbleached All-Purpose Flour

4 teaspoons instant or rapid-rise yeast

2 teaspoons salt

1¾ cups (14 ounces) whole milk, room temperature

¼ cup (1¾ ounces) sugar

3 tablespoons European-style unsalted butter, melted, plus 24 tablespoons (12 ounces) chilled

1 large egg, lightly beaten with 1 tablespoon water and pinch salt

why this recipe works Part pastry, part bread, a croissant has a crisp, deeply golden crust wrapped around tender, pillow-soft, buttery layers. We wanted to create an approachable but authentic croissant recipe for home bakers. The layered structure that characterizes croissants is formed through a process called lamination. First, a basic dough of flour, milk, yeast, sugar, salt, and a small amount of butter is made. Then, a larger amount of butter is formed into a block and encased in the relatively lean dough. This dough-and-butter package is rolled out and folded multiple times (called a "turn") to form paper-thin layers of dough separated by paper-thin layers of butter. These layers are what make baked croissants so flaky and decadent. For our recipe, we found that more turns didn't necessarily produce more layers—we stopped at three turns. We gave the dough a 30-minute super chill in the freezer to firm it up before rolling, cutting, and shaping, to minimize the risk of tears. After letting the croissants rise until they doubled in size, we brushed them with an egg wash and slid them into a very hot oven. When the croissants emerged, they possessed crisp, delicate tiers of pastry that made the process worth the effort. If you can't find King Arthur all-purpose flour, you can substitute bread flour, though the dough may be more difficult to roll. Our favorite European-style butter is Plugrá. Do not attempt to make these croissants in a room that is warmer than 80 degrees. If at any time during rolling the dough retracts or softens, dust it lightly with flour, fold it loosely into thirds, cover it, and return it to the freezer to rest for 10 to 15 minutes. Be sure to reduce the temperature immediately after putting the croissants in the oven. This recipe yields 12 baked croissants and 10 croissants for freezing and baking at a later time.

continued

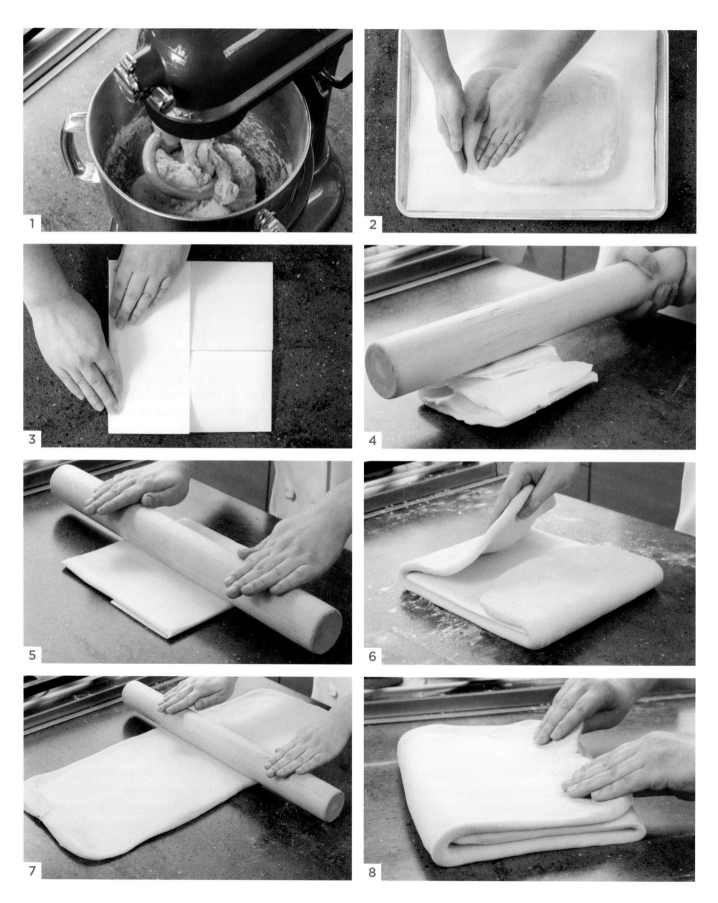

croissants, continued

1 Whisk flour, yeast, and salt together in bowl of stand mixer. Whisk milk, sugar, and melted butter in 4-cup liquid measuring cup until sugar has dissolved. Using dough hook on low speed, slowly add milk mixture to flour mixture and mix until cohesive dough starts to form and no dry flour remains, about 2 minutes, scraping down bowl as needed. Increase speed to medium-low and knead for 1 minute. Cover bowl tightly with plastic wrap and let dough rest for 30 minutes.

2 Transfer dough to parchment paper–lined rimmed baking sheet and press into 10 by 7-inch rectangle, about 1 inch thick. Wrap tightly with greased plastic and refrigerate for 2 hours.

3 Meanwhile, fold 24-inch length of parchment in half to create 12-inch rectangle. Fold over 3 open sides of rectangle to form 8-inch square with enclosed sides. Crease folds firmly.

4 Place chilled butter directly on counter and beat with rolling pin until butter is just pliable but not warm, about 60 seconds, then fold butter in on itself using bench scraper. Beat into rough 6-inch square.

5 Unfold parchment envelope. Using bench scraper, transfer butter to center of parchment, refolding at creases to enclose. Turn packet over so that flaps are underneath, and gently roll until butter fills parchment square, taking care to achieve even thickness. Refrigerate for at least 45 minutes.

6 Transfer dough to freezer and chill for 30 minutes. Transfer dough to lightly floured counter and roll into 17 by 8-inch rectangle, with long side parallel to counter edge. Unwrap butter square and place in center of rectangle. Fold 2 sides of dough over butter so they meet in center. Press seam together with your fingertips.

7 Using rolling pin, press firmly on each open end of dough packet. Roll dough into 24 by 8-inch rectangle, with short side parallel to counter edge. Fold bottom third of dough over middle, then fold upper third over it like business letter to form 8-inch square. Turn dough 90 degrees counter-clockwise and repeat rolling and folding into thirds. Return dough to parchment-lined sheet, wrap tightly with greased plastic, and return to freezer for 30 minutes.

8 Transfer dough to lightly floured counter so that top flap of dough is facing right. Roll dough into 24 by 8-inch rectangle, with short side parallel to counter edge, and fold into thirds. Return dough to baking sheet, wrap tightly with plastic, and refrigerate for at least 2 hours or up to 24 hours.

continued

troubleshooting

problem The croissants are squat.

solution Use higher-protein King Arthur all-purpose flour.

Using all-purpose flour with a higher protein content makes the dough more elastic and less resistant to tearing during rolling, rising, and baking, so it maintains the thin sheets necessary for distinct layering.

problem The crumb is dense.

solution Use high-fat European-style butter.

Standard butter has a higher water content than European-style butter, and excess water can glue the layers together and result in bready pastries. Higher-fat butter is also more pliable when cold, making rolling easier.

9 Transfer dough to freezer and chill for 30 minutes. Transfer dough to lightly floured counter and roll into 18 by 16-inch rectangle, with long side parallel to counter edge. Fold upper half of dough over lower half. Using ruler, mark dough at 3-inch intervals along bottom edge with bench scraper (you should have 5 marks). Move ruler to top of dough, measure in 1½ inches from left, then use this mark to measure out 3-inch intervals (you should have 6 marks).

10 Starting at lower left corner, use pizza cutter or chef's knife to cut dough into triangles from mark to mark. You will have 12 single triangles and 5 double triangles; discard scraps.

11 Unfold double triangles and cut into 10 single triangles (making 22 equal-size triangles in total). If dough begins to soften, return to freezer for 10 minutes. Cover all triangles loosely with greased plastic.

12 Cut ½ inch slit in center of short end of 1 dough triangle (keep remaining triangles covered). Grasp triangle by 2 corners on either side of slit and stretch gently.

13 Grasp bottom point of triangle and stretch. Place triangle on counter so point is facing toward you and fold both sides of slit down.

14 Positioning palms on folds, roll partway toward point. Gently grasp point again and stretch. To finish, continue to roll, tucking point underneath. Curve ends gently toward one another to create crescent shape. Repeat with remaining triangles.

15 Place 12 croissants on 2 parchment-lined rimmed baking sheets, spaced about 2½ inches apart, 6 croissants per sheet. Cover loosely with greased plastic and let rise until nearly doubled in size, 2½ to 3 hours. (Unrisen croissants can be refrigerated for up to 18 hours; let rise at room temperature for 3 to 3½ hours before baking.) Place remaining 10 croissants on separate parchment-lined rimmed baking sheet, spaced about 1 inch apart. Wrap tightly with greased plastic and freeze until solid, about 2 hours. Transfer frozen croissants from baking sheet to zipper-lock bag and return to freezer. (Frozen croissants can be stored in freezer for up to 2 months. Arrange on 2 sheets as directed and increase rising time by 1 to 2 hours.)

16 Adjust oven racks to upper-middle and lower-middle positions and heat oven to 425 degrees. Gently brush croissants with egg mixture. Place croissants in oven and reduce temperature to 400 degrees. Bake for 12 minutes, then switch and rotate baking sheets. Continue to bake until deep golden brown, 8 to 12 minutes. Transfer croissants to wire rack and let cool for 15 minutes. Serve warm or at room temperature.

troubleshooting

problem The dough is hard to work with.

solution Put your freezer to work.

Be sure to chill the dough between turns two and three for the full 30 minutes to keep the butter and flour at exactly the same degree of malleability during rolling. And pop the dough in the freezer anytime it becomes too soft to work with.

kouign-amann

makes 12
resting time 5 hours
rising time 2½ to 3 hours
baking time 25 minutes
total time 9½ to 10 hours, plus 10 minutes cooling time
key equipment rimmed baking sheet, rolling pin, 12-cup muffin tin, pastry brush

3 cups (15 ounces) King Arthur Unbleached All-Purpose Flour

2¾ teaspoons instant or rapid-rise yeast

1½ teaspoons salt

1¼ cups (10 ounces) whole milk, room temperature

1 cup plus 2 tablespoons (7¾ ounces) sugar

4 tablespoons European-style unsalted butter, melted, plus 16 tablespoons (8 ounces) chilled

½ teaspoon coarse sea salt (optional)

why this recipe works *Kouign-amann* originated more than a century ago in Brittany, where it was made with leftover bread dough that was layered with local salted butter and sugar to create a rich, caramelized cake. (*Kouign* means "butter" and *amann* means "cake" in Breton.) Contemporary bakers have created a flaky caramel-crusted interpretation that has taken the pastry world by storm. Our goal was to come up with a clear, straightforward method to prepare these exquisite pastries. The process is similar to that of making croissants, where butter is folded and rolled into yeasted dough in "turns." Our challenge was to determine the best method for incorporating the sugar so that it would produce a delicate caramel crust without burning. We achieved the best texture when we first completed two turns of dough with only butter, followed by two turns in which we incorporated sugar; this ensured that the sugar didn't puncture our dough and compromise the pastry's distinct layers. To work the sugar into the layers, we dusted the counter and the dough with it, as we would with flour, when we rolled out the dough. As we shaped individual dough pieces into bundles, we gave them a fine coating of sugar. And, finally, we sprinkled sugar and sea salt over the tops before baking. Many bakeries use ring molds to shape individual kouign-amann, but we scaled our recipe to fit into a 12-cup muffin pan. If you can't find King Arthur all-purpose flour, you can substitute bread flour, though the dough may be more difficult to roll. Our favorite European-style butter is Plugrá. Do not attempt to make these kouign-amann in a room that is warmer than 80 degrees. If at any time during rolling the dough retracts or softens, dust it lightly with flour, fold it loosely into thirds, cover it, and return it to the freezer to rest for 10 to 15 minutes.

continued

1 Whisk flour, yeast, and salt together in bowl of stand mixer. Whisk milk, 2 tablespoons sugar, and 2 tablespoons melted butter in 4-cup liquid measuring cup until sugar has dissolved. Using dough hook on low speed, slowly add milk mixture to flour mixture and mix until cohesive dough starts to form and no dry flour remains, about 2 minutes, scraping down bowl as needed. Increase speed to medium-low and knead for 1 minute. Cover bowl tightly with plastic wrap and let dough rest for 30 minutes.

2 Transfer dough to parchment paper–lined rimmed baking sheet and press into 9 by 6-inch rectangle, about 1 inch thick. Wrap tightly with greased plastic and refrigerate for 2 hours.

3 Meanwhile, fold 24-inch length of parchment in half to create 12-inch rectangle. Fold over 3 open sides of rectangle to form 6-inch square with enclosed sides. Crease folds firmly. Place chilled butter directly on counter and beat with rolling pin until butter is just pliable but not warm, about 60 seconds, then fold butter in on itself using bench scraper. Beat into rough 6-inch square.

4 Unfold parchment envelope. Using bench scraper, transfer butter to center of parchment, refolding at creases to enclose. Turn packet over so that flaps are underneath, and gently roll until butter fills parchment square, taking care to achieve even thickness. Refrigerate for at least 45 minutes.

5 Transfer dough to lightly floured counter and roll into 13 by 7-inch rectangle, with long side parallel to counter edge. Unwrap butter square and place in center of dough. Fold 2 sides of dough over butter so they meet in center. Press seam together with your fingertips.

6 Using rolling pin, press firmly on each open end of packet. Roll dough into 18 by 6-inch rectangle, with short side parallel to counter edge. Fold bottom third of dough over middle, then fold upper third over it like business letter to form 6-inch square. Turn dough 90 degrees counter-clockwise and repeat rolling and folding into thirds. Return dough to parchment-lined sheet, wrap tightly with greased plastic, and return to refrigerator for 30 minutes.

7 Sprinkle 2 tablespoons sugar into rough 6-inch square on clean counter. Place dough on top of sugar so that top flap of dough is facing right, and sprinkle evenly with 2 tablespoons sugar.

8 Roll into 18 by 6-inch rectangle, with short side parallel to counter edge, gently flipping dough and redistributing sugar on counter as needed.

continued

troubleshooting

problem The sugar doesn't melt.

solution Make sure to tap excess sugar out of the pan.

Sugar in the bottom of the pan gives the pastries a crackly exterior. But if there's too much sugar in the pan it will fail to liquefy and caramelize in the time the pastries take to bake, and it will stick to the bottoms in clumps.

problem The bottoms are pale.

solution Press the dough into the corners of the muffin tin cups.

When the layers expand, they can lift the pastries out of the muffin cups. To make sure every surface of dough is in contact with the pan for even caramelization, press the dough into the bottoms and corners of the muffin cups.

9 Fold bottom third of dough over middle, then fold upper third over it like business letter to form 6-inch square. Turn dough 90 degrees counterclockwise and repeat rolling and folding into thirds with ¼ cup sugar. Return dough to parchment-lined sheet, wrap tightly with greased plastic, and refrigerate for at least 2 hours or up to 24 hours. (Some moisture may appear around seams.)

10 Grease 12-cup muffin tin with 1 tablespoon melted butter. Coat bottom and sides of muffin cups with 2 tablespoons sugar and tap out excess.

11 Transfer dough to lightly floured counter so that top flap of dough is facing right. Roll dough into 16½ by 12½-inch rectangle, with short side parallel to counter edge, gently flipping dough and reflouring counter as needed.

12 Using pizza cutter or chef's knife, trim ¼ inch of dough from each edge and discard. Reshape dough as needed; remaining rectangle should measure 16 by 12 inches. Cut dough vertically into 3 (16 by 4-inch) strips, then cut horizontally into twelve 4-inch squares.

13 Spread ¼ cup sugar onto bottom of shallow dish. Working with 1 dough square at a time, coat both sides with sugar, pressing gently to adhere. Fold four corners of square into center and press firmly on pointed ends to seal.

14 Place squares into muffin cups, folded side up, pressing dough gently into corners. Cover loosely with greased plastic and let rise until nearly doubled in size, 2½ to 3 hours. (Unrisen kouign-amann can be refrigerated for up to 18 hours; let rise at room temperature for 3 to 3½ hours before baking.)

15 Adjust oven rack to middle position and heat oven to 350 degrees. Gently press down on any pointed ends in center of kouign-amann that have become unsealed. Brush tops with remaining 1 tablespoon melted butter and sprinkle with remaining 2 tablespoons sugar and sea salt, if using.

16 Bake until deep golden brown, 25 to 30 minutes, rotating muffin tin halfway through baking. Let kouign-amann cool in muffin tin for 3 minutes, then invert individually onto wire rack and let cool, still inverted, for 10 minutes. Serve warm or at room temperature.

troubleshooting

problem The pastries stick to the pan.

solution Let the pastries cool in the muffin tin for exactly 3 minutes.

Do not let the baked kouign-amann sit in the pan to cool. The melted sugar will harden and glue the pastries to the pan. To ensure that the sugar sticks to the pastries and not to the pan, let them cool in their muffin cups for 3 minutes—any sooner and they will be too fragile to remove. And invert the pastries onto a wire rack to finish cooling to preserve the shattering, caramelized finish and to keep the kouign-amann from adhering to the wire rack.

conversions and equivalents

Some say baking is a science and an art. We would say that geography has a hand in it, too. Flours and sugars manufactured in the United Kingdom and elsewhere will feel and taste different from those manufactured in the United States. So we cannot promise that the bread you bake in Canada or England will taste the same as bread baked in the States, but we can offer guidelines for converting weights and measures. We also recommend that you rely on your instincts when making our recipes. Refer to the visual cues provided. If the dough hasn't "come together," as described, you may need to add more water—even if the recipe doesn't tell you to. You be the judge.

The recipes in this book were developed using standard U.S. measures following U.S. government guidelines. The charts below offer equivalents for U.S. and metric measures. All conversions are approximate and have been rounded up or down to the nearest whole number.

example

1 teaspoon	=	4.9292 milliliters, rounded up to 5 milliliters
1 ounce	=	28.3495 grams, rounded down to 28 grams

volume conversions	
U.S.	METRIC
1 teaspoon	5 milliliters
2 teaspoons	10 milliliters
1 tablespoon	15 milliliters
2 tablespoons	30 milliliters
¼ cup	59 milliliters
⅓ cup	79 milliliters
½ cup	118 milliliters
¾ cup	177 milliliters
1 cup	237 milliliters
1¼ cups	296 milliliters
1½ cups	355 milliliters
2 cups (1 pint)	473 milliliters
2½ cups	591 milliliters
3 cups	710 milliliters
4 cups (1 quart)	0.946 liter
1.06 quarts	1 liter
4 quarts (1 gallon)	3.8 liters

weight conversions	
OUNCES	GRAMS
½	14
¾	21
1	28
1½	43
2	57
2½	71
3	85
3½	99
4	113
4½	128
5	142
6	170
7	198
8	227
9	255
10	283
12	340
16 (1 pound)	454

conversion for common baking ingredients

Baking is an exacting science. Because measuring by weight is far more accurate than measuring by volume, and thus more likely to produce reliable results, in our recipes we provide ounce measures in addition to cup measures for many ingredients. Refer to the chart below to convert these measures into grams.

INGREDIENT	OUNCES	GRAMS
flour		
1 cup all-purpose flour*	5	142
1 cup bread flour	5½	156
1 cup whole-wheat flour	5½	156
1 cup rye flour	5½	156
1 cup cornmeal	5	142
1 cup wheat germ	3	8
liquid		
1 cup water	8	227
1 cup whole milk	8	227
1 cup beer	6½	227
sweetener		
1 cup granulated (white) sugar	7	198
1 cup packed brown sugar (light or dark)	7	198
1 cup confectioners' sugar	4	113
1 cup honey	12	340
1 cup molasses	12	340
cocoa powder		
1 cup cocoa powder	3	85
fat		
4 tablespoons (½ stick, or ¼ cup) butter†	2	57
8 tablespoons (1 stick, or ½ cup) butter†	4	113
16 tablespoons (2 sticks, or 1 cup) butter†	8	227
1 cup shortening	6½	184

* U.S. all-purpose flour does not contain leaveners, as some European flours do. These leavened flours are called self-rising or self-raising. If you are using self-rising flour, take this into consideration before adding leavening to a recipe.

† In the United States, butter is sold both salted and unsalted. We generally recommend unsalted butter. If you are using salted butter, take this into consideration before adding salt to a recipe.

converting temperatures from an instant-read thermometer

We include doneness temperatures in the recipes in this book. We recommend an instant-read thermometer for the job. To convert Fahrenheit degrees to Celsius, use this simple formula:

Subtract 32 degrees from the Fahrenheit reading, then divide the result by 1.8 to find the Celsius reading.

example

"Bake until loaf registers 205 to 210 degrees, 30 to 35 minutes." To convert:

(1) $205°F - 32 = 173°$
$173° \div 1.8 = 96.11°C$, rounded down to 96°C

(2) $210°F - 32 = 178°$
$178° \div 1.8 = 98.89°C$, rounded up to 99°C

oven temperatures		
FAHRENHEIT	CELSIUS	GAS MARK
225	105	¼
250	120	½
275	135	1
300	150	2
325	165	3
350	180	4
375	190	5
400	200	6
425	220	7
450	230	8
475	245	9

index

NOTE Page references in *italics* indicate photographs of finished recipes.

a

b